BIG BOOK OF ANIMAL RHYMES, FINGERPLAYS, AND SONGS

Elizabeth Cothen Low

LIBRARIES

UNLIMITED

A Member of the Greenwood Publishing Group

Westport, Connecticut • London

Library of Congress Cataloging-in-Publication Data

Big book of animal rhymes, fingerplays, and songs / [compiled by] Elizabeth Cothen Low.
   p. cm.
  Includes bibliographical references and indexes.
  ISBN 978-1-59158-630-2 (alk. paper)
  1. Animals—Juvenile poetry. 2. Children's poetry, English. 3. Children's poetry, American. 4. Finger play. 5. Children's songs, English. 6. Children's libraries—Activity programs. I. Low, Elizabeth Cothen, 1977–
  PR1195.A64B54   2009
  821.008'0362—dc22   2008032664

British Library Cataloguing in Publication Data is available.

Library of Congress Catalog Card Number: 2008032664
ISBN: 978-1-59158-630-2

First published in 2009

Libraries Unlimited, 88 Post Road West, Westport, CT 06881
A Member of the Greenwood Publishing Group, Inc.
www.lu.com

Printed in the United States of America

∞™

The paper used in this book complies with the
Permanent Paper Standard issued by the National
Information Standards Organization (Z39.48–1984).

10 9 8 7 6 5 4 3 2 1

Illustrations created by Kai-Siang Douglas Low. Used with permission.

To my little muses: Josie and Isaac
And my loving husband Douglas

Contents

Introduction

Are you looking for a fingerplay about monkeys, a song about snails, or a poem featuring camels? This book is intended to help anyone who works with children find interesting and age-appropriate material to enrich their programming or curriculum. Included are 653 entries about animals, starting with alligators and ending with zebras. The text also features musical notations for 94 songs, instructions for performing 125 action rhymes and fingerplays, and 10 Spanish entries.

Motivation

As a children's librarian, I have spent a lot of time assembling material for programming. Many of these programs, particularly preschool storytime, revolved around a particular topic, such as snow or clothing. I would typically read three or four books interspersed with nursery rhymes, fingerplays and songs that I would present to the children and have them repeat. It usually wasn't difficult to find picture books to read about that week's subject; the online library catalog, along with resources such as *A to Zoo: Subject Access to Children's Picture Books* (Lima and Lima, 2001), usually allowed me to locate a sizable stack that I could then comb through to find the best options.

However, I often found locating supplemental material—the rhymes and songs that are so important to maintaining small children's attention—more difficult. It was not that good resources didn't exist; the bibliography at the end of this book lists more than a hundred books and several Web sites that focus on fingerplays, action rhymes, nursery rhymes, songs, and poems for children. The problem was that most of the books were not very extensive, and the ones that were focused only on one of these topics, such as nursery rhymes. Fewer still were thematically organized or included melodies for songs with which I wasn't familiar. Others were indexes that referred users to other sources, many of which were not available in my small collection. The Internet was somewhat useful, as long as I knew what I was looking for. Many of the Web sites I visited were difficult to navigate and featured material of varying quality. All in all, I spent a lot of time rummaging through sources to put together an interesting program.

When I took a leave of absence from my profession to raise children, I decided to focus on creating a truly comprehensive resource for commonly known English language fingerplays/action rhymes (rhymes with movement included), nursery rhymes (traditional rhymes, including those commonly known as Mother Goose rhymes), folksongs, and poems. I chose animals as a focal point because many picture books feature them and because children naturally gravitate toward animals. Some of my best received programs featured creatures such as dogs, ducks, or cows.

It is my hope that this book be useful for children's librarians, teachers, and child-care providers, interested in thematic programming, as well as a reference tool for librarians and patrons seeking fingerplays, action rhymes, nursery rhymes, songs, and poems about animals.

Importance of Rhymes and Songs

[T]hese trivial verses have endured where newer and more ambitious compositions have become dated and forgotten. They have endured often for nine, or ten generations, sometimes considerably more, and scarcely altered in their journey. (Opie and Opie, 1997, p. 1)

Nursery rhymes and folksongs have long been an important tool for educating children. They teach early literacy skills such as phonological awareness and expand children's vocabulary. They can be used to support lessons about history, science, and manners. Yet most important, rhymes and songs encourage a love of language and foster imaginative thinking.

The entries in this collection can be used with people of every age, from infants to adults. In fact, simple Mother Goose songs have been used for generations to calm and entertain even very small babies. Older infants and toddlers love bouncing rhymes and toe-counting rhymes. Preschoolers enjoy learning fingerplays and acting out simple rhymes, as well as singing funny songs. Grade-schoolers are ready for more complex rhymes, such as tongue twisters, and teens can appreciate rhymes and poems with more sophisticated vocabulary and content, such as satire. To assist educators, I have included the following age guidelines for each entry:

B/T Babies/Toddlers

PreS Preschool

K–5 Kindergarten – 5th Grade

6+ 6th Grade and above

It is important to remember that many of these rhymes are very old—in many cases, they were written two or three hundred years ago. In an attempt to be inclusive, I have included some material that may be inappropriate for young children. And although I excluded the most blatantly sexist and racist rhymes, some of the entries are probably not culturally sensitive or politically correct by today's standards. It also may be difficult to understand some of the language, so I have also included definitions for many of the more archaic terms used in this book. These are listed at the bottom of the relevant entries.

Methodology and Copyright Issues

I used a wide variety of print and electronic sources for this project, including books, databases, indexes, and Web sites. In some cases, I found numerous versions of the same rhyme. I tried to go with the most common version (or the most appropriate for children). If I could not find a most common version, I merged together several variations. All of the entries in this book are thoroughly cross-referenced, so that all entries that mention ducks will be referenced in the "Ducks" chapter.

I have also been extremely careful to include only works that are not under current copyright. I was able to use a number of pre-1922 sources, which are in the public domain in the United States, for most of the nursery rhymes, songs, and poems. Fingerplays and action rhymes are trickier, because many have been passed around for decades in the oral tradition, without any clue to authorship. Regardless, I did not include anything in this collection that I did not find published at least three times without any information regarding authorship (unless the source itself was known to be in the public domain). I also did not include musical notation unless I had access to several scores with similar melodies or I was able to piece out the melody myself. For this reason, I chose not to solicit fingerplays or songs from other librarians, who would probably be unaware of the copyright status of particular works. Any inclusion of copyrighted material is completely unintentional and will be corrected in future editions. I have written or adapted all instructions for fingerplays and action rhymes.

Organization

I tried to compile a collection that could be searched quickly and efficiently, so I organized the chapters by subject (e.g., "Frogs"), and each chapter is broken down into four possible subsections: Fingerplays/Action Rhymes (for rhymes with movement), Nursery Rhymes, Songs (with music included), and Poetry (authored rhymes). So if a reader wants to find a song about ducks, he or she can go to the "Ducks" chapter and look under "Songs." The reader will also find cross-references for songs in other chapters that mention ducks. Rhymes and songs featuring more than one animal are found in the "Multiple Animals" chapter.

Acknowledgments

I would like to thank the children's librarians at Donnell Library Center in Manhattan for their help finding public domain resources, the people at Libraries Unlimited (especially my editor, Barbara Ittner) for their belief in this book and endless brainstorming, and my family for their tireless support and ideas.

References

Lima, Carolyn W., and John A. Lima. *A to Zoo: Subject Access to Children's Picture Books*. Westport, CT: Greenwood, 2001.

Opie, Iona, and Peter Opie, eds. *Oxford Dictionary of Nursery Rhymes*. Rev. ed. Oxford, UK: Oxford University Press, 1997.

ALLIGATORS AND CROCODILES

Fingerplays and Action Rhymes

Five Little Monkeys Swinging From a Tree

See "Multiple Animals" chapter, Fingerplays and Action Rhymes section.

If You Should Meet a Crocodile (Traditional, K–5/6+)

If you should meet a crocodile,
Don't take a stick and poke him. (Poke outstretched left hand with right finger.)
Ignore the welcome of his smile,
Be careful not to stroke him, (Stroke left hand.)
For as he sleeps upon the Nile,
He gets thinner and thinner; (Place hands further apart, then closer together.)
And whene'er you meet a crocodile,
He's ready for his dinner. (Place palms flat, one on top of the other and raise and lower top hand,
     keeping wrists together to mimic a crocodile's mouth.)

She Sailed Away on One Fine Day (Traditional, K–5/6+)

She sailed away on one fine day,
On the back of a crocodile. (Place left hand palm down and place right index finger on top of it.)
"You see," said she,
"He's as tame as he can be;
I'll ride him down the Nile."

The croc winked his eye
As she bade goodbye,
Wearing a happy smile.
At the end of the ride
The lady was inside, (Place right index finger under left palm.)
And the smile was on the crocodile. (Smile and rub belly.)

Nursery Rhymes

The Lady with the Alligator Purse (Traditional, PreS/K–5)

Miss Lucy had a baby,
His name was Tiny Tim.
She put him in the bathtub,
To see if he could swim.

He drank up all the water.
He ate up all the soap.
He tried to eat the bathtub,
But it wouldn't fit down his throat.

Miss Lucy called the doctor,
Miss Lucy called the nurse,

Miss Lucy called the lady with the alligator purse.
"Measles," said the doctor.
"Mumps," said the nurse.
"Nothing," said the lady with the alligator purse.

Out went the doctor.
Out went the nurse.
Out went the lady with the alligator purse.

Poetry

The Crocodile (Hilaire Belloc, 6+)

Whatever our faults, we can always engage
That no fancy or fable shall sully our page,
So take note of what follows, I beg.
This creature so grand and august in its age,
In its youth is hatched out of an egg.
And oft in some far Coptic* town
The Missionary sits him down
To breakfast by the Nile:
The heart beneath his priestly gown
Is innocent of guile;
When suddenly the rigid frown
Of Panic is observed to drown
His customary smile.
Why does he start and leap again,
And scour the sandy Libyan plain
Like one that wants to catch a train
Or wrestles with internal pain?

Because he finds his egg contains—
Green, hungry, horrible and plain—
An Infant Crocodile.

* Coptic: The Coptic church was a form of Christianity practiced in Egypt.

ANTS

Fingerplays and Action Rhymes

Once I Saw an Ant Hill (Emilie Poulsson, PreS/K–5)

Once I saw an ant-hill
With no ants about; (Place right fist inside left fist.)
So I said, "Dear little ants,
Won't you please come out?"
Then as if the little ants
Had heard my call—
One! Two! Three! Four! Five came out! (Have right hand fingers pop out of left fist.)
And that was all!

Songs

The Ants Go Marching (Traditional, PreS/K–5)

Verse 2: The ants go marching two by two
Hurrah, hurrah.
The ants go marching two by two,
Hurrah, hurrah.
The ants go marching two by two,
The little one stops to tie his shoe.

From *The Big Book of Animal Rhymes, Fingerplays, and Songs* by Elizabeth Cothen Low.
Westport, CT: Libraries Unlimited. Copyright © 2009.

And they all go marching down
Into the ground
To get out
Of the rain.
Boom! Boom! Boom!

Verse 3:   The ants go marching three by three . . .
           The little one stops to climb a tree . . .

Verse 4:   The ants go marching four by four . . .
           The little one stops to shut the door . . .

Verse 5:   The ants go marching five by five . . .
           The little one stops to take a dive . . .

Verse 6:   The ants go marching six by six . . .
           The little one stops to pick up sticks . . .

Verse 7:   The ants go marching seven by seven . . .
           The little one stops to pray to heaven . . .

Verse 8:   The ants go marching eight by eight . . .
           The little one stops to shut the gate . . .

Verse 9:   The ants go marching nine by nine . . .
           The little one stops to check the time . . .

Verse 10: The ants go marching ten by ten,
           Hurrah, hurrah.
           The ants go marching ten by ten,
           Hurrah, hurrah.
           The ants go marching ten by ten,
           The little one stops to say, "The End!"

Over in the Meadow

See "Multiple Animals" chapter, Songs section.

From *The Big Book of Animal Rhymes, Fingerplays, and Songs* by Elizabeth Cothen Low.
Westport, CT: Libraries Unlimited. Copyright © 2009.

BADGERS

Nursery Rhymes

The Panther

See "Multiple Animals" chapter, Nursery Rhymes section.

BATS

Nursery Rhymes

Bat, Bat, Come Under My Hat (Traditional, PreS/K–5)

Bat, bat,
Come under my hat,
And I'll give you a slice of bacon;
And when I bake,
I'll give you a cake,
If I am not mistaken.

I Went to the Toad

See "Multiple Animals" chapter, Nursery Rhymes section.

The Moon Is Up

See "Multiple Animals" chapter, Nursery Rhymes section.

Poetry

The Moon

See "Multiple Animals" chapter, Poetry section.

Twinkle, Twinkle, Little Bat (Lewis Carroll, PreS/K–5/6+)*

Twinkle, twinkle, little bat!
How I wonder what you're at!
Up above the world you fly,
Like a tea-tray in the sky.

* Note: This rhyme was recited by the Mad Hatter in the novel "Alice in Wonderland."

A White Hen Sitting

See "Chickens" chapter, Poetry section.

From *The Big Book of Animal Rhymes, Fingerplays, and Songs* by Elizabeth Cothen Low.
Westport, CT: Libraries Unlimited. Copyright © 2009.

BEARS

Fingerplays and Action Rhymes

Bear Hunt (Traditional, PreS/K–5)

(Also known as **Let's Go on a Bear Hunt**)

We're going on a bear hunt! (Have entire group of kids stand up and march in place.)
We're going to catch a bear!
Oh, wait! I see a tree. (Place hand on forehead, palm facing the floor, and peer out.)
Can't go over it. (Hold hand up high.)
Can't go under it. (Touch the floor.)
Better climb up it. (Pretend to climb up tree.)

We're going on a bear hunt! (Have group of kids stand up and march in place.)
We're going to catch a bear!
Oh, wait! I see some water. (Place hand on forehead, palm facing the floor, and peer out.)
Can't go over it. (Hold hand up high.)
Can't go under it. (Touch the floor.)
Better swim through it. (Make swimming motions.)

We're going on a bear hunt! (Have group of kids stand up and march in place.)
We're going to catch a bear!
Oh, wait! I see a mountain. (Place hand on forehead, palm facing the floor, and peer out.)
Can't go under it. (Touch the floor.)
Can't go through it. (Press outward with hand.)
Better go over it. (March with more effort. Wipe head with hand.)

We're going on a bear hunt! (Have group of kids stand up and march in place.)
We're going to catch a bear!
Oh, wait! I see a cave. (Place hand on forehead, palm facing the floor, and peer out.)
Can't go over it. (Hold hand up high.)
Can't go under it. (Touch the floor.)
Better go in it. (March more slowly.)

I think I feel something. (Grope around with hands.)
It has fur, two eyes, and a big wet nose.
It's a bear! Run! (Everyone runs in place.)
Run out of the cave!
Over the mountain! (Run with more effort. Wipe head with hand.)
Through the water! (Make swimming motions.)
Climb up the tree! (Make climbing motions.)
Under the bed! (Collapse in fetal position.)
We made it!

Suggestion: Have children walk through other places, such as mud or a wheat field.

From *The Big Book of Animal Rhymes, Fingerplays, and Songs* by Elizabeth Cothen Low.
Westport, CT: Libraries Unlimited. Copyright © 2009.

Bears in a Cave (Traditional PreS/K–5)

Here is a cave. (Place right fist inside left fist.)
Inside there are bears. (Wiggle right hand fingers under left palm.)
Now they come out (Hold right fingers up, put left hand down.)
To get some fresh air.

They stay out all summer
Its sunshine and heat.
And hunt in the forest
For berries to eat. (Mime eating berries.)

When the snow starts to fall, (Wiggle right hand fingers over left fist.)
They hurry inside (Place right fingers inside left fist again.)
Their warm little cave,
And there they will hide.

Snow covers the cave (Have right hand cover left fist.)
Like a fluffy white rug.
Inside the bears sleep, (Place palms together and place on side of head.)
All cozy and snug.

Fuzzy Wuzzy Was a Bear (Traditional, B/T/PreS)

Fuzzy wuzzy was a bear (Cup hands to ears to make bear ears.)
Fuzzy wuzzy had no hair (Touch head.)
If fuzzy wuzzy had no hair,
He wasn't fuzzy, was he? (Shake head "no.")

Round and Round the Garden (Traditional, B/T)

Round and round the garden (Have your fingers go round child's wrist.)
Like a Teddy Bear.
One step, (Have your fingers walk up child's arm.)
Two steps,
Tickly under there. (Tickle child under armpit.)

Teddy Bear, Teddy Bear Turn Around (Traditional, B/T/PreS/K–5)

Teddy bear, teddy bear,
Turn around. (Stand up and turn around.)
Teddy bear, teddy bear,
Touch the ground. (Touch floor.)
Teddy bear, teddy bear,
Touch your shoe. (Touch shoe.)
Teddy bear, teddy bear,
That will do.

Teddy bear, teddy bear,
Go upstairs. (Pretend to climb stairs.)
Teddy bear, teddy bear,
Say your prayers. (Place palms together.)
Teddy bear, teddy bear,

8

Turn out the light. (Pretend to pull cord.)
Teddy bear, teddy bear,
Say good night. (Place palms together and place on side of head.)

Nursery Rhymes

The Man in the Moon (Traditional, PreS/K–5)

The Man in the Moon as he sails the sky
Is a very remarkable skipper,
But he made a mistake when he tried to take
A drink of milk from the Dipper.

He dipped right out of the Milky Way,
And slowly and carefully filled it,
The Big Bear growled, and the Little Bear howled
And frightened him so that he spilled it!

Songs

The Bear Went Over the Mountain (Traditional, B/T/PreS/K–5)

Second Verse: Oh, the bear went over the mountain,
The bear went over the mountain,
The bear went over the mountain,
To see what he could see.

And all that he could see,
And all that he could see,
Was the other side of the mountain,
The other side of the mountain,
The other side of the mountain,
The other side of the mountain,
Was all that he could see.

Poetry

Kindness to Animals

See "Multiple Animals" chapter, Poetry section.

The Polar Bear (Hilaire Belloc, K–5/6+)

The Polar Bear is unaware
Of cold that cuts me through:
For why? He has a coat of hair,
I wish I had one too!

There Was an Old Person of Ware (Edward Lear, K–5/6+)

There was an old person of Ware
Who rode on the back of a bear;
When they said, "Does it trot?"
He said: "Certainly not,
It's a Moppsikon Floppsikon bear."

BEES

Fingerplays and Action Rhymes

Bumblebee (Traditional, B/T)

Bumblebee was in the barn, (Make circles with finger in the air.)
Carrying his dinner under his arm.
Bzzzzz . . . . (Poke or tickle child.)

Here Is a Nest for the Robin

See "Multiple Animals" chapter, Fingerplays and Action Rhymes section

Here Is the Beehive (Emilie Poulsson, PreS/K–5)

Here is the beehive; (Loosely fold hands together.)
Where are the bees? (Peek inside hands.)
Hidden away where nobody sees.
Soon they come creeping out of the hive—
One, two, three, four, five! (Have fingers of right hand push through cupped left hand, starting with
    index finger and ending with thumb.)
Buzz-z-z-z-z-z-z-z-z! (Have fingers fly away.)

What Do You Suppose? (Traditional, PreS/K–5)

What do you suppose?
A bee sat on my nose. (Place right finger on nose.)
Then what do you think?
He gave me a wink (Wink.)
And said, "I beg your pardon,
I thought you were the garden." (Have finger "fly" away from nose.)

Nursery Rhymes

As I Was Going Over Tipple Tine (Traditional, Riddle, K–5/6+)

As I was going over Tipple Tine,
I met a flock of bonny swine;
Some green-lapped,
Some green-backed,
They were the very bonniest swine
That ever went over Tipple Tine.

Answer: A Swarm of Bees

Burnie Bee (Traditional PreS/K–5)

Burnie bee, burnie bee,
Tell me when your wedding be?
If it be tomorrow day,
Take your wings and fly away.

If Bees Stay at Home (Traditional, Saying, PreS/K–5)

If bees stay at home,
Rain will soon come;
If they fly away,
Fine will be the day.

Puss Came Dancing

See "Multiple Animals" chapter, Nursery Rhymes section.

Rockabye, Lullaby (Traditional, PreS/K–5)

Rockaby, lullaby, bees on the clover!
Crooning so drowsily, crying so low,
Rockaby, lullaby, dear little rover!
Down into wonderland,
Down to the under-land,
Go, oh go!
Down into wonderland, go!

A Swarm of Bees in May (Traditional, PreS/K–5/6+)

A swarm of bees in May,
Is worth a load of hay;
A swarm of bees in June,
Is worth a silver spoon;
A swarm of bees in July,
Isn't worth a fly.

Uprising See the Fitful Lark

See "Multiple Animals" chapter,
Nursery Rhymes section.

Songs

Down by the Bay

See "Multiple Animals" chapter, Songs section.

I'm Bringing Home a Baby Bumblebee (Traditional, PreS/K–5/6+)

Verse 2: I'm squishing up the baby bumblebee,
Won't my mommy be so proud of me.
I'm squishing up a baby bumblebee
Spoken: "Ooh! Yucky, it's all over me!"

Verse 3: I'm wiping off the baby bumblebee,
Won't my mommy be so proud of me.
I'm wiping off the baby bumblebee,
"And there's mommy!"

Over in the Meadow

See "Multiple Animals" chapter, Songs section.

Poetry

When the Cows Come Home the Milk Is Coming

See "Multiple Animals" chapter, Poetry section.

 BIRDS

See also the following chapters:
"Chickens," "Ducks," "Geese," "Owls," "Parrots," "Peacocks," Penguins"

Fingerplays and Action Rhymes

As Little Jenny Wren (Traditional, PreS/K–5)

As Little Jenny Wren (Stay seated for rhyme.)
Was sitting by her shed,
She waggled with her tail, (Place palms together in back of body. Move them back and forth like a tail.)
And nodded with her head. (Nod head.)

She waggled with her tail, (Place palms together in back of body. Move them back and forth like a tail.)
And nodded with her head, (Nod head.)
As little Jenny Wren
Was sitting by the shed.

Can You Hop Like a Rabbit?

See "Multiple Animals" chapter, Fingerplays and Action Rhymes section.

The Dove Says, "Coo" (Traditional, PreS/K–5)

The dove says, "Coo,
What shall I do?
I can scare maintain two." (Show two fingers.)
"Pooh, pooh," says the wren,
"I've got ten (Hold up all ten fingers.)
And keep them all like gentlemen!"

Five Little Birds without Any Home (Traditional, PreS/K–5)

Five little birds without any home (Hold up five fingers on right hand.)
Five little trees in a row (Hold up five fingers on left hand.)
Come build your nests in our branches tall
We'll rock them to and fro. (Cup hands together and rock back and forth.)

Five Little Chickadees Peeping at the Door (Traditional, B/T/PreS)

(Also known as Five Little Chickadees Sitting at the Door)

Five little chickadees
Peeping at the door; (Hold up all five fingers.)
One flew away,
And then there were four. (Fold down one finger at a time, starting with thumb.)
Four little chickadees
Sitting on a tree;

One flew away,
Then there were three.
Three little chickadees
Looking at you;
One flew away,
And then there were two.
Two little chickadees
Sitting in the sun;
One flew away,
And then there was one.
One little chickadee
Left all alone;
One flew away,
And then there were none.

Five Little Robins Lived in a Tree (Traditional, B/T/PreS)

Five little robins lived in a tree,
Father, Mother, (Tug on thumb and index finger.)
And babies three, (Tug on middle and ring fingers, and pinky.)
Father caught a worm, (Tug on thumb.)
Mother caught a bug, (Tug on index finger.)
This one got the bug, (Tug on middle finger.)
This one got the worm, (Tug on ring finger.)
This one said, "Now it's my turn!" (Tug on pinky.)

Frogs Jump

See "Multiple Animals" chapter, Fingerplays and Action Rhymes section.

Here Are Two Telegraph Poles (Traditional, PreS/K–5)

(Also known as **Two Tall Telephone Poles**)
Here are two telegraph poles. (Hold up index fingers.)
Between them a wire strung, (With index fingers still raised, touch middle fingers together.)
Two little birds hopped on (Put thumbs on top of middle fingers.)
To and fro, to and fro,
They hopped on the wire and swung. (Swing hands forward and backward.)

Here Is a Nest for the Robin

See "Multiple Animals" chapter, Fingerplay and Action Rhymes section.

If I Were a Bird, I'd Sing a Song (Traditional PreS/K–5)

If I were a bird, I'd sing a song,
And fly about the whole day long, (Place thumbs together and wiggle rest of fingers, moving hands
     in a circular motion.)
And when the night came,
Go to rest, up in my cozy nest. (Cup hands together and rock back and forth.)

A Little Boy's Walk

See "Multiple Animals" chapter, Fingerplay and Action Rhymes section.

Little Robin Redbreast (Traditional, PreS/K–5)

Little Robin Redbreast,
Sat upon a rail: (Fold down three middle fingers and hold up thumb and pinky.)
Niddle, noddle went his head, (Move thumb back and forth.)
Wibble, wobble went his tail. (Move pinky back and forth.)

My Pigeon House I Open Wide (Traditional, PreS/K–5)

My pigeon house I open wide (Open fingers wide.)
And I set my pigeons free.
They fly around on every side (Place thumbs together and move hands in a circular motion.)
And in the highest tree. (Place hands up high.)
And when they return
From their merry flight, (Close fists, one hand on top on the other.)
They close their eyes
And sing,
Coo, Coo, Coo.

Once I Saw a Little Bird (Traditional, PreS/K–5)

Once I saw a little bird (Make right fist and stick out thumb and pinky.)
Come hop, hop, hop; (Move hand up and down.)
So I cried, "Little bird,
Will you stop, stop, stop?" (Wave right index finger as if scolding.)
I was going to the window
To say, "How do you do?" (Wave.)
But he shook his little tail, (Make right fist and stick out thumb and pinky. Wiggle pinky.)
And far away he flew. (Have right hand "fly" away.)

The Sparrows (Emilie Poulsson, K–5)

"Little brown sparrows,
Flying around, (Place thumbs together and wiggle fingers.)
Up in the treetops, (Raise hands in the air.)
Down on the ground, (Put hands on the ground.)
Come to my window, (Put left and right index fingers and left and right thumbs together to form a box.)
Dear sparrows, come!
See! I will give you
Many a crumb. (Hold palm upward.)

Here is some water, (Cup hands.)
Sparkling and clear;
Come, little sparrows,
Drink without fear.
If you are tired,
Here is a nest; (Interlock left and right fingers, leaving a hollow between palms.)
Wouldn't you like to
Come here to rest?"

All the brown sparrows
Flutter away, (Place thumbs together and wiggle fingers)
Chirping and singing,
"We cannot stay;

For in the treetops,
Among the gray boughs,
There is the sparrows'
Snug little house." (Form tent by placing fingertips of both fingers together.)

Two Little Dicky Birds (Traditional, B/T/PreS/K–5)

Two little dicky birds (Hold up two index fingers.)
Sitting on a wall,
One named Peter, (Wiggle first finger.)
One named Paul. (Wiggle second finger.)
Fly away, Peter! (Hide first finger behind back.)
Fly away, Paul! (Hide second finger behind back.)
Come back, Peter! (Hold up first finger.)
Come back, Paul! (Hold up second finger.)

Two Little Blackbirds (Traditional B/T/PreS/K–5)

Two little blackbirds
Sitting on a hill, (Hold up index fingers.)
One named Jack, (Hold up right index finger.)
One named Jill. (Hold up left index finger.)
Fly away, Jack! (Hide right hand behind back.)
Fly away, Jill! (Hide left hand behind back.)
Come back, Jack! (Hold up right index finger.)
Come back, Jill! (Hold up left index finger.)

When a Robin Cocks His Head (Traditional, PreS/K–5)

When a robin cocks his head (Tilt head to side.)
Sideways in a flower bed,
He can hear the tiny sound (Cup hand around ear.)
Of a worm beneath the ground.

Nursery Rhymes

All in a Row (Traditional, K–5/6+)

All of a row,
Bend the bow,
Shot at a pigeon,
And killed a crow.

As I Walked over the Hill One Day

See "Multiple Animals" chapter, Nursery Rhymes section.

Away, Birds, Away (Traditional, K–5/6+)

Away, birds, away,
Take a little, and leave a little,
And do not come again;
For if you do,
I will shoot you through,
And there is an end of you.

From *The Big Book of Animal Rhymes, Fingerplays, and Songs* by Elizabeth Cothen Low.
Westport, CT: Libraries Unlimited. Copyright © 2009.

Birds of a Feather Flock Together

See "Multiple Animals" chapter, Nursery Rhymes section.

"Bow-Wow," Says the Dog

See "Multiple Animals" chapter, Nursery Rhymes section.

Catch Him, Crow (Traditional, PreS/K–5)

Catch him, crow! Carry him, kite!
Take him away 'til the apples are ripe;
When they are ripe and ready to fall,
Here comes Johnny, apples, and all.

A Carrion Crow Sat on an Oak (Traditional, K–5/6+)

A carrion crow sat on an oak,
Watching a tailor shape his cloak.
"Wife," cried he, "bring me my bow,
That I may shoot yon carrion crow!"

The tailor shot and missed his mark;
And shot his own sow through the heart;
"Wife, bring some brandy in a spoon,
For our old sow is in a swoon."

Cherries (Traditional, K–5/6+)

Under the trees, the farmer said,
Smiling and shaking his wise old head:
"Cherries are ripe! but then, you know,
There's the grass to cut and the corn to hoe;
We can gather the cherries any day,
But when the sun shines we must make our hay;
To-night, when the work has all been done,
We'll muster the boys, for fruit and fun."

Up on the tree a robin said,
Perking and cocking his saucy head,
"Cherries are ripe! and so to-day
We'll gather them while you make the hay;
For we are the boys with no corn to hoe,
No cows to milk, and no grass to mow."
At night the farmer said: "Here's a trick
These roguish robins have had their pick."

The Coming of Spring (Traditional, K–5/6+)

The birds are coming home soon;
I look for them every day;
I listen to catch the first wild strain,
For they must be singing by May.

The bluebird, he'll come first, you know,
Like a violet that has taken wings;
And the red-breast trills while his nest he builds;
I can hum the song that he sings.
And the crocus and wind flower are coming, too;
They're already upon the way;
When the sun warms the brown earth through and through,
I shall look for them any day.

Then be patient, and wait a little, my dear;
"They're coming," the winds repeat;
"We're coming! we're coming!" I'm sure I hear,
From the grass blades that grow at my feet.

Cuckoo, Cuckoo (Traditional, PreS/K–5)

Cuckoo, cuckoo
What do you do?
In April,
I open my bill;
In May,
I sing night and day;
In June,
I change my tune;
In July,
Away I fly;
In August,
Away I must.

Cuckoo, Cuckoo, Cherry Tree (Traditional, PreS/K–5)

Cuckoo, cuckoo, cherry tree,
Catch a bird, and give it to me;
Let the tree be high or low,
Let it hail, or rain, or snow.

The Cuckoo's a Fine Bird (Traditional, PreS/K–5)

The cuckoo's a fine bird,
He sings as she flies;
He brings good tidings.
He tells us no lies.

He sucks little birds' eggs,
To make his voice clear;
And when he sings "cuckoo!"
The summer is near.

Eat, Birds, Eat (Traditional, PreS/K–5)

Eat, birds, eat, and make no waste,
I lie here and make no haste;
If my master chance to come,
You must fly, and I must run.

Elizabeth, Elspeth, Betsey, and Bess (Traditional PreS/K–5)

Elizabeth, Elspeth, Betsy, and Bess,
They all went together to seek a bird's nest;
They found a bird's nest with five eggs in,
They all took one, and left four in.

Every Crow (Traditional, K–5, 6+)

Every crow thinks her own young the whitest.

A Farmer Went Trotting (Traditional, K-5/6+)

(Also known as **The Mischievous Magpie**)
A farmer went trotting upon his gray mare,
Bumpety, bumpety, bump!
With his daughter behind him so rosy and fair;
Lumpety, lumpety, lump!

A raven cried, "Croak!"
And they all tumbled down,
Bumpety, bumpety, bump!
The mare broke her knees, and the farmer his crown,
Lumpety, lumpety, lump!

The mischievous raven flew laughing away,
Bumpety, bumpety, bump!
And vowed he would serve them the same the next day,
Lumpety, lumpety, lump!

Fishes Swim in Water Clear

See "Multiple Animals" chapter, Nursery Rhymes section.

The Friendly Beasts

See "Multiple Animals" chapter, Nursery Rhymes section.

Go to Bed First (Traditional, PreS/K–5)

Go to bed first,
A golden purse;
Go to bed second,
A golden pheasant;
Go to bed third,
A golden bird!

A Grey-Hound Invited a Green-Finch to Tea

See "Multiple Animals" chapter, Nursery Rhymes section.

Jenny Wren Fell Sick (Traditional, 6+)

Jenny Wren fell sick
Upon a merry time,
In came Robin Redbreast
And brought her soup and wine.

"Eat well of the soup, Jenny,
Drink well of the wine."
"Thank you, Robin, kindly,
You shall be mine."

Jenny Wren got well,
And stood upon her feet;
And told Robin plainly,
She loved him not a bit.
Robin he got angry,
And hopped upon a twig,
Saying, "Out upon you, fie* upon you,
Bold faced jig*!"

* Fie: Expression of disapproval
* Jig: Racial slur

I Had Two Pigeons Bright and Gay (Traditional, PreS/K–5)

I had two pigeons bright and gay,
They flew from me the other day;
What was the reason they did go?
I cannot tell for I do not know.

I'm Called by the Name of a Man (Traditional, Riddle, K–5, 6+)

I'm called by the name of a man.
Yet am as little as a mouse;
When winter comes I love to be
With my red target near the house.

Answer: Robin

In the Month of February

See "Multiple Animals" chapter, Nursery Rhymes section.

Little Bob Robin (Traditional, PreS/K–5)

Little Bob Robin,
Where do you live?
Up in yonder wood, sir,
On a hazel twig.

Little Cock Robin (Traditional, PreS/K–5)

Little cock robin peeped out of his cabin,
To see the cold winter come in,
Tit, for tat, what matter for that,
He'll hide his head under his wing!

Little Piggy Wiggy

See "Multiple Animals" chapter, Nursery Rhymes section.

Little Robin Redbreast Sat upon a Tree

See Songs section in this chapter.

A Man of Words and Not of Deeds

See "Multiple Animals" chapter, Nursery Rhymes section.

Mary Had a Pretty Bird

See Songs section in this chapter.

The Moon Is Up

See "Multiple Animals" chapter, Nursery Rhymes section.

My Dame Hath a Lame Tame Crane (Traditional, PreS/K–5)

My dame hath a lame tame crane,
My dame hath a crane that is lame.
Pray, gentle Jane, let my dame's tame crane
Feed and come home again.

Nineteen Birds

See Songs section in this chapter.

The North Wind Doth Blow

See Songs section in this chapter.

On Christmas Eve (Traditional, PreS/K–5)

On Christmas Eve I turned the spit,*
I burnt my fingers, I feel it yet;
The cock sparrow flew over the table;
The pot began to play with the ladle.

* Spit: "Rod for holding meat over a fire" (http://www.merriam-webster.com)

On the First of March (Traditional, PreS/K–5)

On the first of March,
The crows begin to search;
On the first of April
They are sitting still;
By the first of May
They've all flown away,
Coming greedy back again
With October's wind and rain.

The Panther

See "Multiple Animals" chapter, Nursery Rhymes section.

A Pie Sat on a Pear Tree (Traditional, PreS/K–5)

A pie sat on a pear tree,
A pie sat on a pear tree,
A pie sat on a pear tree,
Heigh ho, heigh ho, heigh ho.
Once so merrily hopped she,
Twice so merrily hopped she,
Thrice so merrily hopped she.
Heigh ho, heigh ho, heigh ho.

Pit, Pat, Well-a-Day (Traditional, B/T/ PreS/K–5)

Pit, pat, well-a-day,
Little Robin flew away.
Where can little Robin be?
Gone into the cherry tree.

Polly Piper Plucked a Pigeon

See "Multiple Animals" chapter, Nursery Rhymes section.

Riddle Me, Riddle Me Ree (Traditional, PreS/K–5)

Riddle me, riddle me ree,
A hawk sat up in a tree;
And he says to himself, says he,
Lord! What a fine bird I be!

The Robin and the Redbreast (Traditional, Sayings, K–5/6+)

The robin and the redbreast,
The robin and the wren,
If you take them from their nest,
Ye'll never thrive again.

The robin and the redbreast,
The martin and the swallow,
If you touch one of their eggs,
Ill luck is sure to follow.

The Robin and the Wren (Traditional, PreS/K–5)

The robin and the wren,
They fought upon the parrage˙ pan;
But ere the robin got a spoon,
The wren had eat the parrage down.

˙Parrage: An alternate spelling for porridge

See Saw! (Traditional, K–5, 6+)

See saw! A little Jackdaw,
On the church-steeple, sat crying out "Caw!"
When the bells began to ring,

From *The Big Book of Animal Rhymes, Fingerplays, and Songs* by Elizabeth Cothen Low.
Westport, CT: Libraries Unlimited. Copyright © 2009.

The little Jackdaw he took wing,
And said he thought it vastly wrong,
The noisy bells should spoil his song!

See saw! A little Jackdaw,
Filled his bill with hay and straw!
Up he flew and crammed it tightly,
In the bells that rang so sprightly,
And when he their sound had stopped,
Again up to the steeple hopped!

See saw! The little Jackdaw,
In triumph sat, and cried out "Caw!"
High the wind began to blow,
Which rocked the steeple to and fro,
Till down it fell, with church and all,
And killed the Jackdaw in the fall!

Sing, Little Bird (Traditional, PreS/K–5)

Sing, little bird, when the skies are blue,
Sing, for the world has need of you,
Sing when the skies are overcast,
Sing when the rain is falling fast.

Sing, happy heart, when the sun is warm,
Sing in the winter's coldest storm,
Sing little songs, O heart so true,
Sing, for the world has need of you.

Swallow, Swallow (Traditional, PreS/K–5)

Swallow, Swallow, neighbor Swallow,
Starting on your autumn flight,
Pause a moment at my window,
Twitter softly a good night.

Now the summer days are ended,
All your duties are well done,
And the little homes you've builded
Have grown empty, one by one.
Swallow, Swallow, neighbor Swallow,
Are you ready for your flight?
Are the little coats completed?
Are the feathered caps all right?

Are the young wings strong and steady
For their flight to warmer sky?
Come again in early springtime.
Until then, good-by, good-by.

There Was a Fat Man of Bombay (Traditional, PreS/K–5)

There was a fat man of Bombay,
Who was smoking one sunshiny day
When a bird called a snipe,
Flew away with his pipe,
Which vexed the fat man of Bombay.

There Was a Monkey Climbed a Tree

See "Multiple Animals" chapter, Nursery Rhymes section.

There Was an Old Crow (Traditional, K–5/6+)

There was an old crow
Sat upon a clod;*
That's the end of my song.
That's odd!

* Clod: A mound of dirt

There Was a One-Eyed Gunner (Traditional K–5/6+)

There was a one-eyed gunner,
Who killed all the birds that died last summer.

Tweedledum and Tweedledee (Traditional, PreS/K–5)

Tweedledum and Tweedledee
Agreed to have a battle,
For Tweedledum said Tweedledee
Had spoilt his nice new rattle.

Just then flew by a monstrous crow
As big as a tar-barrel,
Which frightened both the heroes so,
They quite forgot their quarrel.

There Were Two Birds That Once Sat on a Stone

See Songs section in this chapter.

Uprising See the Fitful Lark

See "Multiple Animals" chapter, Nursery Rhymes section.

The Whango Tree (Traditional, Nonsense Verse, 6+).

The woggly bird sat on the whango tree,
Nooping the rinkum corn,
And graper and graper, alas! grew he,
And cursed the day he was born.
His crute was clum and his voice was rum,
As curiously thus sang he,
"Oh, would I'd been rammed and eternally clammed
Ere I perched on this whango tree."

From *The Big Book of Animal Rhymes, Fingerplays, and Songs* by Elizabeth Cothen Low.
Westport, CT: Libraries Unlimited. Copyright © 2009.

Now the whango tree had a bubbly thorn,
As sharp as a nootie's bill,
And it stuck in the woggly bird's umptum lorn
And weepadge, the smart did thrill.
He fumbled and cursed, but that wasn't the worst,
For he couldn't at all get free,
And he cried, "I am gammed, and injustibly nammed
On the luggardly whango tree."

And there he sits still, with no worm in his bill,
Nor no guggledom in his nest;
He is hungry and bare, and gobliddered with care,
And his grabbles give him no rest;
He is weary and sore and his tugmut is soar,
And nothing to nob has he,
As he chirps, "I am blammed and corruptibly jammed,
In this cuggerdom whango tree."

When the Snow Is on the Ground

See Songs section in this chapter.

The White Dove Sat on the Castle Wall (Traditional, K-5/6+)

The white dove sat on the castle wall,
I bend my bow and shoot her I shall;
I put her in my glove both feathers and all;
I laid my bridle upon the shelf,
If you will any more, sing it yourself.

Who Killed Cock Robin? (Traditional, K–5, 6+)

Who killed Cock Robin?
"I," said the Sparrow,
"With my bow and arrow,
I killed Cock Robin."

"Who saw him die?"
"I," said the Fly,
"With my little eye,
I saw him die."

"Who caught his blood?"
"I," said the Fish,
"With my little dish,
I caught his blood."

"Who'll make his shroud?"
"I," said the Beetle,
"With my little needle,
I'll make the shroud."

"Who'll dig his grave?"
"I," said the owl,
"With my spade and shovel,
I'll dig his grave."

"Who'll be the parson?"
"I," said the rook,
"With my little book,
I'll be the parson."

"Who'll be the clerk?"
"I," said the lark,
"If it's not in the dark,
I'll be the clerk."

"Who'll carry the torch?"
"I," said the linnet.
"I'll come in a minute.
I'll carry the torch."

"Who'll carry the coffin?"
"I," said the kite,
"If it's not through the night,
I'll carry the coffin."

"Who'll be the chief mourner?"
"I," said the dove,
"I mourn for my love.
I'll be chief mourner."

"Who will bear the pall?"
"We," said the wren,
"Both the cock and the hen,
We will bear the pall."

"Who'll sing a psalm?"
"I," said the thrush,
"As she sat on a bush,
I'll sing a psalm."

"Who'll toll the bell?"
"I," said the Bull,
"Because I can pull,
I'll toll the bell."

All the birds of the air
Fell to sighing and sobbing,
When they heard the bell toll
For poor Cock Robin.

Who Stole the Bird's Nest? (Traditional, K–5, 6+)

"Tu-whit! Tu-whit! Tu-whee!
Will you listen to me?
Who stole four eggs I laid,
And the nice nest I made?"
"Not I," said the cow, "Moo-oo!
Such a thing I'd never do,
I gave you a wisp of hay,
But didn't take your nest away.
Not I," said the cow, "Moo-oo!
Such a thing I'd never do."

"Tu-whit! Tu-whit! Tu-whee!
Will you listen to me?
Who stole four eggs I laid,
And the nice nest I made?"
"Not I," said the dog, "Bow-wow!
I'm not so mean anyhow!
I gave hairs the nest to make,
But the nest I did not take.
Not I," said the dog, "Bow-wow!
I'm not so mean, I vow."

"Tu-whit! Tu-whit! Tu-whee!
Will you listen to me?
Who stole four eggs I laid,
And the nice nest I made?"
"Coo-coo! Coo-coo! Coo-coo!
Let me speak a few words too!
Who stole that pretty nest
From poor little yellowbreast?"
"Not I," said the sheep, "Oh, no!
I wouldn't treat a poor bird so.
I gave wool the nest to line,
But the nest was none of mine.
Baa! Baa!" said the sheep, "Oh, no!
I wouldn't treat a poor bird so."

"Tu-whit! Tu-whit! Tu-whee!
Will you listen to me?
Who stole four eggs I laid,
And the nice nest I made?"
"Coo-coo! Coo-coo! Coo-coo!
Let me speak a few words too!
Who stole that pretty nest
From poor little yellowbreast?"
"Caw! Caw!" cried the crow;
"I too should like to know
What thief took away
A bird's nest to-day?"

From *The Big Book of Animal Rhymes, Fingerplays, and Songs* by Elizabeth Cothen Low.
Westport, CT: Libraries Unlimited. Copyright © 2009.

"Cluck! Cluck!" said the hen;
"Don't ask me again.
Why, I haven't a chick
Would do such a trick.
We all gave her a feather,
And she wove them together.
I'd scorn to intrude
On her and her brood.
Cluck! Cluck!" said the hen;
"Don't ask me again."

"Chirr-a-whirr! Chirr-a-whirr!
All the birds make a stir!
Let us find out his name,
And all cry, 'For shame!' "
"I would not rob a bird,"
Said little Mary Green;
"I think I never heard
Of anything so mean."

"It is very cruel, too,"
Said little Alice Neal;
"I wonder if he knew
How sad the birds would feel?"

A little boy hung down his head,
And went and hid behind the bed;
For he stole that pretty nest
From poor little yellowbreast;
And he felt so full of shame,
He didn't like to tell his name.

The Winds They Did Blow (Traditional, K–5, 6+)

The winds they did blow,
The leaves they did wag;
Along came a beggar boy,
And put me in his bag.

He took me up to London,
A lady did me buy,
Put me in a silver cage,
And hung me up on high.

With apples by the fire,
And nuts for to crack,
Besides a little feather bed
To rest my little back.

Why Is Pussy in Bed?

See "Multiple Animals" chapter, Nursery Rhymes section.

Songs

Animal Fair

See "Multiple Animals" chapter, Songs section.

The Boy and the Cuckoo (Traditional, K–5/ 6+)

A lit - tle boy went out to sho - ot one day, And carr - ried his ar - rows and bow: For gun - s are dan - ger - ous play - things, they say, In the hands of small chil - dren you know, A lit - tle bird sat on a cher - ry tree, And whist - led and said, "No you can't shoot me." Cuc -koo, cuc - koo, cuc -koo, cuc - koo, cuc -koo, cuc - koo, cuck -oo.

Verse 2:   The little boy drew up his bow to his eye,
And aimed it right straight for a-while:
The little bird laughed and away it did fly,
"A miss is as good as a mile."
The little boy threw down his bow and cried,
The little bird laughed till it almost died.
Cuckoo, cuckoo, cuckoo, cuckoo, cuckoo, cuckoo,
Cuckoo.

Cock Robin and Jenny Wren (Traditional, K–5/ 6+)

(Also known as **Cock Robin Got Up Early**)

"Twas in a mer - ry time, When Jen - ny Wren was you - ng, So

neat - ly as she danc' d And so sweet - ly as she sung, Rob - in Red - breast lost his

hea - rt, He was a gal - lant bird, He doff'd his cap to Jen - ny Wren, re

-quest - ing to be heart.

Verse 2:   "My dearest Jennie Wren,
          If you will but be mine,
          You shall dine on cherry pie,
          And drink nice currant wine;
          I'll dress you like a goldfinch,
          Or like a peacock gay,
          So if you'll have me Jenny, dear,
          Let us appoint the day."

Verse 3:   Jenny blush'd behind her fan
          And thus declared her mind,
          "So let it be tomorrow, Rob,
          I'll take your offer kind
          Cherry pie is very good
          And so is currant wine,
          But I will wear my plain brown gown,
          And never dress up fine."

Verse 4:   Robin Redbreast got up early,
          All at the break of day,
          He flew to Jenny Wren's house,
          And sang a roundelay;
          He sang of Robin Redbreast

From *The Big Book of Animal Rhymes, Fingerplays, and Songs* by Elizabeth Cothen Low.
Westport, CT: Libraries Unlimited. Copyright © 2009.

And pretty Jenny Wren,
And when he came unto the end,
He thus began again.

Cuckoo! (Traditional, K–5/ 6+)

Cuc - koo! Cuc koo! Pret - ty bird say; Cuc - koo! Cuc - koo! Pri - thee so gay? Cuc - koo! Cuc - koo! I loud - ly sing, The near ap -proach of our friend Mis - tress Spring Ah! dear Mis - tress Spring.

Verse 2: Cuckoo! Cuckoo! You at the best,
Cuckoo! Cuckoo! Are but a guest,
Cuckoo! Cuckoo! No sooner here
Than you are gone, till the following year.
Ah! Gone till next year.

Verse 3: Cuckoo! Cuckoo! We almost cry
Cuckoo! Cuckoo! Saying good-bye!
Cuckoo! Cuckoo! Promise, dear, do,
Not to forget us, we shan't forget you!
Ah! Cuckoo! Adieu!

The Green Grass Grew All Around (Traditional, PreS/K–5)

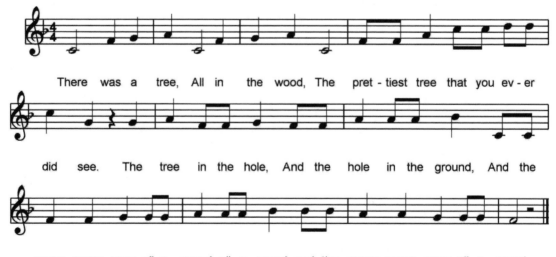

There was a tree, All in the wood, The pret - tiest tree that you ev - er did see. The tree in the hole, And the hole in the ground, And the green grass grew all a -round all a - round and the green grass grew all a -round.

From *The Big Book of Animal Rhymes, Fingerplays, and Songs* by Elizabeth Cothen Low.
Westport, CT: Libraries Unlimited. Copyright © 2009.

Verse 2:   And on that tree,
There was a limb,
The prettiest little limb,
That you ever did see.
The limb on the tree,
And the tree in a hole,
And the hole in the ground
And the green grass grew
All around, all around,
And the green grass grew all around.
And on that limb, (repeat)
There was a branch . . . (continue same as above)

And on that branch, (repeat)
There was a nest . . .

And in that nest, (repeat)
There was an egg . . .
And in that egg, (repeat)
There was a bird . . .

And on that bird, (repeat)
There was a wing . . .

And on that wing, (repeat)
There was a feather . . .

Hush, Little Baby, Don't Say a Word

See "Multiple Animals" chapter, Songs section.

Jaybird (Traditional, African American folksong, 6+)

From *The Big Book of Animal Rhymes, Fingerplays, and Songs* by Elizabeth Cothen Low.
Westport, CT: Libraries Unlimited. Copyright © 2009.

I love them short - en gals! I love them short - en gal! O have mer - cy

on my soul!

Verse 2: That Jaybird a-setting on a swinging limb.
He wink at me and I wink at him.
He laugh at me when my gun 'crack';
It kick me down on the flat of my back.

Verse 3: Next day the Jaybird dance that limb,
I grabbed my gun for to shoot at him.
When I "crack" down, it split my chin.
"Ole Aggie Cunjer" fly like sin.

Verse 4: Way down yonder at the rising sun.
Jaybird a talking with a forked tongue,
He's been down there where the bad men dwell—
"Ole Friday Devil," fare-you-well!

Note: Ole Aggie Cunjer refers to a witch woman. It was believed that jaybirds could not be found on Friday because they went to carry sand to the Devil (Botsford, 1922).

I Know an Old Lady Who Swallowed a Fly

See "Multiple Animals" chapter, Songs section.

A Little Cock Sparrow Sat on a Green Tree (Traditional, K–5/6+)

A lit - tle cock spar - row sat down on a tree, And

he chir - rupped, he chir - rupped, so merry was he; A

lit - tle cock spar - row sat down on a tree, And he chir - rupped, he chir - rupped,

so merry was he.

A naughty boy came with his wee bow and arrow,
Determined to shoot this little cock-sparrow.
A naughty boy came with his wee bow and arrow,
Determined to shoot this little cock-sparrow.
"This little cock-sparrow shall make me a stew,
And his giblets shall make me a little pie, too."
"Oh, no!" said the sparrow, "I won't make a stew."
So he flapped his wings, and away he flew.

Little Robin Redbreast Sat Upon a Tree (Traditional, PreS/K–5)

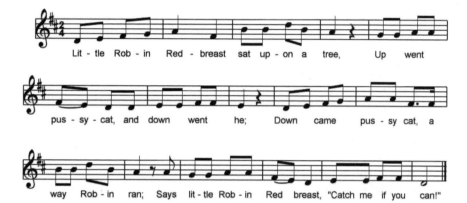

Verse 2:   Little Robin Redbreast jumped upon a wall,
           Pussy cat jumped after him, and almost got a fall;
           Little Robin chirped and sang, and what did pussy say?
           Pussy cat said, "Mew!" and Robin flew away.

Mary Had a Pretty Bird (Traditional, PreS/K–5)

Nineteen Birds (Traditional, PreS/K–5)

Nine - teen birds and one bird more, Just make twen - ty, and that's a score.

To the score, then add but one; Then you'll have just twen - ty one.

Verse 2:   Now add two, and you will see
            You have made up twenty-three.
            If you like these clever tricks,
            Add three more for twenty-six.

Verse 3:   Then three more, if you have time:
            Now you've got to twenty-nine.
            Twenty-nine now quickly take –
            Add one more and Thirty make.

The North Wind Doth Blow (Traditional, PreS/K–5)

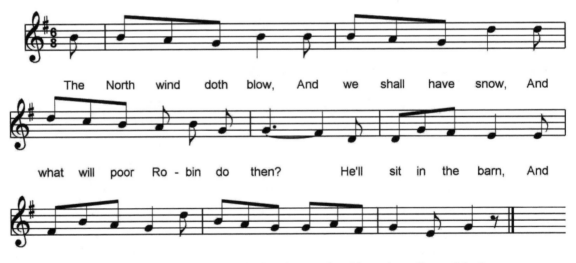

The North wind doth blow, And we shall have snow, And

what will poor Ro - bin do then? He'll sit in the barn, And

keep him - self warm, And tuck his head un - der his wing. Poor thing!

Over in the Meadow

See "Multiple Animals" chapter, Songs section.

Simple Simon

See "Multiple Animals" chapter, Songs section.

Sing a Song of Sixpence (Traditional, PreS/K–5)

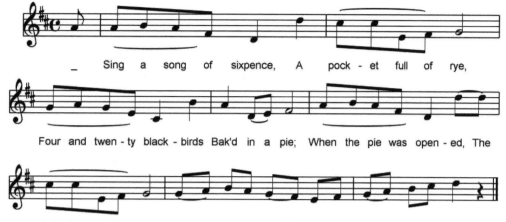
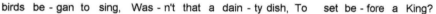

Sing a song of sixpence, A pock-et full of rye,

Four and twen-ty black-birds Bak'd in a pie; When the pie was open-ed, The

birds be-gan to sing, Was-n't that a dain-ty dish, To set be-fore a King?

Verse 2: The king was in his counting-house,
Counting out his money;
The queen was in the parlor,
Eating bread and honey.
The maid was in the garden,
Hanging out the clothes,
When down came a blackbird,
And pecked off her nose.

Skip to My Lou

See "Multiple Animals" chapter, Songs section.

There Were Two Birds That Once Sat on a Stone (Traditional, PreS/K–5)

(Also known as **The Three Crows**)

There were two birds that once sat on a stone, Fa, la, la, la, lal,

de; Then one flew aw-ay and then there was one. Fa, la, la, la, lal,

de; The oth-er bird felt so tim-id a-lone, Fal, la, la, la, la, la, That

he flew a-way, and then there was none, Fal, la, la, la, la, la.

From The Big Book of Animal Rhymes, Fingerplays, and Songs by Elizabeth Cothen Low.
Westport, CT: Libraries Unlimited. Copyright © 2009.

The Twelve Days of Christmas

See "Multiple Animals" chapter, Songs section.

When the Snow Is on the Ground (Traditional, PreS/K–5)

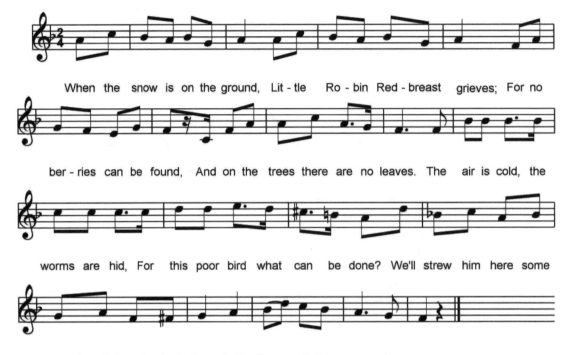

When the snow is on the ground, Lit - tle Ro - bin Red - breast grieves; For no

ber - ries can be found, And on the trees there are no leaves. The air is cold, the

worms are hid, For this poor bird what can be done? We'll strew him here some

crumbs of bread, And then he'll live till the snow is gone.

Poetry

The Bluebird (Emily Huntington Miller, K–5/6+)

I know the song that the bluebird is singing,
Up in the apple tree, where he is swinging.
Brave little fellow! the skies may be dreary,
Nothing cares he while his heart is so cheery.

Hark! how the music leaps out from his throat!
Hark! was there ever so merry a note?
Listen awhile, and you'll hear what he's saying,
Up in the apple tree, swinging and swaying.

"Dear little blossoms, down under the snow,
You must be weary of winter, I know;
Hark! while I sing you a message of cheer,
Summer is coming and springtime is here!

"Little white snowdrop, I pray you arise;
Bright yellow crocus, come, open your eyes;
Sweet little violets hid from the cold,
Put on your mantles of purple and gold;

From *The Big Book of Animal Rhymes, Fingerplays, and Songs* by Elizabeth Cothen Low.
Westport, CT: Libraries Unlimited. Copyright © 2009.

Daffodils, daffodils! say, do you hear?
Summer is coming, and springtime is here!"

Bread and Milk (Christina Rossetti, PreS/K–5)

Bread and milk for breakfast,
And woolen frocks to wear,
And a crumb for robin redbreast
On the cold days of the year.

Dead in the Brush (Christina Rossetti, 6+)

Dead in the cold, a song-singing thrush,
Dead at the foot of a snowberry bush,—
Weave him a coffin of rush,˙
Dig him a grave where the soft mosses grow,
Raise him a tombstone of snow.

* Rush: A kind of marsh plant

The Dinkey-Bird (Eugene Field, Nonsense Verse, 6+)

In an ocean, 'way out yonder
(As all sapient˙ people know),
Is the land of Wonder-Wander,
Whither children love to go;
It's their playing, romping, swinging,
That give great joy to me
While the Dinkey-Bird goes singing
In the Amfalula-tree!

There the gum-drops grow like cherries,
And taffy's thick as peas,—
Caramels you pick like berries
When, and where, and how you please:
Big red sugar-plums are clinging
To the cliffs beside that sea
Where the Dinkey-Bird is singing
In the Amfalula-tree.

So when children shout and scamper
And make merry all the day,
When there's naught to put a damper
To the ardor of their play;
When I hear their laughter ringing,
Then I'm sure as sure can be
That the Dinkey-Bird is singing
In the Amfalula-tree.

For the Dinkey-Bird's bravuras˙
And staccatos˙ are so sweet—
His roulades,˙ appoggiaturas,˙
And robustos so complete,

That the youth of every nation—
Be they near or far away—
Have especial delectation
In that gladsome roundelay.

Their eyes grow bright and brighter,
Their lungs begin to crow,
Their hearts get light and lighter,
And their cheeks are all aglow;
For an echo cometh bringing
The news to all and me.
That the Dinkey-Bird is singing
In the Amfalula-tree.

I'm sure you'd like to go there
To see your feathered friend—
And so many goodies grow there
You would like to comprehend!
Speed, little dreams, your winging
To that land across the sea
Where the Dickey-Bird is singing
In the Amfalula-Tree!

* Sapient: Wise
* Bravuras: Challenging musical passages
* Staccatos: Special way of singing or playing short notes
* Roulades: Several notes sung to one syllable
* Appoggiaturas: Embellishment notes

The Dodo (Hilaire Belloc, K–5/6+)

The Dodo used to walk around,
And take the sun and air.
The sun yet warms his native ground—
The Dodo is not there!

The voice which used to squawk and squeak
Is now for ever dumb—
Yet may you see his bones and beak
All in the Mu-se-um.

The Flamingo (Lewis Gaylord Clark, K–5/6+)

First Voice:
Oh! tell me have you ever seen a red, long-leg'd Flamingo?
Oh! tell me have you ever yet seen him the water in go?

Second Voice:
Oh! yes at Bowling-Green I've seen a red long-leg'd Flamingo,
Oh! yes at Bowling-Green I've there seen him the water in go.

First Voice:

    Oh! tell me did you ever see a bird so funny stand-o

    When forth he from the water comes and gets upon the land-o?

Second Voice:

    No! in my life I ne'er did see a bird so funny stand-o

    When forth he from the water comes and gets upon the land-o.

First Voice:

    He has a leg some three feet long, or near it, so they say, Sir.

    Stiff upon one alone he stands, t'other he stows away, Sir.

Second Voice:

    And what an ugly head he's got! I wonder that he'd wear it.

    But rather more I wonder that his long, thin neck can bear it.

First Voice:

    And think, this length of neck and legs (no doubt they have their uses)

    Are members of a little frame, much smaller than a goose's!

Both:

    Oh! isn't he a curious bird, that red, long-leg'd Flamingo?

    A water bird, a gawky bird, a sing'lar bird, by jingo!

Fly Away, Fly Away Over the Sea (Christina Rossetti, PreS/K–5/6+)

Fly away, fly away over the sea,
Sun-loving swallow, for summer is done;
Come again, come again, come back to me,
Bringing the summer and bringing the sun.

Hear What the Mournful Linnets Say (Christina Rossetti, K–5/6+)

Hear what the mournful linnets say:
"We built our nest compact and warm,
But cruel boys came round our way
And took our summerhouse by storm.
"They crushed the eggs so neatly laid;
So now we sit with drooping wing,
And watch the ruin they have made,
Too late to build, too sad to sing."

I Caught a Little Ladybird (Christina Rossetti, K–5/6+)

I caught a little ladybird
That flies far away;
I caught a little lady wife
That is both staid' and gay.
Come back, my scarlet ladybird,
Back from far away;
I weary of my dolly wife,
My wife that cannot play.
She's such a senseless wooden thing

From *The Big Book of Animal Rhymes, Fingerplays, and Songs* by Elizabeth Cothen Low.
Westport, CT: Libraries Unlimited. Copyright © 2009.

She stares the livelong day;
Her wig of gold is stiff and cold
And cannot change to grey.

* Staid: Serious

If a Mouse Could Fly

See "Multiple Animals" chapter, Poetry section.

If the Sun Could Tell Us Half (Christina Rossetti, K–5/6+)

If the sun could tell us half
That he hears and sees,
Sometimes he would make us laugh,
Sometimes make us cry:
Think of all the birds that make
Homes among the trees;
Think of cruel boys who take
Birds that cannot fly.

Kindness to Animals

See "Multiple Animals" chapter, Poetry section.

A Linnet in a Gilded Cage (Christina Rossetti, K–5/6+)

A linnet in a gilded cage,—
A linnet on a bough,—
In frosty winter one might doubt
Which bird is luckier now.
But let the trees burst out in leaf,
And nests be on the bough,
Which linnet is the luckier bird,
Oh who could doubt it now?

* Bough: Branch of a tree

The Little Maiden and the Little Bird (Lydia Maria Child, K–5/6+)

"Little bird! little bird! come to me!
I have a green cage ready for thee—
Beauty bright flowers I'll bring thee anew,
And fresh, ripe cherries, all wet with dew."
"Thanks, little maiden, for all thy care,—
But I love dearly the clear, cool air,
And my snug little nest in the old oak tree."
"Little bird! little bird! stay with me!"
"Nay, little damsel! away I'll fly
To greener fields and warmer sky;
When spring returns with pattering rain,
You'll hear my merry song again."
"Little bird! little bird! who'll guide thee
Over the hills and over the sea?

Foolish one! come in the house to stay,
For I'm very sure you'll lose your way."

"Ah, no, little maiden! God guides me
Over the hills and over the sea;
I will be free as the rushing air
And sing of sunshine everywhere."

The Monkey's Glue

See "Multiple Animals" chapter, Poetry section.

The Moon

See "Multiple Animals" chapter, Poetry section.

My Robin (Kate Greenaway, K–5/6+)

Under the window is my garden
Where sweet, sweet flowers grow;
And in the pear tree dwells a robin—
The dearest bird I know.

Though I peep out betimes* in the morning
Still the flowers are up the first;
Then I try and talk to the robin
And perhaps he'd chat—if he durst.

* Betimes: Early

Nest Eggs (Robert Louis Stevenson, K–5/6+)

Birds all the sunny day
Flutter and quarrel
Here in the arbour-like
Tent of the laurel.

Here in the fork
The brown nest is seated;
Four little blue eggs
The mother keeps heated.

While we stand watching her
Staring like gabies,*
Safe in each egg are the
Bird's little babies.

Soon the frail eggs they shall
Chip, and upspringing
Make all the April woods
Merry with singing.

From *The Big Book of Animal Rhymes, Fingerplays, and Songs* by Elizabeth Cothen Low.
Westport, CT: Libraries Unlimited. Copyright © 2009.

Younger than we are,
O children, and frailer,
Soon in the blue air they'll be,
Singer and sailor.

We, so much older,
Taller and stronger,
We shall look down on the
Birdies no longer.

They shall go flying `
With musical speeches
High overhead in the
Tops of the beeches.

In spite of our wisdom
And sensible talking,
We on our feet must go
Plodding and walking.

* Gabies: Simpletons

The Robin (Lawrence Alma-Tadema, K–5/6+)

When father takes his spade to dig,
Then Robin comes along.
He sits upon a little twig
And sings a little song.

Or, if the trees are rather far,
He does not stay alone,
But comes up close to where we are
And bobs upon a stone.

Rushes in a Watery Place (Christina Rossetti, K–5/6+)

Rushes in a watery place,
And reeds in a hollow;
A soaring skylark in the sky,
A darting swallow;
And where pale blossom used to hang
Ripe fruit to follow.

Sage Counsel

See "Multiple Animals" chapter, Poetry section.

Singing (Robert Louis Stevenson, K–5/6+)

Of speckled eggs the birdie sings,
And nests among the trees;
The sailor sings of ropes and things
In ships upon the seas.

The children sing in far Japan,
The children sing in Spain;
The organ with the organ man
Is singing in the rain.

Snow Bird (F. C. Woodworth, K–5/6+)

The ground was all covered with snow one day,
And two little sisters were busy at play
When a snow bird was sitting close by on a tree,
And merrily singing his chick-a-de-dee,
Chick-a-de-dee, chick-a-de-dee,
And merrily singing his chick-a-de-dee.

He had not been singing his tune very long
Ere Emily heard him, so loud was his song;
"Oh, sister, look out of the window," said she.
"Here's a dear little bird singing chick-a-de-dee,
Chick-a-de-dee, chick-a-de-dee,
Here's a dear little bird singing chick-a-de-dee.

"Oh, mother, do get him some stockings and shoes,
And a nice little frock, and a hat if he choose,
I wish he'd come into the parlor and see
How warm we would make him, poor chick-a-de-dee.
Chick-a-de-dee, chick-a-de-dee.
How warm we would make him, poor chick-a-de-dee."

"There is One, my dear child, though I cannot tell who,
Has clothed me already, and warm enough, too;
Good-morning! Oh, who are as happy as we?"
And away he went singing his chick-a-de-dee;
Chick-a-de-dee, chick-a-de-dee;
And away he went singing his chick-a-de-dee.

Sir Robin (Lucy Larcom, K–5/6+)

Rollicking Robin is here again.
What does he care for the April rain?
Care for it? Glad of it! Doesn't he know
That the April rain carries off the snow,
And coaxes out leaves to shadow his nest,
And washes his pretty red Easter vest!
And makes the juice of the cherry sweet,
For his hungry little robins to eat?
"Ha! ha! ha!" Hear the jolly bird laugh.
"That isn't the best of the story, by half."

The Summer Nights Are Short (Christina Rossetti, K–5/6+)

The summer nights are short
Where northern days are long:
For hours and hours lark after lark

From *The Big Book of Animal Rhymes, Fingerplays, and Songs* by Elizabeth Cothen Low.
Westport, CT: Libraries Unlimited. Copyright © 2009.

Trills out his song.
The summer days are short
Where southern nights are long:
Yet short the night when nightingales
Trill out their song.

Swift and Sure the Swallow

See "Multiple Animals" chapter, Poetry section.

There Was a Little Robin (Wilhelmina Seegmuller, PreS/K–5)

There was a little robin
Sat singing in a tree;
From early morn till dark he sang—
"The world was made for me."

There Was an Old Man with a Beard (Edward Lear, PreS/K–5/6+)

There was an old man with a beard,
Who said, "It is just as I feared!
Two owls and a hen,
Four larks and a wren,
Have all built their nests in my beard!"

There Was an Old Man Who Said, "Hush!" (Edward Lear, PreS/K–5/6+)

There was an Old Man who said, "Hush!
I perceive a young bird in this bush!"
When they said, "Is it small?"
He replied, "Not at all;
It is four times as big as the bush!"

Time to Rise (Robert Louis Stevenson, K–5/6+)

A birdie with a yellow bill
Hopped upon the window-sill;
Cocked his shining eye, and said,
"Ain't you 'shamed, you sleepy-head?"

The Vulture (Hilaire Belloc, K–5/6+)

The vulture eats between his meals,
And that's the reason why
He very, very rarely feels
As well as you and I.

His eye is dull, his head is bald,
His neck is growing thinner.
Oh! What a lesson for us all
To only eat at dinner.

What Does the Donkey Bray About?

See "Multiple Animals" chapter, Poetry section.

When a Mounting Skylark Sings (Christina Rossetti, K–5/6+).

When a mounting skylark sings
In the sunlit summer morn,
I know that heaven is up on high,
And on earth are fields of corn.
But when a nightingale sings
In the moonlit summer even,
I know not if earth is merely earth,
Only that heaven is heaven.

A White Hen Sitting

See "Chickens" chapter, Poetry section.

The Wind Blows East (Henry W. Longfellow, PreS/K–5/6+)

The wind blows east,
The wind blows west,
The blue eggs in robin's nest
Will soon have wings
And flutter and fly away.

Wrens and Robins (Christina Rossetti, PreS/K–5)

Wrens and robins in the hedge,
Wrens and robins here and there;
Building, perching, pecking, fluttering,
Everywhere!

BISON

Nursery Rhymes

The Panther

See "Multiple Animals" chapter, Nursery Rhymes section.

Songs

Home on the Range

See "Multiple Animals" chapter, Songs section.

Poetry

The Bison (Hilaire Belloc, 6+)

The Bison is vain,
And (I write it with pain)
The Door-mat you see on his head

Is not as some learned professors maintain,
The opulent growth of a genius' brain;
But is sewn on with needle and thread.

BUTTERFLIES AND CATERPILLARS

Fingerplays and Action Rhymes

A Caterpillar Crawled to the Top of a Tree (Traditional, PreS/K–5)

A caterpillar crawled, to the top of a tree. (Have fingers creep up one arm to shoulder.)
"I think I'll take a nap," said he. (Place hands next to head to signify sleep.)
So under a leaf he began to creep (Have fingers on right hand creep under left palm.)
To spin his cocoon, and fall asleep.

All winter long he slept in his bed,
'Til spring came along one day and said,
"Wake up, wake up, little sleepy head, (Have left hand shake right hand.)
Wake up, it's time to get out of bed."
So he opened his eyes that sunshiny day. (Place thumbs together and spread fingers on both hands out.)
Lo! He was a butterfly, and flew away. (Wiggle fingers and keeping thumbs together have hands move upward.)

Fuzzy Little Caterpillar (Emilie Poulsson, B/T/PreS/K–5)

Fuzzy little caterpillar (Make fist with thumb sticking out.)
Crawling, crawling on the ground! (Move thumb along.)
Fuzzy little caterpillar,
Nowhere, nowhere to be found, (Put thumb in fist.)
Though we've looked and looked and hunted
Everywhere around!

When the little caterpillar
Found his furry coat too tight,
Then a snug cocoon he made him
Spun of silk so soft and light;
Rolled himself away within it—
Slept there day and night.

See how this cocoon is stirring! (Shake hand.)
Now a little head we spy— (Have thumb peep out.)
What! Is this our caterpillar
Spreading gorgeous wings to dry? (Place thumbs together and stretch out fingers.)
Soon the free and happy creature
Flutters gaily by. (Maintaining last pose, wiggle fingers and move arms in a circular motion.)

Frogs Jump

See "Multiple Animals" chapter, Finger Plays and Action Rhymes section.

From *The Big Book of Animal Rhymes, Fingerplays, and Songs* by Elizabeth Cothen Low.
Westport, CT: Libraries Unlimited. Copyright © 2009.

Fuzzy Wuzzy Caterpillar (Traditional, B/T/PreS/K–5)

Fuzzy wuzzy caterpillar
Into a corner will creep. (Creep index finger along arm.)
He'll spin himself a blanket, (Spin hands around each other.)
And then fall fast asleep. (Place hands together on side of head, close eyes.)

Fuzzy wuzzy caterpillar
Wakes up by and by, (Open eyes and stretch arms.)
To find his lovely wings,
Changed to a butterfly! (Place thumbs together, stretch out fingers and wiggle.)

"Let's Go to Sleep," the Little Caterpillars Said (Traditional, PreS/K–5)

"Let's go to sleep," (Place fingers of right hand onto left palm.)
The little caterpillars said,
As they tucked themselves (Bend fingers of left hand over other fingers.)
Into bed.

They will wake up
By and by, (Gradually unfold fingers on left hand.)
And each one will be
A lovely butterfly. (Flutter hands in the air.)

Little Arabella Miller (Traditional, B/T/PreS/K–5)

Little Arabella Miller
Found a wooly caterpillar.
First it crawled upon her mother,
Then upon her baby brother.
All said, "Arabella Miller,
Take away that caterpillar." (Wave finger in the air.)

Roly-Poly Caterpillar into a Room Crept (Traditional, PreS/K–5)

Roly-poly caterpillar (Hold out right index finger.)
Into a corner crept,
Spun around himself a blanket (Wrap left-hand fingers around right index finger.)
And for a long time slept.
Roly-poly caterpillar
Wakened by and by—
Found himself with beautiful wings,
Changed to a butterfly. (Place thumbs together, stretch out fingers and wiggle.)

Poetry

Billy and the Butterfly (Traditional, 6+)

Billy he mounted a butterfly's back;
Hepity, lepity, lee!
And he flew to the top of a new-made hay-stack,
With a high dumble, dumble, derree!

"Odds bobs!" said a crow, whom they found sitting there;
Hepity, lepity, lee!
"Don't disturb me I beg, for no place can I spare!"
With a high dumble, dumble, derree!

So away they both flew, till at length they did perch,
Hepity, lepity, lee!
On the top of the steeple of Chichester church,
With a high dumble, dumble, derree!

A dozen old jackdaws came pounce round their ears;
Hepity, lepity, lee!
And bid them depart, for the steeple was theirs.
With a high dumble, dumble, derree!

Billy thought it was hard to be thus turned away
Hepity, lepity, lee!
So vowed that in spite of them all, he would stay,
With a high dumble, dumble, derree!

The biggest old jackdaw flew smack at his nose,
Hepity, lepity, lee!
Whilst the others all pecked at his fingers and toes,
With a high dumble, dumble, derree!

Poor Billy called out, in most grievous dismay,
Hepity, lepity, lee!
And was glad to make off, without saying good day,
With a high dumble, dumble, derree!

They rested no more till they came to a star,
Hepity, lepity, lee!
Where they begged they might stop, as they'd traveled so far,
With a high dumble, dumble, derree!

The star could not hold them, so higher they rose,
Hepity, lepity, lee!
Till they came to the sun, who burnt off Billy's clothes
With a high dumble, dumble, derree!

"Alas," says poor Billy, "I'll venture no more!"
Hepity, lepity, lee!
"What business had I from my station to soar,"
With a high dumble, dumble, derree!

Brown and Furry (Christina Rossetti, K–5/6+)

Brown and furry
Caterpillar in a hurry,
Take your walk
To the shady leaf, or stalk,

From *The Big Book of Animal Rhymes, Fingerplays, and Songs* by Elizabeth Cothen Low.
Westport, CT: Libraries Unlimited. Copyright © 2009.

Or what not,
Which may be the chosen spot.
No toad spy you,
Hovering bird of prey pass by you;
Spin and die,
To live again a butterfly.

Kindness to Animals

See "Multiple Animals" chapter, Poetry section.

Hurt No Living Thing

See "Multiple Animals" chapter, Poetry section.

CAMELS

Nursery Rhymes

The Friendly Beasts

See "Multiple Animals" chapter, Nursery Rhymes section.

The Panther

See "Multiple Animals" chapter, Nursery Rhymes section.

Fingerplays and Action Rhymes

Creeping, Creeping, Creeping
See "Multiple Animals" chapter, Fingerplay and Action Rhymes section

Five Little Kittens Sleeping on a Chair (Traditional, B/T/PreS)
Five little kittens
Sleeping on a chair. (Hold up five fingers.)
One rolled off,
Leaving four there. (Fold down fingers one by one.)

Four little kittens,
One climbed a tree,
To look in a bird's nest.
And then there were three.

Three little kittens
Wondered what to do;
One saw a mouse.
And then there were two.

Two little kittens
Playing near a wall;
One little kitten
Chased a red ball.
And then there was one.

One little kitten
With fur soft as silk;
Was left all alone
To drink a dish of milk.

Five Little Kittens Standing in a Row (Traditional, B/T/PreS)
Five little kittens (Hold up five fingers.)
Standing in a row,
They nod their heads (Bend fingers at joints.)
To the children, so.
They run to the left, (Wiggle fingers to the left.)
They run to the right, (Wiggle fingers to the right.)
They stand up and stretch
In the bright sunlight. (Stretch out fingers.)
Along comes a dog,
Who's in for some fun.
Meow! See those
Five kittens run. (Hide fingers behind back.)

Frogs Jump

See "Multiple Animals" chapter, Fingerplay and Action Rhymes section

Hey, My Kitten, My Kitten (Traditional, B/T)

(Also known as O My Kitten a Kitten)

Hey, my kitten, my kitten,
And hey my kitten, my deary!
Such a sweet pet as this
Was neither far nor neary.

He we go up, up, up, (Lift baby up.)
Here we go down, down, downy; (Lower baby down.)
Here we go backwards and forwards, (Go backward and forward.)
And here we go round, round, roundy. (Turn around in a circle.)

A Kitten Is Hiding Under a Chair (Traditional, PreS/K–5)

A kitten is hiding under a chair. (Hide left thumb under right hand.)
I looked and looked for her everywhere. (Peer under hand.)
Under the table and under the bed; (Point different directions.)
I looked in the corner, and when I said,
"Come, Kitty, come, Kitty, here's milk for you." (Cup hands to make dish.)
Kitty came running and calling, "Mew, mew." (Make running motion with fingers.)

Little Robin Redbreast Sat upon a Tree

See "Birds" chapter, Fingerplay and Action Rhymes section.

Mrs. Pussy's Dinner (Emilie Poulsson, K–5)

Mrs. Pussy, sleek and fat, (Hold up thumb.)
With her kittens four, (Hold up fingers.)
Went to sleep upon the mat (Hold out fist, palm facing upwards.)
By the kitchen door.

Mrs. Pussy heard a noise,
Up she jumped in glee: (Have thumb pop up.)
"Kittens, maybe that's a mouse!
Let us go and see!"

Creeping, creeping, creeping on,
Silently they stole; (Have hand creep along floor.)
But the little mouse had gone
Back within its hole. (Interlock left and right fingers to make a hole.)

"Well," said Mrs. Pussy then,
"To the barn we'll go;
We shall find the swallow there
Flying to and fro." (Place thumbs together and wiggle fingers.)

So the cat and kittens four
Tried their very best;
But the swallows flying fast (Place thumbs together and wiggle fingers, moving arms in a circle.)
Safely reached the nest! (Cup hands together.)

Home went hungry Mrs. Puss
And her kittens four;
Found their dinner on a plate (Hold hand palm up.)
By the kitchen door.

As they gathered round the plate,
They agreed 'twas nice
That it could not run away
Like the birds and mice!

Old Gray Cat (Traditional, B/T/PreS/K-5)

Old gray cat is sleeping, sleeping, sleeping. (Pretend to sleep.)
The old gray cat is sleeping in the house.

The little mice are creeping, creeping, creeping. (Slowly walk in place.)
The little mice are creeping through the house.

The old gray cat is waking, waking, waking. (Open eyes wide.)
The old gray cat is waking in the house.

The old gray cat is chasing, chasing, chasing. (Run in place.)
The old gray cat is chasing though the house.

All the mice are squealing, squealing, squealing. (Make squealing sounds.)
All the mice are squealing through the house.

Suggestion: Divide children into two groups: cats and mice.

One Little, Two Little, Three Little Kittens

See "Pets" subsection of "Multiple Animals" chapter, Fingerplay and Action Rhymes section.

Nursery Rhymes

A, B, C, Tumbledown D

See Songs section in this chapter.

Anna Maria She Sat on the Fire (Traditional, PreS/K–5)

Anna Maria she sat on the fire;
The fire was too hot, she sat on the pot;
The pot was too round, she sat on the ground;
The ground was too flat, she sat on the cat;
The cat ran away with Maria on her back.

As I Walked over the Hill One Day

See "Multiple Animals" chapter, Nursery Rhymes section.

As I Was Going to St. Ives (Traditional, Riddle, K–5/6+)

As I was going to St. Ives,
I met a man with seven wives;
Each wife had seven sacks,
Each sack had seven cats,
Each cat had seven kits:
Kits, cats, sacks, and wives,
How many were there going to St. Ives?

Answer: One, all the rest were coming from St. Ives.

"Bow-Wow," says the Dog

See "Multiple Animals" chapter, Nursery Rhymes section.

Bimble, Bamble, Bumble (Traditional, K–5/6+)

There was an old woman who rode on a broom,
With a high gee ho, gee humble,
And she took her old cat along for a groom,
With a bimble, bamble, bumble.

They went along and they came to the sky,
With a high gee ho, gee humble,
But the ride so long made them very hungry,
With a bimble, bamble, bumble.

Said Tom, "I can find not a mouse to eat,"
With a high gee ho, gee humble;
"So let us go back again, I entreat,"
With a bimble, bamble, bumble.

The old woman would not go back so soon,
With a high gee ho, gee humble,
She wanted to visit the man in the moon,
With a bimble, bamble, bumble.

Said Tom, "I will go alone to the house,"
With a high gee ho, gee humble,
"For there I can catch a rat or a mouse,"
With a bimble, bamble, bumble.

"But," said the old woman, "how will you go?"
With a high gee ho, gee humble,
"You shan't have my nag, I protest and vow!
With a bimble, bamble, bumble.

From *The Big Book of Animal Rhymes, Fingerplays, and Songs* by Elizabeth Cothen Low.
Westport, CT: Libraries Unlimited. Copyright © 2009.

"No, no," says old Tom, "I've a plan of my own,
With a high gee ho, gee humble,
So he slid down the rainbow, and left her alone,
With a bimble, bamble, bumble!

So now if you happen to visit the sky,
With a high gee ho, gee humble,
And want to come back, you Tom's method may try,
With a bimble, bamble, bumble!

The Cat Asleep by the Side of the Fire (Traditional, PreS/K–5)

The cat sat asleep by the side of the fire,
The mistress snored loud as a pig:
John took up his fiddle, by Jenny's desire,
And stuck up a bit of a jig.

Come Dance a Jig

See "Pigs" chapter, Nursery Rhymes section.

The Comic Adventures of Old Dame Trot and Her Cat (Traditional, 6+)

Here you behold Dame Trot, and here
Her comic cat you see.
Each seated in an elbow chair
As snug as they can be.

Dame Trot came home one wintry night,
A shivering, starving soul,
But Puss had made a blazing fire,
And nicely trussed a fowl.

The Dame was pleased, the fowl was dressed,
The table set in place.
The wondrous cat began to carve,
And Goody said her grace.

The cloth withdrawn, old Goody cries,
'I wish we'd liquor too.'
Up jumped Grimalkin for some wine,
And soon a cork she drew.

The wine got up in Pussy's head,
She would not go to bed;
But purred and tumbled, leaped and danced,
And stood upon her head.

Old Goody laughed to see the sport,
As though her sides would crack,
When Puss, without a single word,
Leaped on the spaniel's back.

'Ha, ha! Well done!' old Trot exclaims,
'My cat, you gallop well;'
But Spot grew surly, growled and bit,
And down the rider fell.

Now Goody sorely was fatigued,
Nor eyes could open keep.
So Spot and she and Pussy too,
Agreed to go to sleep.

Next morning Puss got up bedtimes,
The breakfast cloth she laid.
And ere* the village clock struck eight,
The tea and toast she made.

Goody awoke and rubbed her eyes,
And drank her cup of tea;
Amazed to see her cat behave
With such propriety.

The breakfast ended, Trot went out
To see old neighbour Hards,
And coming home she found her cat
Engaged with Spot at cards.

Another time the Dame came in,
When Spot demurely sat
Half lathered to the ears and eyes,
Half shaven by the cat.

Grimalkin having shaved her friend,
Sat down before the glass,
And washed her face, and dressed her hair,
Like any modern lass.

A hat and feather then she took,
And stuck it on aside,
And o'er a gown of crimson silk,
A handsome tippet tied.

Just as her dress was all complete,
In came the good old Dame;
She looked, admired, and curtsied low,
And Pussy did the same.

* Ere: Before

Dame Trot and Her Cat (Traditional, K–5/6+)

Dame Trot and her cat
Sat down for a chat;

From *The Big Book of Animal Rhymes, Fingerplays, and Songs* by Elizabeth Cothen Low.
Westport, CT: Libraries Unlimited. Copyright © 2009.

The Dame sat on this side
And puss sat on that.

"Puss," says the Dame,
"Can you catch a rat
Or a mouse in the dark?"
"Purr," says the cat.

Dame Wiggins of Lee and Her Seven Wonderful Cats (Traditional, 6+)

Dame Wiggins of Lee was a worthy old soul,
As e'er threaded a nee-dle, or wash in a bowl;
She held mice and rats in such antipathy,
That seven fine cats, kept Dame Wiggins of Lee.

The rats and mice scared by this fierce whiskered crew,
The poor seven cats soon had nothing to do;
So, as any one idle, she ne'er loved to see,
She sent them to school, did Dame Wiggins of Lee.

But soon she grew tired, of living alone,
So she sent for her cats, from school to come home;
Each rowing a wherry, returning you see;
The frolic made merry Dame Wiggins of Lee.

To give them a treat, she ran out for some rice;
When she came back, they were skating on ice;
'I shall soon see one down, aye, perhaps two or three,
I'll bet half-a-crown,' said Dame Wiggins of Lee.

While, to make a nice pudding, she went for a sparrow,
They were wheeling a sick lamb, home, in a barrow.
'You shall all have some sprats, for your humanity,
My seven good cats,' said Dame Wiggins of Lee.

While she ran to the field, to look for its dam,
They were warming the bed, for the poor sick lamb;
They turned up the clothes, as neat as could be;
'I shall ne'er want a nurse,' said Dame Wiggins of Lee.

She wished them good night, and went up to bed;
When lo! In the morning, the cats were all fled.
But soon, what a fuss! 'Where can they all be?
Here, pussy, puss, puss!', cried Dame Wiggins of Lee.

The Dame's heart was nigh broke, so she sat down to weep;
When she saw them come back, each riding a sheep.
She fondled and patted, each purring Tom-my:
'Ah! Welcome my dears,' said Dame Wiggins of Lee.

The Dame was unable, her pleasure to smother,
To see the sick lamb, jump up to his mother;
In spite of the gout, and a pain in her knee,
She went dancing about, did Dame Wiggins of Lee.

The Farmer soon heard, where his sheep went astray,
And arrived at Dame's door, with his faithful dog Tray.
He knocked with his crook, and, the stranger to see,
Out of window did look, Dame Wiggins of Lee.
For their kindness he had them, all drawn by his team,
And gave them some field-mice, and raspberry cream;
Said he, 'All my farm, you shall presently see,
For I honour the cats, of Dame Wiggins of Lee.'

For the care of his lamb, and their comical pranks,
He gave them a ham, and abundance of thanks.
'I wish you good day, my fine fellows,' said he;
'My compliments, pray, to Dame Wiggins of Lee.'

* Wherry: A kind of boat

Diddlety, Diddlety, Dumpty (Traditional, K–5/6+)

Diddlety, diddlety, dumpty,
The cat ran up the plum tree;
I'll lay you a crown
I'll fetch you down;
Diddlety, diddlety, dumpty.

Ding, Dong, Bell

See Songs section in this chapter.

Dingle Dingle Doosey

See "Pets" subsection of "Multiple Animals" chapter, Nursery Rhymes section.

Feedum, Fiddledum Fee (Traditional, K-5/6+)

Feedum, fiddledum fee,
The cat's got into the tree.
Pussy, come down,
Or I'll crack your crown,
And toss you into the sea.

Five Little Pussy Cats (Traditional, K–5/6+)

Five little pussy cats,
Invited out to tea,
Cried, Mother, let us go.
Oh do! For good we'll surely be.

We'll wear our bibs and hold our things
As you have shown us how—

Spoons in right paws, cups as well—
And make a pretty bow.

We'll always say, "Yes, if you please,"
And, "Only half of that."
"Then go, my darling children,"
Said the happy Mother Cat.

The five little pussy cats
Went out that night to tea,
Their heads were smooth and glossy,
Their tails were swinging free.

They held their thing as they had learned,
And tried to be polite.
With snowy bibs beneath their chins
They were a pretty sight.

But, alas for manners beautiful,
And coats as soft as silk!
The moment that the little kits
Were asked to take some milk,

They dropped their spoons, forgot to bow,
And—oh, what do you think?
They put their noses in the cups
And all began to drink!

Yes, every naughty little kit
Set up a meow for more,
Then knocked the tea-cups over,
And scampered through the door.

Great A, Little a (Traditional, B/T/PreS/K–5)

Great A, little a,
Bouncing B,
The cat's in the cupboard
And can't see me.

A Grey-Hound Invited a Green-Finch to Tea

See "Multiple Animals" chapter, Nursery Rhymes section.

Hie, Hie, Says Anthony (Traditional, PreS/K–5)

Hie, Hie, says Anthony,
Puss is in the pantry,
Gnawing, gnawing,
A mutton mutton-bone;

See how she tumbles it,
She how she mumbles it,

See how she tosses
The mutton mutton-bone.

Higglety, Pigglety, Pop!

See "Farm Animals" subsection of "Multiple Animals" chapter, Nursery Rhymes section.

Hoddley, Poddley, Puddle and Fogs

See "Pets" subsection of "Multiple Animals" chapter, Nursery Rhymes section.

I Carry My Little Cat (Traditional, 6+)

I carry my little cat under my arm,
For fear that the mastiff* should seize her;
'Twould grieve me if she came to any great harm,
And Towzer would terribly squeeze her.

My cat she is useful, and catches the mice,
I cannot but greatly regard her;
Since but for her skill, I could not keep a slice
Of any good thing in my larder.*

* Mastiff: Variety of large dog
* Larder: Pantry

I Have Been to the Market (Traditional, K–5/6+)

I have been to the market, my lady, my lady;
Then you've not been to the fair, says pussy, says pussy;
I bought me a rabbit, my lady, my lady;
Then you did not buy a hare, says pussy, says pussy;
I roasted it, my lady, my lady;
Then you did not boil it, says pussy, says pussy;
I eat it, my lady, my lady;
And I'll eat you, says pussy, says pussy.

I Know a Little Pussy (Traditional, PreS/K–5)

I have a little pussy
Her coat is silver gray.
She lives in a great wide meadow,
And she never runs away.
Although she is a pussy;
She'll never be a cat.
For she's a pussywillow,
Now what do you think of that!

I Love Little Pussy

See Songs section in this chapter.

From *The Big Book of Animal Rhymes, Fingerplays, and Songs* by Elizabeth Cothen Low.
Westport, CT: Libraries Unlimited. Copyright © 2009.

Jack Sprat Had a Cat (Traditional, PreS/K–5)

Jack Sprat
Had a cat,
It had but one ear;
It went to buy butter
When butter was dear.

Little Tommy Titmouse

See "Multiple Animals" chapter, Nursery Rhymes section.

Little Piggy Wiggy

See "Multiple Animals" chapter, Nursery Rhymes section.

Little Puss (Traditional, PreS/K–5)

As pussy sat upon the step,
Taking the nice fresh air,
A neighbour's little dog came by,
Ah, pussy, are you there?

Good morning, Mistress Pussy Cat,
Come, tell me how you do?
Quite well, I thank you, puss replied,
Now, tell me how are you?

Mother Tabbyskins

See Songs section

My Father He Died

See "Multiple Animals" chapter, Nursery Rhymes section.

Old Mother Shuttle (Traditional, PreS/K–5)

Old Mother Shuttle
Lived in a coal-scuttle˙
Along with her dog and her cat;
What they ate I can't tell,
But 'tis known very well
That not one of the party was fat.

Old Mother Shuttle
Scoured out her coal-scuttle,
And washed both her dog and her cat;
The cat scratched her nose,
So they came to hard blows,
And who was the gainer by that?

* Coal-Scuttle: "A metal pail that usually has a bail and a sloped lip and is used especially for carrying coal"
(http://www.merriam-webster.com)

Poor Pussy (Traditional, K–5/6+)

Poor Pussy's dead! Go ring her knell:
Hark! Hark! I hear her funeral bell!
Bim! Bome! Bell!

Let us a hearse and feathers have,
To take poor Pussy to her grave;
With a Bim! Bome! Bell!

Oh! How came she to die, pray tell?
She would not take her physic well;
Bim! Bome! Bell!

And now she must be buried deep,
Which makes her poor old mother weep;
With a Bim! Bome! Bell!

* Knell: The sound of a bell rung for a funeral
* Physic: Medicine

Polly Piper Plucked a Pigeon

See "Multiple Animals" chapter, Nursery Rhymes section.

Puss Came Dancing

See "Multiple Animals" chapter, Nursery Rhymes section.

Pussicat, Wussicat (Traditional, PreS/K–5)

Pussicat, wussicat, with a white foot,
When is your wedding, for I'll come to it.
The beer's to brew, the bread's to bake,
Pussycat, pussycat, don't be too late!

Pussy Cat Ate the Dumplings (Traditional, PreS/K–5)

Pussy cat ate the dumplings,
Pussy cat ate the dumplings.
Mama stood by,
And cried, "Oh, fie!
Why did you eat the dumplings?"

Pussy-Cat Mole (Traditional, PreS/K–5)

Pussy-Cat Mole
Jumped over a coal
And in her best petticoat burnt a great hole.
Poor pussy's weeping, she'll have no more milk,
Until her best petticoat's mended with silk.

Pussy Cat, Pussy Cat

See Songs section in this chapter.

Pussy Sat by the Fire-Side (Traditional, PreS/K–5)

Pussy sat by the fire-side
In a basket full of coal-dust;
Bas-
ket,
Coal-
dust,
In a basket full of coal-dust!

Pussy Sits Behind the Fire (Traditional, PreS/K–5)

Pussy sits behind the fire,
How can she be fair?
In comes the little dog,
Pussy, are you there?
So, so, Mistress Pussy,
Pray how do you do?
Thank you, thank you, little dog,
I'm very well just now.

The Quarrelsome Kittens (Traditional, K–5/6+)

Two little kittens,
One stormy night,
Began to quarrel,
And then to fight;

One had a mouse
And the other had none,
And that's the way
The quarrel begun.

"I'll have that mouse,"
Said the biggest cat,
"You'll have that mouse?
We'll see about that!"

"I will have that mouse,"
said the eldest son;
"You shan't have that mouse,"
Said the little one.

I told you before
'Twas a stormy night
When these two kittens
Began to fight;

From *The Big Book of Animal Rhymes, Fingerplays, and Songs* by Elizabeth Cothen Low.
Westport, CT: Libraries Unlimited. Copyright © 2009.

The old woman seized
Her sweeping broom,
And swept the two kittens
Right out of the room.

The ground was covered
With frost and snow,
And the two little kittens
Had nowhere to go.

So they laid them down
On the mat at the door
While the old woman finished
Sweeping the floor.

Then they crept in,
As quiet as mice,
All wet with snow a
And as cold as ice;

For they found it was better,
That stormy night,
To lie down and sleep
Than to quarrel and fight.

The Robber Kitten (Traditional, 6+)

A kitten once to its mother said,
"I'll never more be good,
But I'll go and be a robber bold
And live in a dreary wood,
Wood, wood, wood,
And live in a dreary wood."

So off he went to a dreary wood,
And there he met a cock,
And blew his head with a pistol off,
Which gave him an awful shock,
Shock, shock, shock,
Which gave him an awful shock.

Soon after that he met a cat.
"Now give to me your purse
Or I'll shoot you through and stab you, too,
And kill you—which is worse,
Worse, worse, worse,
And kill you—which is worse."

At last he met a robber dog
And they sat down to drink;
The dog did joke and laugh and sing,

From *The Big Book of Animal Rhymes, Fingerplays, and Songs* by Elizabeth Cothen Low.
Westport, CT: Libraries Unlimited. Copyright © 2009.

Which made the kitten wink,
Wink, wink, wink,
Which made the kitten wink.

At last they quarreled, then they fought
Beneath the greenwood tree,
And puss was felled with an awful club
Most terrible to see,
See, see, see,
Most terrible to see.

When puss got up his eye was cut
And swelled, and black and blue;
Moreover all his bones were sore,
Which made this kitten mew,
Mew, mew, mew.
Which made this kitten mew.

So up he got and rubbed his head,
And went home very sad.
"O mother dear, behold me here;
I'll never more be bad,
Bad, bad, bad,
I'll nevermore be bad."

Robin and Richard Were Two Pretty Men

See "Multiple Animals" chapter, Nursery Rhymes section.

Sing, Sing, What Shall I Sing? (Traditional, PreS/K–5)

Sing, sing,
What shall I sing?
The cat's run away
With the pudding* string!

Do, do,
What shall I do?
The cat's run away
With the pudding, too!

* Pudding: "Dish often containing suet or having a suet crust and originally boiled in a bag"
(http://www.merriam-webster.com)

There Was a Crooked Man

See Songs section in this chapter.

There Was a Man, and His Name Was Dob

See "Pets" subsection of "Multiple Animals" chapter, Nursery Rhymes section.

There Were Once Two Cats of Kilkenny (Traditional PreS/K–5, 6+)

There were once two cats of Kilkenny.
Each thought there was one cat too many;
So they fought and they fit,
And they scratched and they bit,
Till, excepting their nails,
And the tip of their tails,
Instead of two cats, there weren't any.

There Were Two Cats Sat Over a Well (Traditional, K–5/6+)

There were two cats sat over a well,
And one of them did tumble in;
The cat that sat by
Wept bitterly,
For one cat was the other cat's cousin.

This Is the House That Jack Built

See "Farm Animals" subsection of "Multiple Animals" chapter, Nursery Rhymes section.

Three Little Kittens

See Songs section in this chapter.

Three Young Rats with Black Felt Hats

See "Multiple Animals" chapter, Nursery Rhymes section.

We Make No Spare

See "Horses" chapter, Nursery Rhymes section.

What an Odd Dame

See "Farm Animals" subsection of "Multiple Animals" chapter, Nursery Rhymes section.

"Who's That Ringing at the Front Door Bell?" (Traditional, PreS/K–5)

"Who's that ringing at the front door bell?"
Miau! Miau! Miau!
"I'm a little Pussy Cat and I'm not very well!"
Miau! Miau! Miau!
"Then rub your nose in a bit of mutton fat."
Miau! Miau! Miau!
"For that's the way to cure a little Pussy Cat."
Miau! Miau! Miau!

Why Is Pussy in Bed?

See "Multiple Animals" chapter, Nursery Rhymes section.

Songs

A, B, C, Tumbledown D (Traditional, B/T/PreS/K–5)

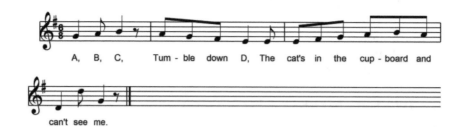

A, B, C, Tum-ble down D, The cat's in the cup-board and

can't see me.

Poor Dog Bright

See "Pets" subsection of "Multiple Animals" chapter, Songs section.

Cat Came Back (Harry S. Miller, K–5/6+)

There was Old Mis-ter John-son, He had troub-les of his own,

He had an old yel-low cat that wouldn't leave its home; He

tri-ed eve-ry-thing he knew to keep the cat a-way Ev-en

sent it to the preach-er and he told it for to stay

But the cat came back, Could-n't stay no long-er, Yes the

cat came back, the ver-y next day; The cat came back,

Thought he was a gon-er, But the cat came back for it

would-n't stay a-way.

Verse 2:   The cat did have some company one night in the yard,
           Someone threw a bootjack,* and they threw it mighty hard,
           Caught the cat behind the ear, he thought it rather slight,
           When along there came a brick bat and it knocked it out of sight.
           Repeat Chorus

* Bootjack: "A device (as with a V-shaped notch) used for pulling off boots" " (http://www.merriam-webster.com)

Ding, Dong, Bell (Traditional, PreS/K–5)

Ding, dong, bell, Pus - sy's in the well; Who put her in?   Lit - tle John - ny Green;

Who pull'd her out? Little Tom - my Stout. What a naugh - ty   boy was that, To

try to drown our   Pus - sy cat!

Extra Lines: Who never did him any harm,
And killed the mice in his father's barn.

Farmer in the Dell

See "Farm Animals" subsection of "Multiple Animals" chapter, Songs section.

Fiddle-I-Fee

See "Farm Animals" subsection of "Multiple Animals" chapter, Songs section.

Hey, Diddle Diddle

See "Farm Animals" subsection of "Multiple Animals" chapter, Songs section.

I Know an Old Lady Who Swallowed a Fly

See "Multiple Animals" chapter, Songs section.

I Love Little Pussy (Traditional, PreS/K–5)

I love lit - tle pus - sy, her coat is so warm, And if I don't hurt her, she'll do me no harm, I'll sit by the fi - re and give her some food, And pus - sy will love me be -cause I am good.

Extra Lines: So I'll not pull her tail,
Nor drive her away,
But pussy and I,
Very gently will play.

The Lazy Cat (Traditional, PreS/K–5)

"Pus - sy, where have you been to - day?" "In the mead - ows a -sleep in the hay." "Pus - sy, you are a la - zy cat, If you have done no more than that."

Mother Tabbyskins (Traditional, PreS/K–5)

Sit - ting at a win - dow, In her cloak and hat, I saw Mo - ther Tab - by - skins The real old cat! Ve - ry old, ve - ry old, Crum - ple - ty and lame; Teach - ing kit - tens how to scold, Is it not a shame?

Old MacDonald

See "Farm Animals" subsection of "Multiple Animals" chapter, Songs section.

Pussy Cat, Pussy Cat (Traditional, PreS/K–5)

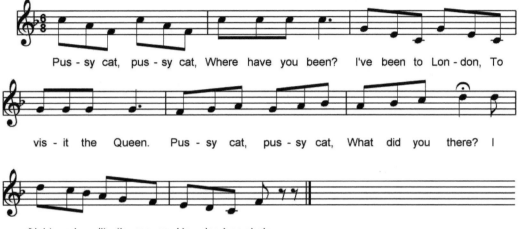

Pus - sy cat, pus - sy cat, Where have you been? I've been to Lon - don, To

vis - it the Queen. Pus - sy cat, pus - sy cat, What did you there? I

fright - ed a lit - tle mouse, Un - der her chair.

Skip to My Lou

See "Multiple Animals" chapter, Songs section.

There Was a Crooked Man (Traditional, PreS/K–5)

There was a crook - ed man, and he went a crook - ed mile, He

found a crook - ed six - pence a -gainst a crook - ed stile; He

bought a crook - ed cat, which caught a crook - ed mouse, And they

all lived to - geth - er in a crook - ed lit - tle house.

Three Little Kittens (Traditional, PreS/K–5)

(Also known as **Once Three Little Kittens**)

Once three lit-tle kit-tens they lost their mit-tens, And they be-gan to

cry, "Oh! mo-ther dear, we sad-ly fear, our mit-tens we have lost." "What,

lost your mit-tens you naugh-ty kit-tens, then you shall have no pie."

"Me - ow, me - ow, me - ow, me - ow, me - ow, me - ow,

Meow."

Verse 2: The three little kittens,
They found their mittens,
And they began to cry,
"Oh, Mother dear,
See here, see here,
Our mittens we have found."
"Put on your mittens,
You silly kittens,
And you shall have some pie."
"Purr-r, purr-r, pur-r,
Oh, let us have some pie."

Verse 3: Three little kittens,
Put on their mittens,
And soon ate up the pie;
"Oh, Mother dear,
We greatly fear,
Our mittens we have soiled."
"What! Soiled your mittens,
You naughty kittens!"
And they began to sigh.
Mee-ow, mee-ow, mee-ow,

Verse 4:   The three little kittens,
            They washed their mittens,
            And hung them out to dry.
            Oh, Mother dear,
            Did you not hear,
            Our mittens we have washed?"
            "What! Washed your mittens,
            Then you're good kittens!
            But I smell a rat close by.
            Mee-ow, mee-ow, mee-ow.

Poetry

Cat of Cats (William Brighty Rands, K–5/6+)

I am the cat of cats. I am
The everlasting cat!
Cunning, and old, and sleek as jam,
The everlasting cat!
I hunt the vermin in the night—
The everlasting cat!
For I see best without the light—
The everlasting cat!

A City Plum Is Not a Plum

See "Multiple Animals" chapter, Poetry section.

The Dog Lies in His Kennel

See "Pets" subsection of "Multiple Animals" chapter, Poetry section.

The Moon

See "Multiple Animals" chapter, Poetry section.

The Owl and the Pussycat

See "Multiple Animals" chapter, Poetry section.

The Peacock Has a Score of Eyes

See "Multiple Animals" chapter, Poetry section.

Pussy Has a Whiskered Face

See "Pets" subsection of "Multiple Animals" chapter, Poetry section.

There Was a Young Man Who Was Bitten (Walter Parke, K–5/6+)

There was a young man who was bitten
By twenty-two cats and a kitten;
Sighed he, "It is clear
My finish is near;
No matter; I'll die like a Briton!"

Winter Night

See "Multiple Animals" chapter, Poetry section.

CHICKENS

Fingerplays and Action Rhymes

Five Eggs and Five Eggs That Makes Ten (Traditional, B/T/PreS/K–5)

Five eggs and five eggs (Hold up all ten fingers.)
That makes ten.
Sitting on top is the Mother Hen. (Make a left fist and place right palm on top of it.)
Cackle, cackle, cackle; (Clap)
What do I see?
Ten fluffy chickens, (Hold up fingers.)
As yellow as can be.

Five Little Chickens (Traditional, PreS/K–5)

(Also known as How to Get Breakfast)

Said the first little chick, (Tug on first finger.)
With a queer little squirm,
"Oh, I wish I could find
A fat little worm!"

Said the second little chick, (Tug on second finger.)
With an odd little shrug,
"Oh, I wish I could find
A fat little bug!"

Said the third little chick, (Tug on fourth finger.)
With a shrill little squeal,
"Oh, I wish I could find
Some nice yellow meal!"

Said the fourth little chick, (Tug on third finger.)
With a small sigh of grief,
"Oh, I wish I could find
A little green leaf!"

Said the fifth little chick, (Tug on fifth finger.)
With a faint little moan,
"Oh, I wish I could find
A wee gravel stone!"

"Now see here," said their mother,
From the near garden patch,
"If you want any breakfast,
You must come here and scratch!" (Pretend to rake ground with fingers.)

Here Sits the Lord Mayor (Traditional, B/T/PreS/K–5)

(Also known as **Here Sits Farmer Giles**)

Here sits the Lord Mayor. (Touch head.)
Here sits his men. (Touch eyes.)
Here sits the cockadoodle. (Touch one cheek.)
Here sits the hen. (Touch the other cheek.)
Here sit the little chickens. (Touch teeth.)
Here they run in, (Open mouth and touch lips.)
Chin chopper, chin chopper
Chin chopper, chin! (Touch chin.)

The Hen and the Chickens (Emilie Poulsson, K–5)

Good Mother Hen sits here on her nest, (Make a left fist and place right palm on top of it.)
Keeps the eggs warm beneath her soft breast,
Waiting, waiting, day after day.
Hark! There's a sound she knows very well:
Some little chickens are breaking the shell, (Tap index finger against chair or floor.)
Pecking, pecking, pecking away.

Now they're all out, Oh, see what a crowd!
Good Mother Hen is happy and proud,
Cluck-cluck, cluck-cluck, clucking away. (Cluck and flap arms.)

Into the coop the mother must go;
But all the chickens run to and fro,
Peep-peep, peep-peep, peeping away. (Peep and run in place.)

Here is some corn in my little dish;
Eat, Mother Hen, eat all that you wish, (Hold palm out, hold index, middle, and thumb together and
    have them peck at hand.)
Picking, picking, picking away.

Happy, we'll be to see you again,
Dear little chicks and good Mother Hen!
Now good-by, good-by for today. (Wave goodbye.)

Oh, My Chicken (Traditional, B/T)

Oh, my chicken, my chicken,
And oh my chicken, my deary!
Such a sweet pet as this
Was neither far nor neary.

He we go up, up, up, (Lift baby up.)
Here we go down, down, downy; (Lower baby down.)
Here we go backwards and forwards, (Go backward and forward.)
And here we go round, round, roundy. (Turn around in a circle.)

From The Big Book of Animal Rhymes, Fingerplays, and Songs by Elizabeth Cothen Low.
Westport, CT: Libraries Unlimited. Copyright © 2009.

Los pollitos (Traditional, Spanish)

Los pollitos dicen—pió, pió, pió—
cuando tienen hambre, (Touch stomach.)
cuando tienen frío. (Hug chest tightly and shiver.)

La gallina busca
el maíz y el trigo, (Have index finger and thumb "peck" at the ground.)
les da la comida, (Point to mouth.)
y les presta abrigo. (Pretend to hug an imaginary person.)
Bajo sus dos alas acurrucaditos
Hasta el otro día duermen los pollitos. (Fold hands next to head and close eyes.)

Translation: The Chicks

The chicks say, cheep, cheep, cheep—
When they are hungry, (Touch stomach.)
When they are cold. (Hug chest tightly and to shiver.)
The hen looks for the corn and the wheat, (Have index to finger and thumb "peck" at the ground.)
    She gives them food, (Point to mouth.)
And she gives them armth. (Pretend to hug an imaginary person.)
Under her two wings they snuggle,
Until the next day, the little chicks sleep. (Fold hands next to head and close eyes.)

See-Saw, Margery Daw (Traditional, B/T)

See-saw, Margery Daw,
The old hen flew over the malt house;
She counted her chickens one by one,
Still she missed the little white one,
And this is it, this is it, this is it. (Wiggle baby's little toe.)

Nursery Rhymes

As I Walked over the Hill One Day

See "Multiple Animals" chapter, Nursery Rhymes section.

Chook, Chook (Traditional, B/T/PreS/K–5)

Chook, chook, chook-chook-chook,
Good Morning, Mrs. Hen.
How many chickens have you got?
Madam, I've got ten.
Four of them are yellow,
And four of them are brown,
And two of them are speckled red,
The nicest in the town.

Cinco pollitos (Traditional, Spanish)

Cinco pollitos
Tiene mi tía
Uno le canta,

From *The Big Book of Animal Rhymes, Fingerplays, and Songs* by Elizabeth Cothen Low.
Westport, CT: Libraries Unlimited. Copyright © 2009.

Otro le pía
Y tres le tocan
La chirimía.

Translation: Five Little Chickens

Five little chickens
Has my aunt.
One sings for her,
The other peeps
And three play
The chirimía.

Cock a Doodle Doo (Traditional, PreS/K–5)

Cock–a-doodle-doo,
My dame has lost her shoe;
My master's lost his fiddling stick
And knows not what to do.

Cock–a-doodle-doo,
What is my dame to do?
Till master finds his fiddling stick,
She'll dance without her shoe.

Cock–a-doodle-doo,
My dame has found her shoe,
And master's found his fiddling stick,
Sing doodle doodle doo.

Cock–a-doodle-doo,
My dame will dance with you
While master fiddles his fiddling stick
For dame and doodle doo.

Cock–a-doodle-doo,
Dame has lost her shoe;
Gone to bed and scratched her head,
And can't tell what to do.

Cock, Cock, Cock, Cock (Traditional, K–5/6+)

Hen says:
"Cock, cock, cock, cock,
I've laid an egg,
Am I to go ba-are foot?"
Cock replies:
"Hen, hen, hen, hen,
I've been up and down,
To every shop in town,
And cannot find a shoe
To fit your foot,
If I'd crow my hea-art out.

Suggestion: This rhyme is an imitation of sounds chickens make. Say lines fast, except for last two lines which should be said very loudly.

The Cock Crows in the Morn (Traditional, PreS/K–5)

The cock crows in the morn
To tell us to rise,
And he that lies late
Will never be wise:

For early to bed,
And early to rise,
Is the way to be healthy,
And wealthy and wise.

The Cock Doth Crow (Traditional, PreS/K–5)

The cock doth crow,
To let you know,
If you be wise,
'Tis time to rise.

The Cock's on the Housetop

See "Multiple Animals" chapter, Nursery Rhymes section.

Dame Duck's First Lecture on Education

See "Ducks" chapter, Nursery Rhymes section.

A Dog and a Cock

See "Multiple Animals" chapter, Nursery Rhymes section.

I Bought a Dozen New-Laid Eggs (Traditional, PreS/K–5)

I bought a dozen new-laid eggs,
Of good old farmer Dickens;
I hobbled home upon two legs,
And found them full of chickens.

I Had a Little Hen (Traditional, PreS/K–5)

I had a little hen,
The prettiest ever seen;
She washed up the dishes
And kept the house clean;
She went to the mill
To fetch me some flour,
She brought it home
In less than an hour;
She baked me my bread,
She brewed me my ale,
She sat by the fire
And told many a fine tale.

The Little Black Dog

See "Multiple Animals" chapter, Nursery Rhymes section.

Live Fowls!—Live Fowls!—Buy a Live Fowl! (Traditional, K–5, 6+)

'Live fowls! Charming fowls in variety see!
Come buy them, kind customers, buy them of me.
The sluggard the cock will arose when 'tis day,
And an egg for the weakly the pullet* will lay.'

* Pullet: A Young Chicken

Lock the Dairy Door (Traditional, PreS/K–5)

The Cock:
> "Lock the dairy door!
> Lock the dairy door!"

The Hen:
> "Chickle! chackle, chee."
> "I haven't got the key."

Hickety, Pickety, My Black Hen (Traditional, PreS/K–5)

(Also known as **Higgledy, Piggledy, My Black Hen**)

Hickety, Pickety, my black hen,
She lays eggs for gentlemen;
Gentlemen come every day
To see what my black hen doth lay;
Sometimes nine and sometimes ten,
Hickety, Pickety, my black hen.

Humpty Dumpty Sat on a Wall

See Song section in this chapter.

Oh, My Pretty Cock, Oh, My Handsome Cock (Traditional, PreS/K–5)

Oh, my pretty cock, oh, my handsome cock,
I pray you, do not crow before day,
And your comb shall be made of the very beaten gold
And your wings of the silver so gray.

One, Two, Buckle My Shoe (Traditional, PreS/K–5)

One, two, buckle my shoe;
Three, four, open the door;
Five, six, pick up sticks;
Seven, eight, lay them straight;
Nine, ten, a big fat hen.

Robin and Richard Were Two Pretty Men

See "Multiple Animals" chapter, Nursery Rhymes section.

This Is the House That Jack Built

See "Farm Animals" subsection of "Multiple Animals" chapter, Nursery Rhymes section.

What an Odd Dame

See "Farm Animals" subsection of "Multiple Animals" chapter, Nursery Rhymes section.

Songs

Fiddle-I-Fee

See "Farm Animals" subsection of "Multiple Animals" chapter, Songs section.

Humpty Dumpty Sat on a Wall (Traditional, PreS/K–5)

Hump-ty Dump-ty sat on a wall, Hump-ty Dump-ty had a great fall,

All the King's hors-es and all the King's men, Could-n't put Hump-ty to

-geth-er a-gain.

The Twelve Days of Christmas

See "Multiple Animals" chapter, Songs section.

Poetry

Before the Barn Door Crowing (John Gay, 6+)

Before the barn door crowing
The cock by hens attended,
His eyes around him throwing,
Stands for a while suspended;
Then one singles from the crew,
And cheers the happy hen,
With how do you do, and how do you do,
And how do you do again.

The Clucking Hen (A. Hawkshawe, K–5/6+)

"Will you take a walk with me,
My little wife, to-day?
There's barley in the barley field,
And hayseed in the hay."

"Thank you;" said the clucking hen;
"I've something else to do;
I'm busy sitting on my eggs,
I cannot walk with you."

"Cluck, cluck, cluck, cluck,"
Said the clucking hen;
"My little chicks will soon be hatched,
I'll think about it then."

The clucking hen sat on her nest,
She made it in the hay;
And warm and snug beneath her breast,
A dozen white eggs lay.

Crack, crack, went all the eggs,
Out dropped the chickens small!
"Cluck," said the clucking hen,
"Now I have you all."

"Come along, my little chicks,
I'll take a walk with you."
"Hallo!" said the barn-door cock,
"Cock–a-doodle-doo!"

H Was an Indigent Hen (Bruce Porter, K–5/6+)

H was an indigent Hen,
Who picked up a corn now and then;
She had but one leg
On which she could peg,
And behind her left ear was a wen.

* Indigent: Poor
* Wen: A Cyst

The Hen (Oliver Herford, 6+)

Alas! my Child, where is the Pen
That can do Justice to the Hen?
Like Royalty, She goes her way,
Laying foundations every day,
Though not for Public Buildings, yet
For Custard, Cake and Omelette.

Or if too Old for such a use
They have their Fling at some Abuse,
As when to Censure Plays Unfit
Upon the Stage they make a Hit,
Or at elections Seal the Fate
Of an Obnoxious Candidate.
No wonder, Child, we prize the Hen,
Whose Egg is Mightier than the Pen.

Kindness to Animals

See "Multiple Animals" chapter, Poetry section.

Kookoorooko! (Christina Rossetti, PreS/K–5)

"Kookoorookoo! kookoorookoo!"
Crows the cock before the morn;
"Kikirikee! kikirikee!"
Roses in the east are born.
"Kookoorookoo! kookoorookoo!"
Early birds begin their singing;
"Kikirikee! kikirikee!"
The day, the day, the day is springing.

Seven Little Chicks (Wilhelmina Seegmuller, PreS/K–5)

Seven little chicks go,
"Peep, peep, peep,"
Hunting where the grasses grow
Deep, deep, deep.

Then the mother hen calls,
"Cluck, cluck, cluck,"
Wishing every little chick
Luck, luck, luck.

There Was an Old Man with a Beard

See "Birds" chapter, Poetry section.

A White Hen Sitting (Christina Rossetti, PreS/K–5)

A white hen sitting
On white eggs three:
Next, three speckled chickens
As plump as plump can be.
An owl, and a hawk,
And a bat come to see:
But chicks beneath their mother's wing
Squat safe as safe can be.

COWS, BULLS, AND OXEN

Fingerplays and Action Rhymes

Did You Feed My Cow? (Traditional, Call and Response Rhyme, PreS/K–5)

1. Did you feed my cow? (Adult calls out this line.)
2. Yes, ma'am! (Children instructed to say this line.)

1. Will you tell me how?
2. Yes, ma'am!

1. What did you feed her?
2. Corn and hay.

1. What did you feed her?
2. Corn and hay.

1. Did you milk her good?
2. Yes, ma'am!

1. Did you milk her like you should?
2. Yes, ma'am!

1. How did you milk her?
2. Swish, swish, swish! (Mimic milking a cow.)

1. How did you milk her?
2. Swish, swish, swish!

This Little Cow Eats Grass (Traditional, B/T)

This little cow eats grass, (Tug on little toe or pinky.)
This little cow eats hay, (Tug on fourth toe or ring finger.)
This little cow drinks water, (Tug on middle toe or finger.)
This little cow runs away, (Tug on second toe or index finger.)
And this BIG cow does nothing at all,
But lie in the fields all day! (Tug on big toe or thumb.)
We'll chase her, we'll chase her, we'll chase her away! (Tickle child.)

Nursery Rhymes

As I Was Going to Banbury

See "Farm Animals" subsection of "Multiple Animals" chapter, Nursery Rhymes section

"Bow-Wow," says the Dog

See "Multiple Animals" chapter, Nursery Rhymes section.

Charley Warlie Had a Cow (Traditional, B/T/PreS)

(Also known as **Bobbie Shaftoe Had a Cow** or **Whooley Foster Had a Cow**)

Charley Warlie had a cow
Black and white about the brow;
Open the gate and let her go through,
Charley Warlie's old cow!

The Cock's on the Housetop

See "Multiple Animals" chapter, Nursery Rhymes section.

Cow and a Calf (Traditional, 6+)

A cow and a calf,
An ox and a half,
Forty good shillings and three;
Is that not enough tocher˙
For a shoemaker's daughter,
A bonny lass with a black eye?

* Tocher: Dowry

Cushy Cow, Bonnie (Traditional, K–5, 6+)

Cushy cow, Bonnie, let down thy milk,
And I will give thee a gown of silk;
A gown of silk and a silver tee,
If thou wilt let down thy milk for me.

A Farmer's Boy (Traditional, K–5, 6+)

They strolled down the lane together,
The sky was studded with stars—
They reached the gate in silence
And he lifted down the bars—
She neither smiled nor thanked him
Because she knew not how;
For he was just a farmer's boy
And she was a jersey cow.

The Friendly Beasts

See "Multiple Animals" chapter, Nursery Rhymes section.

Hurly, Burly, Trumpet Trase (Traditional, PreS/K–5)

Hurly, burly, trumpet trase,
The cow was in the market place,
Some goes far, and some goes near,
But where shall this poor henchman steer.

Hush-a-Bye

See "Farm Animals" subsection of "Multiple Animals" chapter, Nursery Rhymes section.

I Had a Little Cow (Traditional, PreS/K–5)

I had a little cow
Hey-diddle, ho-diddle.
I had a little cow, and it had a little calf.
Hey-diddle, ho-diddle, and there's my song half.

I had a little cow
Hey-diddle, ho-diddle.
I had a little cow and I drove it to the stall.
Hey-diddle, ho-diddle, and there's my song all.

I Had a Little Cow, to Save Her (Traditional, 6+)

I had a little cow, to save her,
I turned her into the meadow to graze her;
There came a heavy storm of rain,
And drove the little cow home again.
The church door they stood open,
And there the little cow was cropen:
The bell-ropes they were made of hay,
And the little cow ate them all away:
The sexton came to toll the bell,
And pushed the little cow into the well!

* Cropen: Tied up

I Never Saw a Purple Cow (Traditional, PreS/K–5/6+)

I never saw a purple cow.
I never hope to see one.
But I can tell you anyhow
I'd rather see than be one.

Johnny Armstrong Killed a Calf (Traditional, 6+)

Johnny Armstrong killed a calf,
Peter Henderson got half,
Willy Wilkinson got the head,
Ring the bell, the calf is dead!

The Little Black Dog

See "Multiple Animals" chapter, Nursery Rhymes section.

Little Maid, Little Maid

See Songs section.

My Father He Died

See "Multiple Animals" chapter, Nursery Rhymes section.

One Old Oxford Ox

See "Multiple Animals" chapter, Nursery Rhymes section.

Over the Hills and Far Away

See "Multiple Animals" chapter, Nursery Rhymes section.

Ring-a-Ring O'Roses (Traditional, B/T/PreS)

Ring-a-ring o'roses,
A pocket full of posies,
A-tishoo! A-tishoo!
We all fall down.

The cows are in the meadow
Lying fast asleep,
A-tishoo! A-tishoo!
We all get up again.

Robin and Richard Were Two Pretty Men

See "Multiple Animals" chapter, Nursery Rhymes section.

Sukey, You Shall Be My Wife

See "Farm Animals" subsection of "Multiple Animals" chapter, Nursery Rhymes section.

There Once Was a Man Who Said, "How" (Traditional, K–5/6+)

There once was a man who said, "How
Shall I manage to carry my cow?
For if I should ask it
To get in my basket,
'Twould make such a terrible row."

There Was an Old Woman Had Three Cows (Traditional, K–5/6+)

There was an old woman had three cows,
Rosy and Colin and Dun;
Rosy and Colin were sold at the fair,
And Dun broke her heart in a fit of despair,
So there was an end of her three cows,
Rosy and Colin and Dun.

There Was an Old Soldier of Bister (Traditional, K–5/6+)

There was an old soldier of Bister,
Went walking one day with his sister,
When a cow at a poke
Tossed her into an oak,
Before the old gentleman missed her.

There Was an Old Miser at Reading (Traditional, K–5/6+)

There was an old miser at Reading,
Had a house, and a yard with a shed in;

'Twas meant for cow,
But so small, that I vow
The poor creature could scarce get her head in.

There Was an Old Woman Sat Spinning (Traditional, K–5/6+)

There was an old woman sat spinning,
And that's the first beginning;
She had a calf,
And that's half,
She took it by the tail,
And threw it over the wall,
And that's all.

Alternate version:

There Was an Old Man (Traditional, K–5/6+)

There was an old man,
And he had a calf;
And that's half.
He took him out of the stall,
And put him on the wall;
And that's all.

There Was a Piper Had a Cow (Traditional, K–5/6+)

There was a piper, he'd a cow,
And he'd no hay to give her
He took his pipes and played a tune,
Consider, old cow, consider!

The cow considered very well,
For she gave the piper a penny,
That he might play the tune again,
Of corn rigs are bonnie!

This Is the House That Jack Built

See "Farm Animals" subsection of "Multiple Animals" chapter, Nursery Rhymes section.

'Tis Midnight

See "Multiple Animals" chapter, Nursery Rhymes section.

Uprising See the Fitful Lark

See "Multiple Animals" chapter, Nursery Rhymes section.

Whistle, Daughter, Whistle

See "Farm Animals" subsection of "Multiple Animals" chapter, Nursery Rhymes section.

Will You Go a Milking? (Traditional, 6+)

Will you go a milking, my dilding, my dalding?
I'll give you syllabubs from the cow,
With sugar and wine,
I will make them so fine,
For my grandmother she taught me how.

Will you go a milking, my dilding, my dalding?
I'll give you syllabubs from the cow,
In the yard she does stand,
Ready come to my hand;
So pray let us go to her now.

* Syllabubs: "Milk or cream that is curdled with an acid beverage (as wine or cider) and often sweetened and served as a drink or topping or thickened with gelatin and served as a dessert" (http://www.merriam-webster.com)

Songs

Fiddle-I-Fee

See "Farm Animals" subsection of "Multiple Animals" chapter, Songs section.

Git Along, Little Dogies (Traditional, K–5/6+)

As I was a-walk-ing one morn-ing for plea-sure, I

spi-ed a cow punch-er rid-ing a-long, His hat was throwed back and his

spurs were a ji-ng-lin', As he approach-ed he was

sing-ing this song: Whoop-ee ti yi yo, git a-long lit-tle dog-ies, It's

you-r mis-for-tune and none of my own. Whoop-ee ti yi yo, git a

-long lit-tle dog-ies, You know that Wy-om-ing will be your new home.

Hey, Diddle Diddle

See "Farm Animals" subsection of "Multiple Animals" chapter, Songs section.

Hush, Little Baby, Don't Say a Word

See "Multiple Animals" chapter, Songs section.

I Know an Old Lady Who Swallowed a Fly

See "Multiple Animals" chapter, Songs section.

Little Boy Blue

See "Farm Animals" subsection of "Multiple Animals" chapter, Songs section.

Little Maid, Little Maid (Traditional, PreS/K–5/6+)

(Also known as: **Little Maid, Pretty Maid**)

"Lit - tle maid, Lit - tle maid, whi - ther goest thou?" "Down to the mea - dow to mi - lk my cow." "Shall I go with thee?" "No, not now." "When I sent for thee, then come thou."

Old MacDonald

See "Farm Animals" subsection of "Multiple Animals" chapter, Songs section.

Simple Simon

See "Multiple Animals" chapter, Songs section.

Poetry

Brownie, Brownie, Let Down Your Milk (Christina Rossetti, K–5/6+)

Brownie, Brownie, let down your milk
White as swans down and smooth as silk,
Fresh as dew and pure as snow:
For I know where the cowslips blow,
And you shall have a cowslip wreath
No sweeter scented than your breath.

The Cow (Oliver Herford, 6+)

The Cow is too well known, I fear,
To need an introduction here.
If She should vanish from earth's face
It would be hard to fill her place;
For with the Cow would disappear
So much that every one holds Dear.
Oh, think of all the Boots and Shoes,
Milk Punches, Gladstone Bags and Stews,
And Things too numerous to count,
Of which, my child, she is the Fount.
Let's hope, at least, the Fount may last
Until our Generation's past.

The Friendly Cow (Robert Louis Stevenson)

The friendly cow all red and white,
I love with all my heart:
She gives me cream with all her might,
To eat with apple-tart.

She wanders lowing here and there,
And yet she cannot stray,
All in the pleasant open air,
The pleasant light of day;

And blown by all the winds that pass
And wet with all the showers,
She walks among the meadow grass
And eats the meadow flowers.

I Would Like You for a Comrade (Judge Parry, K–5/6+)

I would like you for a comrade, for I love you, that I do,
I never met a little calf as amiable as you;
I would teach you how to dance and sing and how to talk and laugh,
If I were not a little girl and you were not a calf.

I would like you for a comrade; you should share my barley meal,
And butt me with your little horns just hard enough to feel;
We would lie beneath the chestnut trees and watch the leaves uncurl,
If I were not a clumsy calf and you a little girl.

Kindness to Animals

See "Multiple Animals" chapter, Poetry section.

When the Cows Come Home the Milk Is Coming

See "Multiple Animals" chapter, Poetry section.

DEER AND ANTELOPE

Fingerplays and Action Rhymes

Frogs Jump
See "Multiple Animals" chapter, Fingerplays and Action Rhymes section.

Nursery Rhymes

Why Is Pussy in Bed?
See "Multiple Animals" chapter, Nursery Rhymes section.

Songs

Home on the Range
See "Multiple Animals" chapter, Songs section.

Poetry

Sage Counsel
See "Multiple Animals" chapter, Poetry section.

When the Cows Come Home the Milk Is Coming
See "Multiple Animals" chapter, Poetry section.

From *The Big Book of Animal Rhymes, Fingerplays, and Songs* by Elizabeth Cothen Low.
Westport, CT: Libraries Unlimited. Copyright © 2009.

DOGS

Fingerplays and Action Rhymes

Can You Hop Like a Rabbit?

See "Multiple Animals" chapter, Fingerplays and Action Rhymes section.

Dog Went to Dover (Traditional, B/T/PreS)

Leg over leg,
As the dog went to Dover,
When he comes to a stile,
Jump! He goes over! (Lift baby up or jump fingers over arm.)

Five Little Kittens Standing in a Row

See "Cats" chapter, Fingerplays and Action Rhymes section.

Frogs Jump

See "Multiple Animals" chapter, Fingerplays and Action Rhymes section.

My Dog Rags (Traditional, PreS/K–5)

I have a dog and his name is Rags. (Point to yourself.)
He eats so much that tummy sags. (Place arms out in front of you as if holding large belly.)
His ears flip-flop, (Place hands in front of ears and flap them up and down.)
And his tail wig-wags, (Have hands wave side-to-side for tail.)
And when he walks he zig-zags! (Move arm in zig-zag motion.)
Flip-flop, wig-wag, zig-zag. (Repeat motions.)

One Little, Two Little, Three Little Kittens

See "Pets" subsection of "Multiple Animals" chapter, Fingerplays and Action Rhymes section.

Nursery Rhymes

Barnaby Bright (Traditional, 6+)

Barnaby Bright he was a sharp cur,*
He always would bark if a mouse did but stir;
But now he's grown old, and can no longer bark,
He's condemned by the parson to be hanged by the clerk.

* Cur: Mutt

"Bow-Wow," says the Dog

See "Multiple Animals" chapter, Nursery Rhymes section.

Bow-Wow-Wow! (Traditional, K–5/6+)

Bow-wow-wow!
It's the great watch dog.
I know by his honest bark,
Bow-wow-wow!
Says the great watch dog,
When he hears a foot in the dark.

Not a breath can stir
But he's up with a whir
And a big bow-wow gives he,
And with tail on end,
He'll the house defend
Far better than lock or key.

Bow, Wow, Wow (Traditional, B/T/PreS)

Bow, wow, wow,
Whose dog art thou?
Little Tom Tinker's dog—
Bow, wow, wow.

Dingle Dingle Doosey

See "Pets" subsection of "Multiple Animals" chapter, Nursery Rhymes section.

A Dog and a Cock

See "Multiple Animals" chapter, Nursery Rhymes section.

The Dog Trim (Traditional, PreS/K–5)

There once was a nice little dog, Trim,
Who never had ill temper or whim;
He could sit up and dance,
Could run, skip, and prance.
Who would not like the little dog Trim?

Doggie, Go Away (Traditional, PreS/K–5)

Go away, doggie, oh dear, oh dear!
Doggie, oh, doggie, please don't come here!
I want my supper myself, I say.
Oh, mother, please come, and send doggie away.

A Gaping Wide-Mouthed Waddling Frog

See "Multiple Animals" chapter, Nursery Rhymes section.

A Grey-Hound Invited a Green-Finch to Tea

See "Multiple Animals" chapter, Nursery Rhymes section.

High, Ding, Cockatoo-Moody (Traditional, 6+)

High, ding, cockatoo-moody,
Make a bed in a barn, I will come to thee;
High, ding, straps of leather,
Two little puppy-dogs tied together;
One by the head, and one by the tail,
And over the water these puppy-dogs sail.

Hark, Hark

See Songs section in this chapter.

Higglety, Pigglety, Pop!

See "Farm Animals" subsection of "Multiple Animals" chapter, Nursery Rhymes section.

High Diddle Doubt

See "Farm Animals" subsection of "Multiple Animals" chapter, Nursery Rhymes section.

Hoddley, Poddley, Puddle and Fogs

See "Pets" subsection of "Multiple Animals" chapter, Nursery Rhymes section.

Hush-a-Bye

See "Farm Animals" subsection of "Multiple Animals" chapter, Nursery Rhymes section.

I Had a Little Dog (Traditional, K–5/6+)

I had a little dog and his name was Bluebell;
I gave him some work and he did it very well.
I sent him upstairs to pick up a pin,
He stepped in the coal-scuttle* up to his chin.
I sent him to the garden to pick some sage,
He tumbled down and fell in a rage;
I sent him to the cellar to draw a pot of beer,
He came up again and said there was none there.

* Coal-scuttle: Container used to store coal

The Little Black Dog

See "Multiple Animals" chapter, Nursery Rhymes section.

Little Piggy Wiggy

See "Multiple Animals" chapter, Nursery Rhymes section.

Little Tommy Titmouse

See "Multiple Animals" chapter, Nursery Rhymes section.

Oh, Where, Oh, Where Has My Little Dog Gone?

See Songs section in this chapter.

Old Mother Hubbard/ The Comic Adventures of Old Mother Hubbard and Her Dog
(Traditional, PreS/K–5/6+)

Old Mother Hubbard
Went to the cupboard,
To fetch her poor dog a bone;
But when she got there
The cupboard was bare,
And so the poor dog had none.

She went to the baker's
To buy him some bread;
But when she came back
The poor dog was dead!

She went to undertaker's
To buy him a coffin;
But when she came back
The poor dog was laughing.

She took a clean dish
To get him some tripe;
But when she came back
He was smoking a pipe.

She went to the alehouse
To get him some beer;
But when she came back
The dog sat in a chair.

She went to the fishmonger's
To buy him some fish,
But when she came back
He was licking the dish.

She went to the tavern
For white wine and red;
But when she came back
The dog stood on his head.

She went to the fruiterer's
To buy him some fruit;
But when she came back
He was playing the flute.

She went to the tailor's
To buy him a coat;
But when she came back
He was riding a goat,
She went to the hatter's
To buy him a hat;

From *The Big Book of Animal Rhymes, Fingerplays, and Songs* by Elizabeth Cothen Low.
Westport, CT: Libraries Unlimited. Copyright © 2009.

But when she came back
He was feeding the cat.

She went to the barber's
To buy him a wig;
But when she came back
He was dancing a jig.

She went to the cobbler's
To buy him some shoes;
But when she came back
He was reading the news.

She went to the seamstress
To buy him some linen;
But when she came back
The dog was a-spinning.

She went to the hosier's
To buy him some hose;
But when she came back
He was dressed in his clothes.

The dame made a curtsey,
The dog made a bow;
The dame said, Your servant,
The dog said, Bow-wow.

Robin and Richard Were Two Pretty Men

See "Multiple Animals" chapter, Nursery Rhymes section.

Tell-Tale Tit (Traditional, K–5/6+)

Tell-Tale Tit!
Your tongue shall be slit,
And all the dogs in the town
Shall have a little bit.

Two Legs Sat Upon Three Legs (Traditional, Riddle, K–5/6+)

Two legs sat upon three legs
With one leg in his lap;
In comes four legs
And runs away with one leg;

Up jumps two legs,
Catch up three legs,
Throws it after four legs,
And makes him bring back one leg.

Answer: Two legs (man), three legs (stool), one leg (meat), four legs (dog)

There Was a Man, and His Name Was Dob

See "Pets" subsection of "Multiple Animals" chapter, Nursery Rhymes section.

There Was an Old Woman (Traditional, 6+)

There was an old woman, as I've heard tell,
She went to market her eggs for to sell;
She went to market all on a market-day,
And she fell asleep on the king's highway.

There came by a peddler whose name was Stout,
He cut her petticoats all round about;
He cut her petticoats up to the knees,
Which made the old woman to shiver and freeze.

When this little woman first did wake,
She began to shiver and she began to shake,
She began to wonder and she began to cry,
"Oh! deary, deary me, this is none of I!

"But if it be I, as I do hope it be,
I've a little dog at home, and he'll know me;
If it be I, he'll wag his little tail,
And if it be not I, he'll loudly bark and wail."

Home went the little woman all in the dark,
Up got the little dog, and he began to bark;
He began to bark, so she began to cry,
"Oh! deary, deary me, this is none of I!"

This Is the House That Jack Built

See "Farm Animals" subsection of "Multiple Animals" chapter, Nursery Rhymes section.

Three Young Rats with Black Felt Hats

See "Multiple Animals" chapter, Nursery Rhymes section.

Two Little Dogs Sat by the Fire (Traditional, K–5/6+)

Two little dogs
Sat by the fire
Over a fender* of coal dust.
Says one little dog
To the other little dog,
If you don't talk, why, I must.

* Fender of coal dust: Fireplace screen

Uprising See the Fitful Lark

See "Multiple Animals" chapter, Nursery Rhymes section.

We Make No Spare

See "Horses" chapter, Nursery Rhymes section.

Wingy, Wongy (Traditional, K–5/6+)

Wingy, wongy,
Days are longy,
Cuckoo and the sparrow;
Little dog has lost his tail,
And he shall be hung to-morrow.

Why Is Pussy in Bed?

See "Multiple Animals" chapter, Nursery Rhymes section.

Whoop, Whoop, and Hollow (Traditional, K–5/6+)

Whoop, whoop, and hollow,
Good dogs won't follow,
Without the hare cries "pee wit."

Songs

Farmer in the Dell

See "Farm Animals" subsection of "Multiple Animals" chapter, Songs section.

Fiddle-I-Fee

See "Farm Animals" subsection of "Multiple Animals" chapter, Songs section.

Hark, Hark (Traditional, PreS/K–5)

Hark! Hark! The dogs do bark, Beg-gars are com-ing to town;

Some in jags, some in rags, and one in a vel-vet gown; Some in jags,

some in rags, and one in a vel-vet gown.

Hey, Diddle Diddle

See "Farm Animals" subsection of "Multiple Animals" chapter, Songs section.

Hush, Little Baby, Don't Say a Word

See "Multiple Animals" chapter, Songs section.

I Had a Little Doggy (Traditional, PreS/K–5)

I had a lit-tle dog-gy that used to sit and beg, But

Dog-gy tumbl-ed down the stairs, and broke his lit-tle leg; Oh!

dog-gy I will nurse you, and try to make you well, And

you shall have a col-lar with a pre-ty lit-tle bell.

Verse 2: Ah! Doggy, don't you think you should very faithful be,
For having such a loving friend to comfort you as me.
And when your leg is better, and you can run and play,
We'll have a scamper in the fields, and see them making hay.

Verse 3: But, Doggy, you must promise (and mind your word you keep)
Not once to tease the little lambs, or run among the sheep.
And then the yellow chicks that play upon the grass,
You must not even wag your tail to scare them as you pass.

I Know an Old Lady Who Swallowed a Fly

See "Multiple Animals" chapter, Songs section.

Oh, Where, Oh, Where Has My Little Dog Gone? (Traditional, PreS/K–5)

Oh, where, oh where has my lit-tle dog gone, Oh where, oh where can he

be? With his ears cut short and his tail cut long, Oh, where, oh where is

he?

Old MacDonald

See "Farm Animals" subsection of "Multiple Animals" chapter, Songs section.

Poor Dog Bright

See "Pets" subsection of "Multiple Animals" chapter, Songs section.

There Was a Farmer Had a Dog (Traditional, PreS/K–5)

(Also known as **BINGO**)

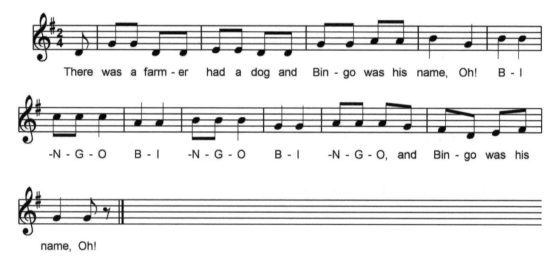

There was a farm-er had a dog and Bin-go was his name, Oh! B-I

-N-G-O B-I -N-G-O B-I -N-G-O, and Bin-go was his

name, Oh!

Verse 2: There was a farmer had a dog,
And Bingo was its name-o.
(Clap) I-N-G-O,
(Clap) I-N-G-O,
(Clap) I-N-G-O,
And Bingo was its name-o.

Verse 3: . . . (Clap, clap) N-G-O . . .
Verse 4: . . . (Clap, clap, clap) G-O . . .
Verse 5: . . .. (Clap, clap, clap, clap) O . . .
Verse 6: . . .. (Clap, clap, clap, clap, clap) . . . .

This Old Man (Traditional, PreS/K–5)

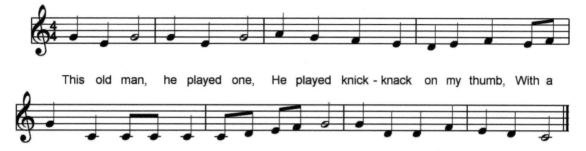

This old man, he played one, He played knick-knack on my thumb, With a
knick-knack pad-dy whack, give the dog a bone, This old man came roll-ing home.

Verse 2: This old man,
He played two,
He played nick-nack
On my shoe . . .

Verse 3: . . . on my knee . . .
Verse 4: . . . on my door . . .
Verse 5: . . . on my hive . . .
Verse 6: . . . on my sticks . . .
Verse 7: . . . up to heaven . . .
Verse 8: . . . on my gate . . .
Verse 9: . . . on my spine . . .
Verse 10: . . . nick-nack once again . . .

What Are Little Boys Made Of?

See "Multiple Animals" chapter, Songs section.

Poetry

The Diner in the Kitchen (James Whitcomb Riley, PreS/K–5)

Our dog Fred
Et the bread

Our dog Dash
Et the hash

Our dog Pete
Et the meat

Our dog Davy
Et the gravy

Our dog Toffy
Et the coffee

Our dog Jake
Et the cake

Our dog Trip
Et the dip

And—the worst,
From the first—

Our dog Fido
Et the pie-dough

The Dog Lies in His Kennel

See "Pets" subsection of "Multiple Animals" chapter, Poetry section.

An Elegy on the Death of a Mad Dog (Oliver Goldsmith, 6+)

Good people all, of every sort,
Give ear unto my song;
And if you find it wondrous short,—
It cannot hold you long.

In Islington there was a man,
Of whom the world might say
That still a godly race he ran,—
Whene'er he went to pray.

A kind and gentle heart he had,
To comfort friends and foes;
The naked every day he clad,—
When he put on his clothes.

And in that town a dog was found,
As many dogs there be,
Both mongrel, puppy, whelp, and hound,
And curs of low degree.

The dog and man at first were friends;
But when a pique began,
The dog, to gain some private ends,
Went mad, and bit the man.

Around from all the neighboring streets,
The wondering neighbors ran,
And swore the dog had lost his wits
To bite so good a man.

The wound it seemed both sore and sad
To every Christian eye;
And while they swore the dog was mad
They swore the man would die.

But soon a wonder came to light,
That showed the rogues they lied;
The man recovered of the bite,
The dog it was that died.

* Whelp: Young dog
* Curs: Mutts
* Pique: Dispute

Hop-o'-My-Thumb (Christina Rossetti, K–5/6+)

Hop-o'-my-thumb and little Jack Horner,
What do you mean by tearing and fighting?
Sturdy dog Trot close round the corner,
I never caught him growling and biting.

Kindness to Animals

See "Multiple Animals" chapter, Poetry section.

The Moon

See "Multiple Animals" chapter, Poetry section.

Old Dog Tray (Stephen Foster, K–5/6+)

The morn of life is past
And evening comes at last,
It brings me a dream of a once happy day,
Of merry forms I've see
Upon the village green,
A-sporting with my old dog Tray.

Old dog Tray's ever faithful.
Grief cannot drive him away.
He's gentle and he's kind,
I'll never, never find
A better friend than old dog Tray.

Pussy Has a Whiskered Face

See "Pets" subsection of "Multiple Animals" chapter, Poetry section.

There Was an Old Man of Leghorn (Edward Lear, K–5/6+)

There was an Old Man of Leghorn,
The smallest that ever was born;
But quickly snapt up he
Was once by a Puppy,
Who devoured that Old Man of Leghorn.

There Was an Old Man of Kamschatka (Edward Lear, K–5/6+)

There was an Old Man of Kamschatka
Who possessed a remarkably fat Cur;*
His gait and his waddle
Were held as a model
To all the fat dogs in Kamschatka.

* Cur: Mutt

DONKEYS

See also the chapter "Horses and Mules."

Nursery Rhymes

Donkey, Donkey, Old and Gray (Traditional, PreS/K–5)

Donkey, donkey, old and gray,
Open your mouth and gently bray;
Lift your ears and blow your horn,
To wake the world this sleepy morn.

Donkey, donkey, do not bray,
But mend your pace and trot away.
Indeed the market's almost done,
My butter's melting in the sun.

The Friendly Beasts

See "Multiple Animals" chapter, Nursery Rhymes section.

If I Had a Donkey (Traditional, PreS/K–5)

If I had a donkey that wouldn't go,
D'you think I'd beat him? Oh, no, no.
I'd put him in a barn and give him some corn,
The best little donkey that ever was born.

The Little Donkey (Traditional, PreS/K–5)

I'm a poor little donkey,
And work very hard;
To my sighs and fatigues
Master pays no regard:

Yet for him would I toil,
And do always my best,
Would he speak to me kindly,
And give me some rest.

Over the Hills and Far Away

See "Multiple Animals" chapter, Nursery Rhymes section.

Sweetly Sings the Donkey (Traditional, PreS/K–5)

Sweetly sings the donkey as he goes to hay.
If you do not hold him, he will run away.
Kee'yi, Kee'yo

From *The Big Book of Animal Rhymes, Fingerplays, and Songs* by Elizabeth Cothen Low.
Westport, CT: Libraries Unlimited. Copyright © 2009.

Kee'yi, Kee'yo, Kee'yay,
Kee'yi, Kee'yo
Kee'yi, Kee'yo, Kee'yay.

Up in the North a Long Way Off (Traditional, PreS/K–5)

Up in the north a long way off,
A donkey caught the whooping cough.
What shall we give to make him better?
Salt, mustard, vinegar, and pepper.

Poetry

What Does the Donkey Bray About?

See "Multiple Animals" chapter, Poetry section.

DUCKS

Fingerplays and Action Rhymes

Can You Hop Like a Rabbit?

See "Multiple Animals" chapter, Fingerplays and Action Rhymes section.

Five Little Ducks

See Songs section in this chapter.

Five Little Ducks Went in for a Swim (Traditional, PreS/K–5)

Five little ducks went in for a swim; (Wiggle all five fingers.)
The first little duck put his head in, (Wiggle thumb.)
The second little duck put his head back; (Wiggle index finger.)
The third little duck said, "Quack, quack, quack." (Wiggle middle finger.)
The fourth little duck with his tiny brother, (Wiggle ring finger and pinky.)
Went for a walk with his father and mother. (Show index and middle fingers on other hand.)

Mr. Duck Went out to Walk (Traditional, PreS/K–5)

(Also known as Mr. Turkey and Mr. Duck)

Mr. Duck went out to walk, (Hold up right index finger.)
One day in lovely weather.
He met Mr. Turkey on the way. (Hold up left index finger.)
They stopped and talked together.
Gobble! Gobble! Gobble! (Bend and unbend left finger at joint.)
Quack! Quack! Quack! (Bend and unbend right finger at joint.)
Gobble! Gobble! Gobble!
Quack! Quack! Quack!
And then they walked on back. (Hide behind back.)

Six Little Ducks

See Songs section.

Nursery Rhymes

"Bow-Wow," says the Dog

See "Multiple Animals" chapter, Nursery Rhymes section.

Charley Barley, Butter and Eggs (Traditional, PreS/K–5)

Charley Barley, butter and eggs,
Sold his wife for three duck eggs.
When the ducks began to lay
Charley Barley flew away.

The Cock's on the Housetop

See "Multiple Animals" chapter, Nursery Rhymes section.

Dame Duck's First Lecture on Education (Traditional, K–5/6+)

Old Mother Duck has hatched a brood
Of ducklings, small and callow;
Their little wings are short, their down
Is mottled gray and yellow.

There is a quiet little stream,
That runs into the moat,
Where tall green sedges spread their leaves,
And water lilies float.

Close by the margin of the brook
The old duck made her nest,
Of straw, and leaves, and withered grass,
And down from her own breast.

And then she sat for four long weeks
In rainy days and fine,
Until the ducklings all came out—
Four, five, six, seven, eight, nine.

One peeped out from beneath her wing,
One scrambled on her back;
"That's very rude," said old Dame Duck,
"Get off! quack, quack, quack, quack!"

" 'Tis close," said Dame Duck, shoving out
The eggshells with her bill;
"Besides, it never suits young ducks
To keep them sitting still."

So, rising from her nest, she said,
"Now, children, look at me;
A well-bred duck should waddle so,
From side to side—d' ye see?"

"Yes," said the little ones, and then
She went on to explain:
"A well-bred duck turns in its toes
As I do—try again."

"Yes," said the ducklings, waddling on:
"That's better," said their mother;
"But well-bred ducks walk in a row,
Straight—one behind another."

"Yes," said the little ducks again,
All waddling in a row:
"Now to the pond," said old Dame Duck—
Splash, splash, and in they go.

"Let me swim first," said old Dame Duck,
"To this side, now to that;
There, snap at those great brown-winged flies,
They make young ducklings fat.

"Now when you reach the poultry yard,
The hen-wife, Molly Head,
Will feed you, with the other fowls,
On bran and mashed-up bread.

"The hens will peck and fight, but mind,
I hope that all of you
Will gobble up the food as fast
As well-bred ducks should do.

"You'd better get into the dish,
Unless it is too small;
In that case, I should use my foot,
And overturn it all."

The ducklings did as they were bid,
And found the plan so good,
That, from that day, the other fowls
Got hardly any food.

* Callow: Immature
* Sedges: A kind of marsh plant

A Duck and a Drake (Traditional, K–5/6+)

A duck and a drake,
And a nice barley cake,
With a penny to pay the old baker;
A hop and a scotch
Is another notch,
Slitherum, slatherum, take her.

A Gentleman of Wales

See "Multiple Animals" chapter, Nursery Rhymes section.

I Saw a Ship a-Sailing

See "Multiple Animals" chapter, Nursery Rhymes section.

There Was a Little Man (Traditional, 6+)

There was a little man,
He had a little gun,
The bullets they were made of lead;
He went to the brook,
He shot a little duck,
And shot it through the head.

He carried it home to his wife Joan,
And a fire he bid her make,
To dress the little duck, while he went to the brook,
And shot, shot, shot the drake.

Three Young Rats with Black Felt Hats

See "Multiple Animals" chapter, Nursery Rhymes section.

Uprising See the Fitful Lark

See "Multiple Animals" chapter, Nursery Rhymes section.

What an Odd Dame

See "Farm Animals" subsection of "Multiple Animals" chapter, Nursery Rhymes section.

Why Is Pussy in Bed?

See "Multiple Animals" chapter, Nursery Rhymes section.

Songs

Be Kind to Your Web-Footed Friends (Traditional, PreS/K–5/6+)

Be kind to your web-foot-ed friends, For a duck may be some-bo-dy's

moth-er, Be kind to the birds in the swamp, For the weath-er is ver-y

damp. Oh, you may think this is the end, Well it is!

Dame, Get Up and Bake Your Pies (Traditional, K–5/6+)

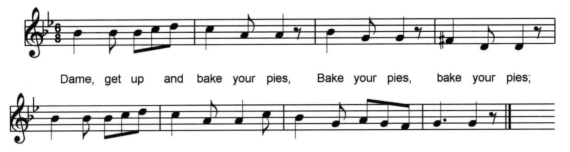

Dame, get up and bake your pies, Bake your pies, bake your pies;

Dame, get up and bake your pies, On Chris-mas day in the morn-ing.

Verse 2:   Dame, what makes your maidens lie,
             Maidens lie, maidens lie;
             Dame, what makes your maidens lie,
             On Christmas day in the morning.

Verse 3:   Dame, what makes your ducks to die,
             Ducks to die, duck to die;
             Dame, what makes your ducks to die,
             On Christmas day in the morning.

Verse 4:   Their wings are cut and they cannot fly,
             Cannot fly, cannot fly;
             Their wings are cut and they cannot fly,
             On Christmas day in the morning.

Fiddle-I-Fee

See "Farm Animals" subsection of "Multiple Animals" chapter, Songs section.

Five Little Ducks (Traditional, B/T/PreS/K–5)

(Also known as **Five Little Ducks Went Out to Play** and **Five Little Ducks Went Swimming One Day**)

Five lit-tle ducks went out one day, Over the hills and far a-way;

Moth-er Duck said, "Quack, quack, quack," and four lit-tle ducks came

run-ning back.

Verse 2: Four little ducks went out one day, (Show five fingers.)
          Over the hills and far away, (Move right hand and arm in curvy up and down motion as if
              following a mountain path.)
          Mother Duck said, "Quack, quack, quack, quack." (Pretend hand is a duck's mouth.)
          But only three little ducks came back. (Show four fingers.)

Verse 3: Three little ducks went out one day... (Repeat same lines for four ducks.)
Verse 4: Two little ducks went out one day . . .
Verse 5: One little duck went out one day,
          Over the hills and far away,
          Mother Duck said, "Quack, quack, quack, quack,"
          And all of the five little ducks came back.

Simple Simon

See "Multiple Animals" chapter, Songs section.

Six Little Ducks (Traditional, B/T/PreS/K–5)

(Also known as Five Little Ducks That I Once Knew)

He led the   oth - ers with a   quack, quack, quack!

Verse 1   (With instructions): Six little ducks that I once knew, (Hold up six fingers.)
          Fat ones, (Hold up thumb.)
          Skinny ones, (Hold up pinky.)
          Fair ones, too. (Hold up three middle fingers.)
          But the one little duck (Hold up index finger.)
          With the feather on his back, (Bend over and place hands on lower back with fingers
              pointing skyward.)

He led the other with a "quack, quack, quack." (Bring thumb and fingers of right hand
     together in "talking" motion.)
Quack, quack, quack, (Continue to "quack" with left hand.)
Quack, quack, quack,
He led the others with a "quack, quack, quack."

Verse 2:   Down to the river they would go,
          Wibble, wobble, wibble, wobble to and fro.
          But the one little duck with the feather on his back,
          He led the others with a "quack, quack, quack."
          Quack, quack, quack, (Continue to "quack" with left hand.)
          Quack, quack, quack,
          He led the others with a "quack, quack, quack."

Verse 3:   Home from the river they would come,
          Wibble, wobble, wibble, wobble, ho-hum-hum!
          But the one little duck with the feather on his back,
          He led the others with a "quack, quack, quack."
          Quack, quack, quack, (Continue to "quack" with left hand.)
          Quack, quack, quack,
          He led the others with a "quack, quack, quack."

Poetry

When the Cows Come Home the Milk Is Coming

See "Multiple Animals" chapter, Poetry section.

Elephants

Fingerplays and Action Rhymes

The Elephant (Traditional, B/T/PreS/K–5)

An elephant goes like this and that. (Get on hands and knees and rock back and forth.)
He's terribly big, and he's terribly fat. (Reach up to the sky, then stretch arms out wide.)
He has no fingers, he has no toes, (Wiggle fingers, point to toes.)
But goodness gracious, what a nose! (Curve arm swing it right and left like an elephant trunk.)

One Elephant Went Out to Play

See Songs section in this chapter.

Nursery Rhymes

The Elephant Carries a Great Big Trunk (Traditional, PreS/K–5)

The elephant carries a great big trunk;
He never packs it with clothes;
It has no lock and it has no key,
But he takes it wherever he goes

Miss Mary Mack (Traditional, Clapping Rhyme, PreS/K–5)

(Also known as I Asked My Mother for Fifty Cents)

Miss Mary Mack, Mack, Mack,
All dressed in black, black, black.
With silver buttons, buttons, buttons
All down her back, back, back.

She asked her mother, mother, mother,
For fifteen cents, cents, cents,
To see the elephant, elephant, elephant,
Jump the fence, fence, fence.

He jumped so high, high, high,
He touched the sky, sky, sky,
And never come back, back, back,
Till the Fourth of July, ly, ly.

The Moon Is Up

See "Multiple Animals" chapter, Nursery Rhymes section.

One Old Oxford Ox

See "Multiple Animals" chapter, Nursery Rhymes section.

From *The Big Book of Animal Rhymes, Fingerplays, and Songs* by Elizabeth Cothen Low.
Westport, CT: Libraries Unlimited. Copyright © 2009.

The Panther

See "Multiple Animals" chapter, Nursery Rhymes section.

Songs

Ain't It Great to Be Crazy?

See "Multiple Animals" chapter, Songs section.

Animal Fair

See "Multiple Animals" chapter, Songs section.

One Elephant Went out to Play (Traditional, PreS/K–5)

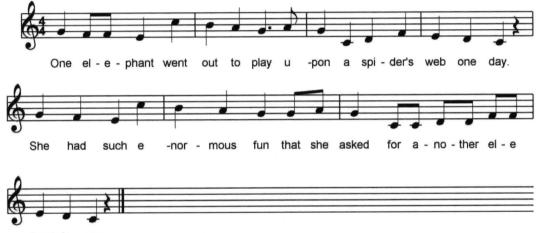

One el-e-phant went out to play u-pon a spi-der's web one day.

She had such e-nor-mous fun that she asked for a-no-ther el-e

-phant to come.

Verse 2:   Two elephants went out to play
            Upon a spider's web one day.
            They had such enormous fun
            That they called for another elephant to come.

Suggestion: Have each child pull another one to the center of a circle. Continue to add verses until all of the children are accounted for.

Spanish version: Los elefantes (Traditional)

Un elefante se balanceaba
sobre la tela de una araña.
Como veía que resistía
fue a llamar a otro elefante.

Verse 2:   Dos elefantes se balanceaban
            sobre la tela de una arena.
            Como veía que resistía
            fueron a llamar a otro elefante.

Verse 3:   Tres...

Poetry

The Elephant (Hilaire Belloc, K–5/6+)

When people call this beast to mind,
They marvel more and more
At such a little tail behind,
So LARGE a trunk before.

FISH

See also the chapter "Jellyfish."

Fingerplays and Action Rhymes

Can You Hop Like a Rabbit?

See "Multiple Animals" chapter, Fingerplays and Action Rhymes section

The Fish Lives in the Brook (Traditional, B/T/PreS)

The fish lives in the brook, (Place hands together and wiggle arms side to side.)
The bird lives in the tree, (Raise both arms, like tree limbs.)
But home's the very nicest place
For a little child like me. (Point to yourself.)

Five Little Fishes Swimming in a Pool (Traditional, B/T/PreS/K–5)

Five little fishes were swimming in a pool.
First one said, "This pool is cool." (Tug on thumb.)
Second one said, "This pool is deep." (Tug on index finger.)
Third one said, "I think I'll sleep." (Tug on middle finger.)
Fourth one said, "Let's swim and dip." (Tug on ring finger.)
Fifth one said, "I see a ship." (Tug on fifth finger.)
Line goes splish, splash, (Pretend to cast a fishing line.)
And away the five little fishes dashed. (Hide fingers behind back.)

Here Is the Sea (Traditional, PreS/K–5)

Here is the sea, the wavy sea. (Make swimming motion with hand.)
Here is a boat, and here is me. (Cup left hand and place palm upward to form "boat." Hold right index
    finger upright and have it sit in boat.)
And all the fishes down below, (Continue to maintain boat position with left hand. Point downward
    with right hand under left hand.)
Wriggle their tails and away they go. (Wiggle hands and place behind back.)

I Hold My Fingers Like a Fish (Traditional, PreS/K–5)

I hold my fingers like a fish, (Place palms together.)
And wave them as I go.
See them swimming with a swish, (Maintaining above position, move wrists side to side.)
So swiftly to and fro.

A Little Boy's Walk

See "Multiple Animals" chapter, Finger Play/Action Rhymes section.

One, Two, Three, Four, Five (Traditional, PreS/K–5)

One, two, three, four, five, (Count out fingers starting with index finger and ending with thumb.)
Once I caught a fish alive. (Wiggle left hand and grab it with right hand.)
Six, seven, eight, nine, ten, (Count out fingers on other hand.)

Then I let it go again. (Close hands together and then release.)
Why did you let him go?
Because he bit my finger so. (Hold right pinky with left hand.)
Which finger did he bite?
This little finger on the right. (Hold up right pinky.)

Nursery Rhymes

Dance to Your Daddy (Traditional, B/T/PreS)

Dance to your daddy,
My little laddie.
Dance to your daddy,
My little lamb.

You shall have a fishy
In a little dishy;
You shall have a fishy
When the boat comes in.
Dance to your daddy, my little laddie,

Dance to your daddy, my little lamb.
You shall have an apple,
You shall have a plum,
You shall have an apple
When your dad comes home.

Fishy, Fishy in the Brook (Traditional, B/T/PreS/K–5)

(Also known as **Little Fishy in the Brook**)

Fishy, fishy in the brook,
Daddy catch him on a hook,
Mommy fry him in a pan,
Johnny eat him like a man.

Fishes Swim in Water Clear

See "Multiple Animals" chapter, Nursery Rhymes section.

Flounders! Jumping Alive! Fine Flounders! (Traditional, PreS/K–5/6+)

"Come buy my live flounders! All jumping, ho!"
"Alive?' 'Yes, all jumping, Ma'am, two hours ago;
From sea just arrived, else may truth never thrive!
Fine flounders! Fresh flounders! All jumping alive!"

Ickle, Ockle, Blue Bockle (Traditional, PreS/K–5)

Ickle, ockle, blue bockle,
Fishes in the sea,
If you want a pretty maid,
Please choose me.

In Fir Tar Is

See "Multiple Animals" chapter, Nursery Rhymes section.

The Man in the Wilderness Asked Me (Traditional, PreS/K–5/6+)

The man in the wilderness asked me,
How many strawberries grew in the sea?
I answered him, as I thought good,
As many as red herrings grew in the wood.

One Old Oxford Ox

See "Multiple Animals" chapter, Nursery Rhymes section.

Terence McDiddler (Traditional, PreS/K–5)

Terence McDiddler,
The three-stringed fiddler,
Can charm, if you please,
The fish from the seas.

When the Wind Is in the East (Traditional, Sayings, K–5/6+)

When the wind is in the east,
'Tis good for neither man nor beast;

When the wind is in the north,
The skillful fisher goes not forth;

When the wind is in the south,
It blows the bait in the fishes' mouth;

When the wind is in the west,
Then it is at its very best.

Songs

Over in the Meadow

See "Multiple Animals" chapter, Songs section.

Poetry

If a Mouse Could Fly

See "Multiple Animals" chapter, Poetry section.

Kindness to Animals

See "Multiple Animals" chapter, Poetry section.

The Learned Fish (Hilaire Belloc, K–5/6+)

This learned Fish has not sufficient brains
To go into the water when it rains.

Minnie and Mattie (Christina Rossetti, K–5/6+)

Minnie and Mattie
And fat little May,
Out in the country,
Spending a day.

Such a bright day,
With the sun glowing,
And the trees half in leaf,
And the grass growing.

Pinky-white pigling
Squeals through his snout,
Woolly-white lambkin
Frisks all about.

Cluck! Cluck! the nursing hen
Summons her folk,—
Ducklings all downy soft,
Yellow as yolk.

Cluck! Cluck! the mother hen
Summons her chickens
To peck the dainty bits
Found in her pickings.

Minnie and Mattie
And May carry posies,
Half of sweet violets,
Half of primroses.

Give the sun time enough,
Glowing and glowing,
He'll rouse the roses
And bring them blowing.

Don't wait for roses,
Losing to-day,
O Minnie, O Mattie,
And wise little May.

Violets and primroses
Blossom to-day,
For Minnie and Mattie
And fat little May.

The Peacock Has a Score of Eyes

See "Multiple Animals" chapter, Poetry section.

Timid Hortense (Peter Newell, K–5/6+)

"Now, if the fish will only bite, we'll have some royal fun."
"And do fish bite? The horrid things! Indeed, I'll not catch one!"

When Fishes Set Umbrellas Up

See "Multiple Animals" chapter, Poetry section.

Wynken, Blynken, and Nod (Eugene Field, K–5/6+)

Wynken, Blynken, and Nod one night
Sailed off in a wooden shoe.
Sailed on a river of crystal light
Into a sea of dew.
"Where are you going, and what do you wish?"
The old moon asked the three.
"We have come to fish for the herring fish
That lives in this beautiful sea.
Nets of silver and gold have we!"
Said Wynken, Blynken, and Nod.

The old moon laughed and sang a song,
As they rocked in the wooden shoe,
And the wind that sped them all night long,
Ruffled the waves of dew.
The little stars were the herring fish
That lived in that beautiful sea.
"Now cast your net wherever you wish—
Never afeared are we."
So cried the stars to the fisherman three:
Wynken, Blynken, and Nod.

All night long their nets they threw
To the stars in the twinkling foam;
Then down from the skies came the wooden shoe,
Bringing the fisherman home.
'Twas all so pretty a sail, it seemed
As if it could not be;
And some folks thought 'twas a dream they'd dreamed
Of sailing that beautiful sea:
But I shall name you the fisherman three:
Wynken, Blynken, and Nod.

Wynken and Blynken are two little eyes,
And Nod is a little head;
And the wooden shoe that sailed the skies
Is a wee one's trundle-bed.
So shut your eyes while Mother sings
Of wonderful sights that be,
And you shall see the beautiful things
As you rock in the misty sea,
Where the old shoe rocked the fisherman three:
Wynken, Blynken, and Nod.

From The Big Book of Animal Rhymes, Fingerplays, and Songs by Elizabeth Cothen Low.
Westport, CT: Libraries Unlimited. Copyright © 2009.

FOXES

Fingerplays and Action Rhymes

Put Your Finger in Foxy's Hole (Traditional, B/T/PreS/K–5)

Put your finger in Foxy's hole. (Have child place finger in adult's loose fist.)
Foxy's not at home.
Foxy's at the back door,
Picking on a bone! (Tighten grip around child's finger.)

Nursery Rhymes

A Dog and a Cock

See "Multiple Animals" chapter, Nursery Rhymes section.

A-Hunting We Will Go

See Song section.

Fox a Fox (Traditional, Game, K–5/6+)

Fox a fox, a brummalary,
How many miles to Lummaflary? Lummabary.
Eight and eight, and a hundred and eight.
How shall I get home tonight?
Spin your legs, and run fast. (Children run from "fox.")

The Fox Went Out on a Chilly Night (Traditional, K–5, 6+)

The fox went out on a chilly night.
He prayed to the moon to give him light.
For he'd many a mile to go that night
Before he'd reach the town-o, town-o, town-o
He'd many a mile to go that night
Before he reached the town-o.

He ran till he came to a great big bin,
The ducks and the geese were kept therein;
A couple of you will grease my chin
Before I leave this town-o . . . (Repeat refrain as in previous verse.)
So he grabbed a gray goose by the neck
And threw a duck across his back;
He didn't mind their "quack, quack, quack"
And their legs dangling down-o . . . (Repeat refrain as in first verse.)

Then old Mother Flipper-flopped jumped out of bed
And out of the window she stuck her head;
Said, "John, John, the gray goose is gone,
And the fox is in the town-o . . . (Repeat refrain as in first verse.)

So John he ran to the top of the hill
And he blew his horn both loud and shrill;
The fox said, "I'd better flee with my kill
Or they'll soon be on my trail-o . . . (Repeat refrain as in first verse.)

He ran till he came to his cozy den
And there were his little ones, eight, nine, and ten;
They said, "Daddy, you better go back again
'Cause it must be a mighty fine town-o . . . (Repeat refrain as in first verse.)

So the fox and wife, without any strife,
They cut up the goose with a fork and a knife;
They never had such a supper in their lives
And the little ones chewed on the bones-o . . . (Repeat refrain as in first verse.)

One Moonshiny Night (Traditional, K–5/6+)

One moonshiny night
As I sat high,
Waiting for one
To come by;
The boughs did bend,
My heart did ache
To see what hole the fox did make.

The Peacock Has a Score of Eyes

See "Multiple Animals" chapter, Poetry section.

Songs

A-Hunting We Will Go (Traditional, B/T/PreS/K–5)

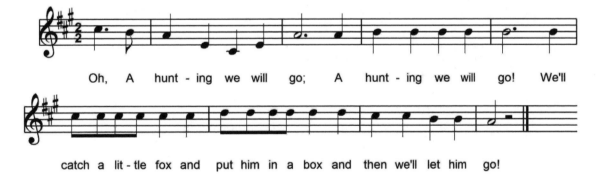

Oh, A hunt - ing we will go; A hunt - ing we will go! We'll

catch a lit - tle fox and put him in a box and then we'll let him go!

From *The Big Book of Animal Rhymes, Fingerplays, and Songs* by Elizabeth Cothen Low.
Westport, CT: Libraries Unlimited. Copyright © 2009.

FROGS AND TOADS

Fingerplays and Action Rhymes

Can You Hop Like a Rabbit?

See "Multiple Animals" chapter, Fingerplays and Action Rhymes section.

Five Little Froggies (Traditional, B/T/PreS/K–5)

Five little froggies sat on the shore, (Hold up five fingers.)
One went for a swim, and then there were four. (Fold down one finger each time a frog leaves.)

Four little froggies looked out to sea,
One went swimming, and then there were three.

Three little froggies said, "What can we do?"
One jumped in the water, and then there were two.

Two little froggies sat in the sun.
One swam off, and then there was one.

One lonely froggie said, "This is no fun."
He dived in the water, and then there was none.

Five Little Froggies Sitting on a Well (Traditional, B/T/PreS/K–5)

Five little froggies sitting on a well (Hold up five fingers.)
One looked up, and down he fell. (Look up and fold down one finger.)
Froggies jumped high. (Point finger on other hand up.)
Froggies jumped low. (Point finger down.)
Four little froggies dancing to and fro. (Close fists and sway side to side.)

Four little froggies sitting on a well . . . (Repeat same lines and movement.)
Three little froggies sitting on a well . . .
Two little froggies sitting on a well . . .

One little froggy sitting on a well. (Hold up last finger.)
He looked up and down he fell. (Look up and fold down one finger.)
Froggies jumped high. (Point finger on other hand up.)
Froggies jumped low. (Point finger down.)
No little froggies sitting on a well. (Shake head.)

Five Little Speckled Frogs (Traditional, B/T/PreS/K–5)

Five little speckled frogs, (Hold up five fingers.)
Sat on a speckled log,
Eating some most delicious bugs.
Yum! Yum! (Rub tummy.)
One jumped into the pool, (Point index finger downwards.)
Where it was nice and cool,

Then there were four little speckled frogs. (Hold up four fingers.)
Glub, glub.
Verse 2: Four little speckled frogs . . . (Repeat refrain as in previous verse.)
Verse 3: Three little speckled frogs . . . (Repeat refrain as in first verse.)
Verse 4: Two little speckled frogs . . . (Repeat refrain as in first verse.)

Verse 5: One little speckled frog
Sat on a speckled log,
Eating some most delicious bugs.
Yum! Yum!
One jumped into the pool,
Where it was nice and cool,
Then there were no little speckled frogs.
Glub, glub.

Frogs Jump

See "Multiple Animals" chapter, Fingerplays and Action Rhymes section.

Mr. Bullfrog (Traditional, B/T/PreS/K–5)

Here's Mr. Bullfrog (Place fist on palm.)
Sitting on a rock.
Along comes a little boy.
Mr. Bullfrog jumps, KERPLOP! (Have fist "jump" off of palm.)

I Am a Little Toad Staying by the Road (Traditional, PreS/K–5)

I am a little toad
Staying by the road. (Stand up.)
Just listen to my song; (Cup hand around ear.)
I sleep all winter long. (Place palms together, rest head on hands.)
When spring comes, I peek out (Peer under outstretched palm.)
And then I jump about; (Leap in the air.)
And now I catch a fly. (Stick out tongue.)
And now I wink my eye (Wink.)
And now and then I hop (Hop.)
And now and then I stop. (Freeze and sit down.)

A Little Frog in a Pond Am I (Traditional, B/T/PreS)

A little frog in a pond am I, (Stand up.)
Hippity, hippity, hop.
And I can jump up so high, (Leap up into the air.)
Hippity, hippity, hop.

Nursery Rhymes

"Croak!" Said the Toad (Traditional, K–5/6+)

"Croak!" said the toad, "I'm hungry, I think;
Today I've had nothing to eat or to drink;
I'll crawl to a garden and jump through the pales,

From The Big Book of Animal Rhymes, Fingerplays, and Songs by Elizabeth Cothen Low.
Westport, CT: Libraries Unlimited. Copyright © 2009.

And there I'll dine nicely on slugs and on snails."
"Ho, ho!" quoth the Frog, "Is that what you mean?
Then I'll hop away to the next meadow stream;
There I will drink, and eat worms and slugs too,
And then I shall have a good dinner like you."

A Gaping Wide-Mouthed Waddling Frog

See "Multiple Animals" chapter, Nursery Rhymes section.

I Went to the Toad

See "Multiple Animals" chapter, Nursery Rhymes section.

My Dream (Traditional, 6+)

I dreamed a dream next Tuesday week,
Beneath the apple-trees;
I thought my eyes were big pork-pies,
And my nose was Stilton cheese.
The clock struck twenty minutes to six,
When a frog sat on my knee;
I asked him to lend me eighteen pence,
But he borrowed a shilling of me.

La rana (Traditional, Spanish, K–5/6+)

Cucú, cucú, cantaba la rana.
Cucú, cucú, debajo del agua.
Cucú, cucú, pasó un caballero.
Cucú, cucú, con capa y sombrero.
Cucú, cucú, pasó una señora.
Cucú, cucú, con traje de cola.
Cucú, cucú, paso un marinero,
Cucú, cucú, vendiendo romero,
Cucú, cucú, pidió un ramito,
Cucú, cucú, no le quiso dar,
Cucú, cucú, y se echó a llorar.

Translation: The Frog

Cucú, cucú, sang the frog.
Cucú, cucú, underneath the water.
Cucú, cucú, a gentleman passed by.
Cucú, cucú, with a cape and hat.
Cucú, cucú, a lady passed by.
Cucú, cucú, with a formal dress.
Cucú, cucú, then came a sailor,
Cucú, cucú, selling rosemary,
Cucú, cucú, the frog requested some,
Cucú, cucú, he did not want to give any,
Cucú, cucú, and so he lay down and cried.

Ribbit, Ribbit Went the Little Green Frog One Day (Traditional, B/T/PreS/K–5)

(Also known as Gung, Gung Went the Little Green Frog or Glunk, Glunk Went the Little Green Frog)

Ribbit, ribbit went the little green frog one day.
Ribbit, ribbit went the little green frog!
Ribbit, ribbit went the little green frog one day.
And his eyes went blink, blink, blink.

Sana, sana (Traditional, Spanish, B/T/PreS)

Sana, sana,
Colita de rana.
Si no sanas hoy,
Sanarás mañana.

Translation: It Heals, It Heals

It heals, it heals,
Little frog bottom.
If you don't heal today,
You will heal tomorrow.

Suggestion: This rhyme is read or sung to children with boo-boos.

There Was a Frog (Traditional, 6+)

There was a frog swum in the lake,
The crab came crawling by:
"Wilt thou," coth the frog, "be my make?"
Coth the crab, "No, not I."
"My skin is sooth and dappled fine,
I can leap far and nigh.
Thy shell is hard: so is not mine."
Coth the crab, "No, not I."
"Tell me," then spake the crab, "therefore,
Or else I thee defy:
Give me thy claw, I ask no more."
Coth the frog, "That will I."
The crab bit off the frog's fore-feet;
The frog then he must die.
To woo a crab it is not meet:
If any do, it is not I.

'Tis Midnight

See "Multiple Animals" chapter, Nursery Rhymes section.

We Make No Spare

See "Horses" chapter, Nursery Rhymes section,

Songs

A Frog He Would A-Wooing Go (Traditional, 6+)

(Similar version known as Frog Went A-Courtin')

A Frog he would a -woo-ing go, Heigh Ho! said Row-ly, A
Frog, he would a -woo-ing go, Whe-ther his mo-ther would
let him or no, with a Row-ly Pow-ly Gam-mon and Spin-age, Heigh
ho! said An-tho-ny Row-ly.

Verse 2: So off he set with his opera hat,
Heigh-ho! said Rowley,
So off he set with his opera hat,
And on the road he met with a Rat.
With a Rowley, Powley. Gammon and Spinach,
Heigh ho! said Anthony Rowley.

Verse 3: Pray, Mister Rat, will you go with me?
Heigh-ho! said Rowley,
Pray, Mister Rat, will you go with me?
Kind Mistress Mousey for to see? *(Repeat refrain as in previous verse.)*

Verse 4: They soon arrived at the Mouses hall,
Heigh-ho! said Rowley,
They gave a loud tap, and they gave a loud call . . . *(Repeat refrain as in first verse.)*

Verse 5 : Pray, Mistress Mouse, are you within?
Heigh-ho! said Rowley,
Oh yes, kind sirs, I'm sitting to spin . . . *(Repeat refrain as in first verse.)*

Verse 6: Come, Mistress Mouse, now give us some beer?
Heigh-ho! said Rowley,
That Froggy and I may have some cheer . . . *(Repeat refrain as in first verse.)*

Verse 7: Pray, Mister Frog, will you give us a song?
Heigh-ho! said Rowley,
Let the subject be something that's not very long . . . *(Repeat refrain as in first verse.)*

Verse 8: Indeed, Mistress Mouse, replied Mister Frog,
Heigh-ho! said Rowley,
A cold has made me as hoarse as a dog . . . *(Repeat refrain as in first verse.)*

Verse 9: Since you have a cold, Mister Frog, Mousey said,
Heigh-ho! said Rowley,
I'll sing you a song that I have just made . . . *(Repeat refrain as in first verse.)*

Verse 10: As they were in glee and a merry making,
Heigh-ho! said Rowley,
A Cat and her Kittens came tumbling in . . . *(Repeat refrain as in first verse.)*

Verse 11: The Cat she seized the Rat by the crown,
Heigh-ho! said Rowley,
The Kittens they pulled the little mouse down . . . *(Repeat refrain as in first verse.)*

Verse 12: This put Mister Frog in a terrible fright,
Heigh-ho! said Rowley,
He took up his Hat and he wished them good-night . . . *(Repeat refrain as in first verse.)*

Verse 13: But Froggy was crossing it over a brook,
Heigh-ho! said Rowley,
A lily-white Duck came and gobbled him up . . . . *(Repeat refrain as in first verse.)*

Verse 14: So there is an end of one, two, three,
Heigh-ho! said Rowley,
The Rat, the Mouse, and the little Frog-ee . . . *(Repeat refrain as in first verse.)*

Over in the Meadow (Lyrics by Olive A. Wadsworth)

See "Multiple Animals" chapter, Songs section.

There's a Hole in the Bottom of the Sea (Traditional, PreS/K–5,6+)

(Also known as: There's a Hole in the Middle of the Sea)

There's a hole in the bot-tom of the sea, There's a

hole in the bot-tom of the sea, There's a hole, there's a hole, there's a

hole in the bot-tom of the sea.

From The Big Book of Animal Rhymes, Fingerplays, and Songs *by Elizabeth Cothen Low.*
Westport, CT: Libraries Unlimited. Copyright © 2009.

Verse 2:   There's a log in the hole
In the bottom of the sea,
There's a log in the hole
In the bottom of the sea,
There's a log, there's a log,
There's a log in the hole in the bottom of the sea.

Verse 3:   There's a bump on the log in the hole . . . (Repeat refrain as in previous verse.)

Verse 4:   There's a frog on the bump on the log . . . (Repeat refrain as in previous verse.)

Verse 5:   There's a fly on the frog on the bump on the log . . . (Repeat refrain as in previous verse.)

Verse 6:   There's a wing on the fly on the frog on the bump on the log . . . (Repeat refrain as in previous verse.)

Verse 7:   There's a flea, on the wing, on the fly, on the frog,
On the bump, on the log, in the hole in the bottom of the sea,
There's a flea, on the wing, on the fly, on the frog,
On the bump, on the log, in the hole in the bottom of the sea,
There's a flea, there's a flea,
On the wing, on they fly, on the frog, on the bump, on the log
In the hole in the bottom of the sea.

What Are Little Boys Made Of?

See "Multiple Animals" chapter, Songs section.

Poetry

A City Plum Is Not a Plum

See "Multiple Animals" chapter, Poetry section.

The Frog (Hilaire Belloc, K–5/6+)

Be kind and tender to the Frog
And do not call him names,
As "Slimy skin," or "Polly-wog,"
Or likewise "Ugly James,"
Or "Gap-a-grin," or "Toad-gone-wrong,"
Or "Bill Bandy-knees":
The Frog is justly sensitive
To epithets like these.
No animal will more repay
A treatment kind and fair
At least so lonely people say
Who keep a frog (and, by the way,
They are extremely rare.)

Hopping Frog (Christina Rossetti, 6+)

Hopping frog, hop here and be seen,
I'll not pelt you with stick or stone:
Your cap is laced and your coat is green;
Good bye, we'll let each other alone.
Plodding toad, plod here and be looked at,
You the finger of scorn is crooked at:
But though you're lumpish, you're harmless too;
You won't hurt me, and I won't hurt you.

Kindness to Animals

See "Multiple Animals" chapter, Poetry section.

GEESE

Fingerplays and Action Rhymes

May My Geese Fly Over Your Barn? (Traditional, Call, and Response, PreS/K–5)

"May my geese fly over your barn?" (Adults call out this line.)
"Yes, if they'll do no harm." (Children instructed to respond with this line.)
"Fly over his barn and eat all his corn." (Children pretend to fly and eat corn.)

Wire, Brier, Limberlock (Traditional, PreS/K–5)

(Also known as Intery, Mintery, Country Corn)

Wire, brier, limberlock,
Three geese in a flock;
One flew east and one flew west, (Count out on fingers.)
And one flew over the cuckoo's nest.

Nursery Rhymes

Buy a Live Goose!—Buy a Live Goose! (Traditional, K–5/6+)

'Buy a live goose!—from my flock pick and choose,
All fat from the farm, in high order for use;
Five shillings apiece, young and tender the whole,
As e'er flapped a wing, at the end of my pole.'

Cackle, Cackle Mother Goose (Traditional, PreS/K–5)

Cackle, cackle Mother Goose,
Have you any feathers loose?
Truly have I, pretty fellow,
Quite enough to fill a pillow.
Here are quills, take one or two,
And down to make a bed for you.

Christmas Is Coming, the Geese Are Getting Fat (Traditional, PreS/K–5)

Christmas is coming,
The geese are getting fat.
Please to put a penny
In the old man's hat.
If you haven't got a penny,
A ha'penny will do;
If you haven't got a ha'penny,
Then God bless you!

Gaffer Gilpin Got a Goose and Gander (Traditional, Tongue Twister, PreS/K–5/6+)

Gaffer Gilpin got a goose and gander;
Did Gaffer Gilpin get a goose and gander?

If Gaffer Gilpin got a goose and gander,
Where's the goose and gander Gaffer Gilpin got?

Goosey, Goosey, Gander (Traditional, K–5)

Goosey, goosey, gander,
Who stands yonder?
Little Betsy Baker;
Take her up and shake her.

Gray Goose and Gander (Traditional, PreS/K–5)

Gray goose and gander,
Waft your wings together,
And carry the good king's daughter
Over the one-strand river.

Hyder Iddle Diddle Dell (Traditional, K–5/6+)

Hyder iddle diddle dell,
A yard of pudding's not an ell;*
Not forgetting tweedle-dye,
A tailor's goose will never fly.

* Ell: Unit of length about 45 inches

Intery, Mintery, Cutery-Corn (Traditional, PreS/K–5)

Intery, mintery, cutery-corn,
Apple seed and apple thorn;
Wire, briar, limber-lock,
Five geese in a flock,
Sit and sing by a spring,
O-U-T, and in again.

Old Mother Goose (Traditional, PreS/K–5/6+)

Old Mother Goose,
When she wanted to wander,
Would ride through the air
On a very fine gander.

Mother Goose had a house,
'Twas built in a wood,
Where an owl at the door
For sentinel stood.

She had a son Jack,
A plain-looking lad,
He was not very good,
Nor yet very bad.
She sent him to market,
A live goose he bought,
Here, mother, says he,
It will not go for nought.

Jack's goose and her gander
Grew very fond;
They'd both eat together,
Or swim in the pond.

Jack found one morning,
As I have been told,
His goose had laid him
An egg of pure gold.

Jack ran to his mother
The news for to tell,
She called him a good boy,
And said it was well.

Jack sold his gold egg
To a merchant untrue,
Who cheated him out of
A half of his due.

Then Jack went a-courting
A lady so gay,
As fair as the lily,
And sweet as the May.

The merchant and squire
Soon came at his back,
And began to belabour
The sides of poor Jack.

Then old Mother Goose
That instant came in,
And turned his son Jack
Into famed Harlequin.

She then with her wand
Touched the lady so fine,
And turned her at once
Into sweet Columbine.

The gold egg in the sea
Was thrown away then,
When an odd fish brought her
The egg back again.

The merchant then vowed
The goose he would kill,
Resolving at once
His pockets to fill.

Jack's mother came in,
And caught the goose soon,
And mounting its back,
Flew up to the moon.

Three Gray Geese (Traditional, Tongue Twister, PreS/K–5)

Three gray geese in a green field grazing;
Gray were the geese and green was the grazing.

Songs

Fiddle-I-Fee

See "Farm Animals" subsection of "Multiple Animals" chapter, Songs section.

Go Tell Aunt Rhody (Traditional, K–5/6+)

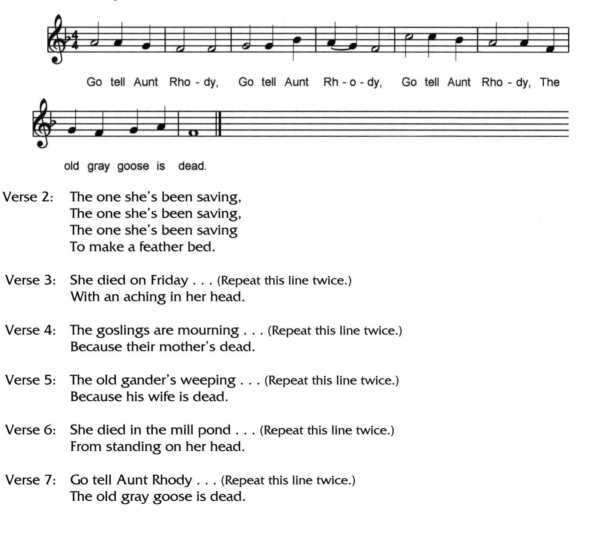

Go tell Aunt Rho-dy, Go tell Aunt Rh-o-dy, Go tell Aunt Rho-dy, The

old gray goose is dead.

Verse 2:   The one she's been saving,
           The one she's been saving,
           The one she's been saving
           To make a feather bed.

Verse 3:   She died on Friday . . . (Repeat this line twice.)
           With an aching in her head.

Verse 4:   The goslings are mourning . . . (Repeat this line twice.)
           Because their mother's dead.

Verse 5:   The old gander's weeping . . . (Repeat this line twice.)
           Because his wife is dead.

Verse 6:   She died in the mill pond . . . (Repeat this line twice.)
           From standing on her head.

Verse 7:   Go tell Aunt Rhody . . . (Repeat this line twice.)
           The old gray goose is dead.

Goosey, Goosey, Gander (Traditional, PreS/K–5)

Goo - sey, goo - sey gan - der, Whith - er shall I wan - der?

Up - stairs and down - stairs, And in my la - dy's cham - ber;

There I met an old man, Who would not say his prayers; I

took him by the left leg; And threw him down the stairs.

The Twelve Days of Christmas

See "Multiple Animals" chapter, Songs section.

Poetry

Kindness to Animals

See "Multiple Animals" chapter, Poetry section.

Some Geese (Oliver Herford, 6+)

Ev-er-y child who has the use
Of his sen-ses knows a goose.
See them un-der-neath the tree
Gath-er round the goose-girl's knee,
While she reads them by the hour
From the works of Scho-pen-hau-er.

How pa-tient-ly the geese at-tend!
But do they re-al-ly com-pre-hend
What Scho-pen-hau-er's driv-ing at?
Oh, not at all; but what of that?
Nei-ther do I; nei-ther does she;
And, for that mat-ter, nor does he.

* Schopenhauer: A nineteenth-century German philosopher

What Does the Donkey Bray About?

See "Multiple Animals" chapter, Poetry section.

GIRAFFES

Poetry

Camelopard (Hilaire Belloc, 6+)

The Camelopard,˙ it is said
By travelers (who never lie),
He cannot stretch out straight in bed
Because he is so high.
The clouds surround his lofty head,
His hornlets touch the sky.
How shall I hunt this quadruped?˙
I cannot tell! Not I!
I'll buy a little parachute
(A common parachute with wings),
I'll fill it full of arrowroot
And other necessary things,
And I will slay this fearful brute
With stones and sticks and guns and slings.

* Camelopard: Archaic word for giraffe
* Quadruped: Animal with four feet

GOATS

Nursery Rhymes

A Gentleman of Wales

See "Multiple Animals" chapter, Nursery Rhymes section.

In Fir Tar Is

See "Multiple Animals" chapter, Nursery Rhymes section.

'Tis Midnight

See "Multiple Animals" chapter, Nursery Rhymes section.

Songs

Bill Grogan's Goat (Traditional, K–5/6+)

There was a man, There was a man, Now please take note, Now please take note, There was a man, There was a man, Who had a goat, Who had a goat, He loved that goat, He loved that goat, In-deed he did, In-deed he did, He loved that goat, He loved that goat, Just like a kid, Just like a kid.

Verse 2:   One day that goat, (Echo each line.)
            Felt frisk and fine . . .
            Ate three red shirts . . .
            Right off the line . . .
            The man, he grabbed . . .
            Him by the back . . .
            And tied him to . . .
            A railroad track . . .

Verse 3:   Now, when that train . . .
           Hove into sight . . .
           That goat grew pale . . .
           And green with fright . . .
           He heaved a sigh . . .
           As if in pain . . .
           Coughed up those shirts . . .
           And flagged the train . . .

Hush, Little Baby, Don't Say a Word

See "Multiple Animals" chapter, Songs section.

GUINEA PIGS

Nursery Rhymes

There Was a Little Guinea-Pig (Traditional, K–5/6+)

There was a little guinea-pig,
Who, being little, was not big,
He always walked upon his feet,
And never fasted when he ate.

When from a place he ran away,
He never at that place did stay;
And while he ran, as I am told,
He ne'er stood still for young or old.

He often squeaked and sometimes vi'lent,
And when he squeaked he ne'er was silent;
Though ne'er instructed by a cat,
He knew a mouse was not a rat.

One day, as I am certified,
He took a whim and fairly died;
And as I'm told by men of sense,
He never has been living since.

HEDGEHOGS

Nursery Rhymes

As I Went over Lincoln Bridge (Traditional, Riddle, K–5/6+)

As I went over Lincoln Bridge
I met Mister Rusticap;
Pins and needles on his back,
A-going to Thorney Fair.

Answer: A Hedgehog

Humphrey Hunchback Had a Hundred Hedgehogs (Traditional, Tongue Twister, K–5/6+)

Humphrey Hunchback had a hundred hedgehogs;
Did Humphrey Hunchback have a hundred hedgehogs?
If Humphrey Hunchback had a hundred hedgehogs,
Where's the hundred hedgehogs Humphrey Hunchback had?

HIPPOS

Poetry

The Hippopotamus (Hilaire Belloc, K–5/6+)

I shoot the Hippopotamus
With bullets made of platinum,
Because if I use leaden ones
His hide is sure to flatten 'em.

HORSES AND MULES

See also the chapter "Donkeys."

Fingerplays and Action Rhymes

Frogs Jump

See "Multiple Animals" chapter, Fingerplays and Action Rhymes section.

Shoe a Little Horse (Traditional, B/T)

Shoe a little horse, (Pat baby's feet while saying this rhyme.)
Shoe a little mare,
But let the little colt
Go bare, bare, bare.

Shoe the Colt (Traditional, B/T)

Shoe the colt, (Pat baby's feet while saying this rhyme.)
Shoe the colt,
Shoe the wild mare;
Here a nail,
There a nail,
Yet she goes bare.

Pitty Patty Polt (Traditional, B/T)

Pitty Patty Polt, (Pat baby's feet while saying this rhyme.)
Shoe the wild colt.
Here a nail,
And there a nail,
Pitty Patty Polt.

This Is the Way the Ladies Ride (Traditional, B/T)

This is the way the ladies ride,
Tri, tre, tre, tree,
Tri, tre, tre, tree;
This is the way the ladies ride,
Tri, tre, tre, tre, tri-tre-tre-tree! (Bounce baby gently on knee.)

This is the way the gentlemen ride,
Gallop-a-trot,
Gallop-a-trot;
This is the way the gentlemen ride,
Gallop-a-gallop-a-trot! (Bounce baby faster.)

This is the way the farmers ride,
Hobbledy-hoy,
Hobbledy-hoy;

This is the way the farmers ride,
Hobbledy hobbledy-hoy! (Bounce baby from knee to knee.)

This Is the Way the Ladies Ride, Nim, Nim, . . . (Traditional, B/T)

This is the way the ladies ride,
Nim, nim, nim, nim. (Bounce baby gently on knee.)

This is the way the gentlemen ride,
Trim, trim, trim, trim. (Bounce baby a little faster.)

This is the way the farmers ride,
Trot, trot, trot, trot. (Bounce baby high up and down.)

This is the way the huntsmen ride,
A-gallop, a-gallop, a-gallop, a-gallop. (Bounce baby fast.)

This is the way the ploughboys ride,
Hobble-dy-gee, hobble-dy-gee. (Bounce baby from knee to knee.)

Trot, Trot to Boston, Trot Trot to Lynn (Traditional, B/T)

Trot, trot to Boston, trot, trot to Lynn, (Bounce baby on knee.)
Watch out, Baby, don't fall in! (Have baby slip through legs.)

Nursery Rhymes

As I Was Going to Banbury

See "Farm Animals" subsection of "Multiple Animals" chapter, Nursery Rhymes section.

Bell Horses, Bell Horses (Traditional, B/T/PreS/K–5)

Bell horses, bell horses,
What time of day?
One o'clock, two o'clock,
Three and away.

Caballito blanco (Traditional, Spanish, PreS/K–5/6+)

Caballito blanco
sácame de aquí,
llévame hasta el pueblo
donde yo nací.

Translation: White Pony

White pony
Take me away from here,
Take me to the town
Where I was born.

Daniel and Dick Rode the Horse to the Fair

See "Multiple Animals" chapter, Nursery Rhymes section.

Father and Mother and Uncle John (Traditional, B/T/PreS/K–5)

Father and Mother and Uncle John,
Went to market one by one;
Father fell off—!
And Mother fell off—!

But Uncle John—
Went on, and on,
And on, and on . . .
And on, and on, and on . . .

For Want of a Nail (Traditional, K–5, 6+)

For want of a nail,
The shoe was lost;
For want of a shoe,
The horse was lost;
For want of a horse,
The rider was lost;
For want of a rider,
The battle was lost;
For want of a battle,
The kingdom was lost;
And all for the want
Of a horseshoe nail.

The Friendly Beasts

See "Multiple Animals" chapter, Nursery Rhymes section.

A Gaping Wide-Mouthed Waddling Frog

See "Multiple Animals" chapter, Nursery Rhymes section.

Gee-up, Neddy, To the Fair (Traditional, PreS/K–5)

(Also known as **Giddyap, Horsey**)

Gee-up, Neddy, the fair.
What shall I buy when I get there?
A ha've penny apple, a penny pear,
Gee-up Neddy to the fair.

A Gentleman of Wales

See "Multiple Animals" chapter, Nursery Rhymes section.

Here Goes My Lord (Traditional, B/T/PreS/K–5)

Here goes my lord,
A trot! A trot! A trot! A trot!
Here goes my lady,
A canter! A canter! A canter! A canter!

From The Big Book of Animal Rhymes, Fingerplays, and Songs by Elizabeth Cothen Low.
Westport, CT: Libraries Unlimited. Copyright © 2009.

Here goes my young master,
Jockey-hitch! Jockey-hitch! Jockey-hitch! Jockey-hitch!

Here goes my young miss,
An amble! An amble! An amble! An amble!

The footman lags behind to tipple ale and wine,
And goes gallop, a gallop, a gallop to make up his time.

The Hobby Horse

See Songs section in this chapter.

Horsie, Horsie, Don't You Stop (Traditional, B/T/PreS/K–5)

Horsie, horsie, don't you stop,
Just let your feet go clippety clop;
Your tail goes swish, and the wheels go round –
Giddyup, you're homeward bound!

Hussy, Nussy, Where's Your Horse? (Traditional, B/T/PreS/K–5)

Hussy, nussy, where's your horse?
Hussy, nussy, gone to grass!
Hussy, nussy, fetch him home,
Hussy, nussy, let him alone.

I Had a Little Hobby Horse (Traditional, PreS/K–5)

I had a little hobby horse,
His name was Tommy Gray,
His head was made of pease straw.
His body made of hay;
I saddled him and bridled him,
And rode him up to town,
There came a little puff of wind
And blew him up and down.

I Had a Little Hobby Horse, It Was Well Shod (Traditional, K–5/6+)

I had a little hobby horse, it was well shod,
It carried me to the mill-door, trod, trod, trod;
When I got there I gave a great shout,
Down came the hobby horse and I cried out.
Fie* upon the miller, he was a great beast,
He would not come to my house, I made a little feast,
I had but little, but I would give him some,
For playing of his bag-pipes and beating his drum.

* Fie: Curses

I Had a Little Pony (Traditional, PreS/K–5/6+)

I had a little pony,
His name was Dapple Gray;
I lent him to a lady

To ride a mile away.
She whipped him, she slashed him,
She called it through the mire;
I would not lend my pony now,
For all the lady's hire.

I Lost My Mare in Lincoln Lane (Traditional, PreS/K–5)

I lost my mare in Lincoln Lane,
And couldn't tell where to find her,
Till she came home both lame and blind,
With never a tail behind her.

If Wishes Were Horses (Traditional, PreS/K–5)

If wishes were horses
Beggars would ride;
If turnips were watches
I would wear one by my side.

In Fir Tar Is

See "Multiple Animals" chapter, Nursery Rhymes section.

Is John Smith Within? (Traditional, PreS/K–5)

Is John Smith within?
Yes, that he is.
Can he set a shoe?
Aye, marry, two.
Here a nail, and there a nail.
Tick, tack, too.

John Cook Had a Little Grey Mare (Traditional, PreS/K–5)

John Cook had a little grey mare,
He, haw, hum!
Her back stood up and her bones were bare,
He, haw, hum!

John Cook was riding up Shuter's Bank,
He, ha, hum!
And there his nag did kick and prank,
He, haw, hum!

John Cook was riding up Shuter's Hill,
He, haw, hum!
His mare fell down and she made her will,
He, haw, hum!

The bridle and saddle he laid on the shelf,
He, haw, hum!
If you want any more you may sing it yourself,
He, haw, hum!

From *The Big Book of Animal Rhymes, Fingerplays, and Songs* by Elizabeth Cothen Low.
Westport, CT: Libraries Unlimited. Copyright © 2009.

Lend Me Your Mare (Traditional, K–5/6+)

1: "Lend me your mare to ride a mile?"
2: "She is lame leaping over a stile."
1: "Alack! And I must get to the fair,
I'll give thee money for thy mare."
2: "Oh, oh! Say you so?
Money will make the mare to go."

Little John Jiggy Jag (Traditional, K–5/6+)

Little John Jiggy Jag,
He rode a penny nag,
And went to Wigan to woo:
When he came to a beck,
He fell and broke his neck,
Johnny, how dost thou now?

I made him a hat,
Of my coat lap,
And stocking of pearly blue;
A hat and a feather,
To keep out of cold weather,
So, Johnny, how dost thou now?

Matthew, Mark, Luke, and John (Traditional, PreS/K–5/6+)

Matthew, Mark, Luke, and John,
Hold my horse 'till I leap on;
Hold him steady; hold him sure,
And I'll get over the misty moor.

Moss Was A Little Man (Traditional, 6+)

Moss was a little man, and a little mare did buy,
For kicking and for sprawling none her could come nigh;
She could trot, she could amble, and could canter here and there.
But one night she strayed away—so Moss lost his mare.

Moss got up next morning to catch her fast asleep,
And round about the frosty fields so nimbly he did creep.
Dead in a ditch he found her, and glad to find her there,
So I'll tell you by and bye, how Moss caught his mare.

"Rise! Stupid, rise!" He thus to he did say;
"Arise, you beast, you drowsy beast, get up without delay,
For I must ride you to the town, so don't lie sleeping there;"
He put the halter round her neck—so Moss caught his mare.

My Father He Died

See "Multiple Animals" chapter, Nursery Rhymes section

A Nimble! An Amble! (Traditional, K-5/6+)

A nimble, an amble! A nimble, an amble!
My lady is coming this way;
She likes better to ride on her pony, than ramble
Upon her ten toes all the day.

A trot—a trot—a trot—a trot,
My lord sits his horse by her side;
Do you see what a fine hat and feather he's got,
To ride with his beautiful bride?

A canter—a canter—a canter's the pace,
The groom rides behind on his mare;
With his livery trimmed with a handsome gold lace,
And his neat little cropped head of hair.

A gallop—a gallop—a gallop—a gallop,
Here comes the old farmer behind;
Now he goes down the hill, and see here he comes up
Till his nag has quite broken his wind.

One to Make Ready (Traditional, PreS/K–5)

One to make ready,
Two to prepare;
Good luck to the rider,
And away goes the mare!

Ride a Cock-Horse to Banbury Cross

See Songs section in this chapter.

Ride a Cock-Horse to Banbury Cross, To Buy . . . (Traditional, PreS/K–5)

Ride a cock-horse to Banbury Cross
To buy little Johnny a galloping horse.
It trots on behind, and it ambles before,
And Johnny shall ride till he can ride no more.

Ride a Cock-Horse to Banbury Cross, to See What . . . (Traditional, PreS/K–5)

Ride a cock-horse
To Banbury Cross,
To see what
Tommy can buy;
A penny white loaf,
A penny white cake,
And a two-penny apple pie.

Ride a Cock-Horse to Coventry Cross (Traditional, PreS/K–5)

Ride a cock-horse to Banbury Cross
To buy little Johnny a galloping horse.

It trots on behind, and it ambles before,
And Johnny shall ride till he can ride no more.

Ride a cock-horse to Coventry-cross;
To see what Emma can buy;
A penny white cake I'll buy for her sake,
And a twopenny tart or a pie.

Ride Away, Ride Away (Traditional, PreS/K–5)

Ride away, ride away,
Johnny shall ride,
He shall have a pussy cat
Tied to one side;
He shall have a little dog
Tied to the other,
And Johnny shall ride
To see his grandmother.

Ride, Baby, Ride, Baby Shall Ride (Traditional, B/T/PreS)

Ride, baby, ride,
Pretty baby shall ride,
And have a little puppy-dog tied to her side,
And little pussy-cat tied to the other,
And away she shall ride to see her grandmother,
To see her grandmother,
To see her grandmother.

Robert Barnes, Fellow Fine (Traditional, PreS/K–5)

"Robert Barnes, fellow fine,
Can you shoe this horse of mine?"
"Yes, good sir, that I can,
As well as any other man.
There's a nail, and there's a prod,
And now, good sir, your horse is shod."

Rory Rumpus Rode a Raw-Boned Racer (Traditional, Tongue Twister, PreS/K–5/6+)

Rory Rumpus rode a raw-boned racer;
Did Rory Rumpus ride a raw-boned racer?
If Rory Rumpus rode a raw-boned racer,
Where's the raw-boned racer Rory Rumpus rode?

See, See! What Shall I See? (Traditional, PreS/K–5)

See, see, what shall I see?
A horse's head where his tail should be.

Said a Very Proud Farmer at Ryegate (Traditional, PreS/K–5)

(Alternate version: **A Man Went a-Hunting at Reigate**)

Said a very proud farmer at Ryegate,

When the squire rode up to his high gate,
'With your horse and your hound
You had better go round,
For, I say, you shan't jump over my gate.'

There Was a Little Nobby Colt (Traditional, PreS/K–5)

There was a little nobby colt,
His name was Nobby Gray;
His head was made of pouce straw,
His tail was made of hay;
He could ramble, he could trot,
He could carry a mustard-pot,
Round the town of Woodstock,
Hey, Jenny, hey!

There Was a Monkey Climbed a Tree

See "Multiple Animals" chapter, Nursery Rhymes section.

There Was an Old Man (Traditional, 6+)

There was an old man, who lived in a wood,
As you may plainly see;
He said he could do as much work in a day,
As his wife could do in three.
With all my heart, the old woman said,
If that you will allow,
Tomorrow, you'll stay at home in my stead,
And I'll go drive the plough:

But you must milk the Tidy cow,
For fear that she go dry;
And you must feed the little pigs
That are within the sty;
And you must mind the speckled hen,
For fear she lay away;
And you must reel the spool of yarn
That I spun yesterday.

The old woman took a staff in her hand,
And went to drive the plough:
The old man took a pail in his hand,
And went to milk the cow;
But Tidy hinched, and Tidy flinched,
And Tidy broke his nose,
And Tidy gave him such a blow,
That the blood ran down to his toes.

High! Tidy! Ho! Tidy! High!
Tidy! Do stand still;
If ever I milk you, Tidy, again,
'Twill be sore against my will!

He went to feed the little pigs,
That were within the sty;
He hit his head against the beam,
And he made the blood to fly.

He went to mind the speckled hen,
For fear she'd lay astray,
And he forgot the spool of yarn
His wife spun yesterday.

So he swore by the sun, the moon, and the stars,
And the green leaves on the tree,
If his wife didn't do a day's work in her life,
She should ne'er be ruled by he.

Thirty White Horses (Traditional, Riddle, K–5/6+)

Thirty white horses
Upon a red hill,
Now they stamp,
Now they champ,
Now they stand still.

Answer: Teeth

Up Hill Spare Me (Traditional, Riddle, K–5/6+)

Up hill spare me,
Down hill ware me,
On level ground spare me not,
And in the stable forget me not.

Answer: Horse

We Make No Spare (Traditional, 6+)

We make no spare
Of John Hunkes' mare;
And now I
Think she will die;
He thought it good
To put her in the wood,
To seek where she mightly dry;
If the mare should chance to fail,
Then the crownes would for her sale.

The rose is red, the grass is green.
Serve Queen Bess our noble queen;
Kitty the spinner
Will sit down to dinner,
And eat the leg of a frog;
All good people

Look over the steeple,
And see the cat play with the dog.

Why Is Pussy in Bed?

See "Multiple Animals" chapter, Nursery Rhymes section.

Songs

Ain't It Great to Be Crazy?

See "Multiple Animals" chapter, Songs section.

All the Pretty Little Horses (Traditional, B/T/PreS)

(Also known as **Hush-a-bye, Don't You Cry**)

Hush - a - by don't you cry, Go to sleep - y lit - tle ba - by, When you wake,

you shall have, All the pret - ty lit - tle hor - ses. Dap - ples and bays, tans and bays,

All the pret - ty lit - tle hor - ses.

Verse 2: Hush-a-bye, don't you cry,
Go to sleepy, little baby;
When you wake,
You shall have cake,
Coach and six white horses,
All the pretty little horses.

Camptown Races (Stephen Foster, K–5/6+)

The Camp - town lad - ies sing this song, Doo - dah! Doo - dah! The

Camp - town race - track's five miles long, Oh! Doo - dah day! I

come down there with my hat caved in Doo - dah! Doo - dah! I

go back home with a poc - ket full of tin, Oh! Doo - dah day!

Going to run all night! Going to run all day! I'll bet my mon - ey on the

bob - tail nag. Some - bo - dy bet on the bay.

Verse 2:   The longtail filly* and the big black horse,
           Doo-dah!, doo-dah!
           They fly the tract and they both cut across,
           Oh, doo-dah day!
           The blind horse stick-in' in a big mud-hole,
           Doo-dah!, doo-dah!
           Can't touch bottom with a ten-foot pole,
           Oh, doo-dah day!

Repeat Chorus

Verse 3:   See them flying on a ten mile heat
           Doo-dah! Doo-day!
           Round de race-track, then repeat
           Oh! Doo-day day!
           I win my money on de bob-tail* nag
           Doo-dah! Doo-day!
           I keep my money in an old tow-bag
           Oh! Doo-day day!

* Filly: Young female horse
* Bob-tail: Short tail

The Erie Canal (Thomas S. Allen, K–5/6+)

I've got an old mule, her name's Sal, Fif - teen miles on the
Er - ie Can - al. She's a good old wor - ker and a good old pal,
Fif - teen miles on the Er - ie Can - al. We've hauled some bar - ges in our day,
filled with lum - ber coal and hay, And ev - ery inch of the way we know from
Al - ban - y to Buff a - lo,
Oh, low bridge ev - ery - bo - dy down, Low bridge for we're
com - ing in to town, And you'll al - ways known your neigh - bor, you'll
al - ways know your pal; If you've ev - er na - vi - gat - ed on the E
-rie Can - al.

Verse 2: We'd better get along on our way, old gal,
Fifteen miles on the Erie Canal,
'Cause you bet your life I'd never part with Sal,
Fifteen miles on the Erie Canal,
Git up there mule, here comes a lock,
We'll make Rome 'bout six o'clock,
One more trip and back we'll go,
Right back home to Buffalo
Repeat Chorus

Verse 3: Oh, where would I be if I lost my pal?
Fifteen miles on the Erie Canal,
Oh, I'd like to see a mule as good as Sal,
Fifteen miles on the Erie Canal,
A friend of mine once got her sore,
Now he's got a busted jaw,
Cause she let fly with her iron toe,
And kicked him in to Buffalo
Repeat Chorus

Verse 4: Don't have to call when I want my Sal,
Fifteen miles on the Erie Canal,
She trots from her stall like a good old gal,
Fifteen miles on the Erie Canal,
I eat my meals with Sal each day,
I eat beef and she eats hay,
And she ain't so slow if you want to know,
She put the "Buff" in Buffalo
Repeat Chorus

Fiddle-I-Fee

See "Farm Animals" subsection of "Multiple Animals" chapter, Songs section.

The Hobby Horse (Traditional, B/T/PreS/K-5)

(Also known as **Trot, Trot, Trot**)

Hop, hop, hop! Nim - ble as a top, Where 'tis smooth and
where 'tis ston - y, trudge a - long, my lit - tle po - ny, Hop, hop, hop, hop, hop!
Nim - ble as a top.

Verse 2: Whoa, whoa, whoa!
How like fun you go,
Very well, my little pony,
Safe's our jaunt
Tho' rough and stony,
Spare, spare, spare, spare, spare!
Sure enough we're there.

Hush, Little Baby, Don't Say a Word

See "Multiple Animals" chapter, Songs section.

I Know an Old Lady Who Swallowed a Fly

See "Multiple Animals" chapter, Songs section.

Jingle Bells (Traditional, B/T/PreS/K–5)

Verse 1: Dashing through the snow
In a one-horse open sleigh
O'er the fields we go
Laughing all the way
Bells on bobtail ring
Making spirits bright
What fun it is to ride and sing
A sleighing song tonight!

Verse 2: A day or two ago
I thought I'd take a ride;
And soon Miss Fannie Bright
Was seated by my side.
The horse was lean and lank;
Misfortune seemed his lot;
He got into a drifted bank,
And we, we got upset.

Repeat Chorus

Verse 3: Now the ground is white,
          Go it while you're young;
          Take the girls tonight,
          And sing this sleighing song.
          Just get a bobtailed bay,*
          Two-forty for his speed;
          Then hitch him to an open sleigh,
          And crack! You'll take the lead.

        Repeat Chorus

* Bay: A reddish-brown horse

Mules (Traditional, K--5/6+)

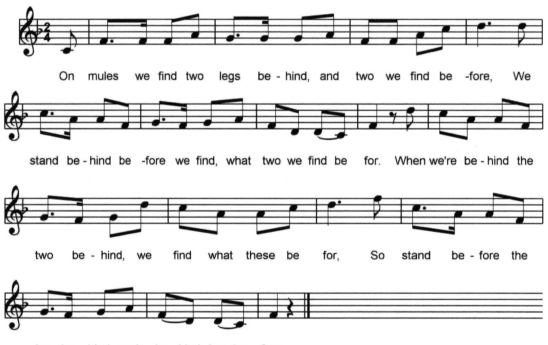

On mules we find two legs be-hind, and two we find be-fore, We

stand be-hind be-fore we find, what two we find be for. When we're be-hind the

two be-hind, we find what these be for, So stand be-fore the

two be-hind, and be-hind two be-fore.

From *The Big Book of Animal Rhymes, Fingerplays, and Songs* by Elizabeth Cothen Low.
Westport, CT: Libraries Unlimited. Copyright © 2009.

Old Gray Mare (Traditional, PreS/K–5)

The old gray mare, she ain't what she used to be,

Ain't what she used to be, Ain't what she used to be, The old gray mare she

ain't what she used to be, man - y long years a -go. Man - y long years a

-go, Man - y long years a -go, The old gray mare she

ain't what she used to be man - y long years a -go.

Old MacDonald

See "Farm Animals" subsection of "Multiple Animals" chapter, Songs section.

Over the River and Through the Wood (Lydia Maria Child, PreS/K–5/6+)

Ov - er the riv - er and through the wood, to grand - fath - er's house we

go; The horse knows the way to car - ry the sleigh through the

white and drift - ed snow, oh! Ov - er the riv - er and through the wood, Oh!,

how the wind does blow, It stings the toes and bites the nose as

ov - er the ground we go.

From *The Big Book of Animal Rhymes, Fingerplays, and Songs* by Elizabeth Cothen Low.
Westport, CT: Libraries Unlimited. Copyright © 2009.

Verse 3:   Over the river and through the wood,
To have a first rate play;
Oh, hear the bell ring,
"Ting-a-ling-ling!" Hurrah for
Thanksgiving Day-ay!

Verse 4:   Over the river and through the wood,
Trot fast my dapple˙ gray!
Spring over the ground,
Like a hunting hound!
For this is Thanksgiving Day.

Verse 5:   Over the river and thru the wood,
And straight through the barnyard gate.
We seem to go extremely slow
It is so hard to wait!

Verse 6:   Over the river and through the woods,
Now Grandmother's face I spy.
Hurray for the fun, is the pudding done?
Hurrah for the pumpkin pie.

* Dapple: Spotted

Ride a Cock-Horse to Banbury Cross (Traditional, B/T/PreS/K–5)

Ride a Cock - horse to Ban - bur-y Cross, To see a fine la - dy up

-on a white horse, Rings on her fin - gers, and bells on her toes.

She shall have mu - sic wh -er - ever she goes.

Yankee Doodle (Traditional, PreS/K–5/6+)

Yank - ee Doo - dle came to town, a rid - ing on a pon - y; He

stuck a feath - er in his cap and called it mac - a -ro - ni.

Chorus:

Yank - ee Doo - dle keep it up, Yank - ee Doo - dle Dan - dy, Mind the mus - ic

and the step and with the girls be hand - y.

Father and I went down to camp
Along with Captain Gooding,
And there we saw the men and boys
As thick as hasty puddin'.*

Repeat Chorus

And there was Captain Washington
Upon a strappin' stallion,
And all the men and boys around,
I guess there was a million.

Repeat Chorus

* Hasty pudding: Cornmeal mush

Poetry

Windy Nights (Robert Louis Stevenson, 6+)

Whenever the moon and stars are set,
Whenever the wind is high,
All night long in the dark and wet,
A man goes riding by.
Late in the night when the fires are out,
Why does he gallop and gallop about?

Whenever the trees are crying aloud,
And ships are tossed at sea,
By, on the highway, low and loud,
By at the gallop goes he.
By at the gallop he goes, and then
By he comes back at the gallop again.

INSECTS

Fingerplays and Action Rhymes

Frogs Jump

See "Multiple Animals" chapter, Fingerplays and Action Rhymes section.

A Little Boy's Walk

See "Multiple Animals" chapter, Fingerplays and Action Rhymes section.

Nursery Rhymes

Buz! Buz! (Traditional, PreS/K–5)

Buz! Buz! Quote the great blue fly,
Who is so happy, so happy as I?
I whisk through the air,
Without thought, without care,
And no king is so happy as I, as I!
And no king is so happy as I.

Buzz, Quoth the Blue Fly (Traditional, PreS/K–5)

Buzz, quoth the blue fly,
Hum, quoth the bee,
Buzz and hum they cry,
And so do we:

In his ear, in his nose,
Thus do you see?
He ate the dormouse,
Else it was he.

Daniel and Dick Rode the Horse to the Fair

See "Multiple Animals" chapter, Nursery Rhymes section.

Fiddle-de-dee, Fiddle-de-dee

See Songs section in the chapter.

A Gaping Wide-Mouthed Waddling Frog

See "Multiple Animals" chapter, Nursery Rhymes section.

Good Night, Sleep Tight (Traditional, PreS/K–5)

Good night, sleep tight,
Don't let the bed bugs bite.

Grasshopper Green (Traditional, K–5/6+)

Grasshopper Green is a comical chap;
He lives on the best of fare.
Bright little trousers, jacket and cap,
These are his summer wear.
Out in the meadow he loves to go,
Playing away in the sun;
Its hopperty, skipperty, high and low—
Summer's the time for fun.

Grasshopper Green has a dozen wee boys,
And soon as their legs grow strong
Each of them joins in his frolicsome joys,
Singing his merry song.
Under the hedge in a happy row
Soon as the day has begun
Its hopperty, skipperty, high and low—
Summer's the time for fun.

Grasshopper Green has a quaint little house.
It's under the hedge so gay.
Grandmother Spider, as still as a mouse,
Watches him over the way.
Gladly he's calling the children, I know,
Out in the beautiful sun;
It's hopperty, skipperty, high and low—
Summer's the time for fun.

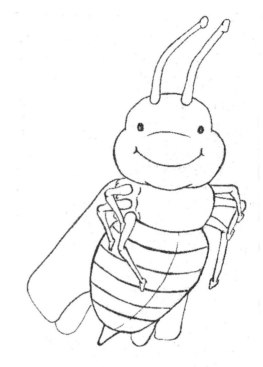

A Grey-Hound Invited a Green-Finch to Tea

See "Multiple Animals" chapter, Nursery Rhymes section.

Ladybug, Ladybug, Fly Away Home (Traditional, PreS/K–5)

(Also known as Ladybird, Ladybird)

Ladybug, ladybug,
Fly away home,
Your house is on fire
And your children all gone;
All except one
And that's little Ann
And she has crept under
The warming pan.

Little Miss Tuckett (Traditional, PreS/K–5)

Little Miss Tuckett
Sat on a bucket,
Eating some peaches and cream.
Along came a grasshopper
And tried hard to stop her,
But she said, "Go away, or I'll scream."

Little Tommy Torment (Traditional, K–5/6+)

Little Tommy Torment
Did very cruel things!
He caught the flies to play with,
And then pulled off their wings.

Mamma was very angry,
And gave him to the sweep;
Who up and down the chimney,
Makes Tommy Torment creep!

Old Dame Cricket (Traditional, K–5/6+)

Old Dame Cricket, down in a thicket,
Brought up her children nine,—
Queer little chaps, in glossy black caps
And brown little suits so fine.

"My children," she said,
"The birds are abed:
Go and make the dark earth glad!
Chirp while you can!"
And then she began,—
Till, oh, what a concert they had!
They hopped with delight,
They chirped all night,
Singing, "Cheer up! cheer up! cheer!"
Old Dame Cricket,
Down in the thicket,
Sat awake till dawn to hear.

"Nice children," she said,
"And very well bred.
My darlings have done their best.
Their naps they must take:
The birds are awake;
And they can sing all the rest."

One Old Oxford Ox

See "Multiple Animals" chapter, Nursery Rhymes section.

"Spider, Spider! What Do You Spin?"

See "Spiders" chapter, Nursery Rhymes section.

There Was a Jolly Miller (Traditional, K–5/6+)

There was a jolly miller
Lived on the river Dee,
He looked upon his pillow,
And there he saw a flea.
"Oh! Mr. Flea,

You have been biting me,
And you must die."
So he cracked his bones
Upon the stones,
And there he let him lie.

Why Is Pussy in Bed?

See "Multiple Animals" chapter, Nursery Rhymes section.

Songs

Ain't It Great to Be Crazy?

See "Multiple Animals" chapter, Songs section.

Baby Bye, Here's a Fly (Traditional, B/T/PreS/K–5)

Ba - by bye, here's a fly, We will watch him, you and I. How he

crawls up the walls, Yet he nev - er fall! I be -lieve, with those six

legs; You and I could walk on eggs! There he goes, on his toes, Tick - ling

ba - by's nose.

Fiddle Dee Dee (Traditional, PreS/K–5)

Fid - dle - de - dee, Fid - dle - de dee, The fly has mar - ried the bum - ble - bee. Says the fly, says he, "Will you mar ry me? And live with me, sweet bum ble - bee?" Fid - dle de - dee, Fid - dle de - dee, The fly has mar - ried the bum - ble - bee.

Verse 2:   Said the bee, said she,
"I'll live under your wing,
And you'll never know I carry a sting."
Fiddle-de-dee, fiddle-de-dee,
The fly has married the bumblebee.

Jimmy Crack Corn (Traditional, K–5/6+)

When I was young, I used to wait on Mas - ter and hand him the plate, Pass down the bot - tle when he git dry, and brush a - way the blue tail fly.

Chorus:

Jim crack corn I don't care, Jim crack corn I don't care, Jim crack corn, I don't care, Old Mas - ter's gone a -way.

From *The Big Book of Animal Rhymes, Fingerplays, and Songs* by Elizabeth Cothen Low.
Westport, CT: Libraries Unlimited. Copyright © 2009.

169

Verse 2:   After dinner my master sleep,
           He bid for me to vigil keep:
           And when he went to shut his eyes,
           He told me to watch the blue tail fly.

           Repeat Chorus

Verse 3:   And when he rode in the afternoon,
           I followed with a hickory broom;
           The pony being very shy,
           When bitten by the blue tail fly.

           Repeat Chorus

Verse 4:   One day he rode around the farm.
           The flies so numerous they did swarm;
           One chanced to bite him on the thigh,
           A trouble-making blue tail fly.

           Repeat Chorus

Verse 5:   The pony ran, he jump and pitched,
           And tumbled master into the ditch;
           He died and the jury wondered why
           The verdict was the blue tail fly.

   Repeat Chorus

Verse 6:   They laid him under a persimmon tree,
           His epitaph is there to see:
           "Beneath this stone I'm forced to lie,
           All by means of the blue tail fly."

           Repeat Chorus

I Know an Old Lady Who Swallowed a Fly

See "Multiple Animals" chapter, Songs section.

Over in the Meadow

See "Multiple Animals" chapter, Songs section.

Skip to My Lou

See "Multiple Animals" chapter, Songs section.

From *The Big Book of Animal Rhymes, Fingerplays, and Songs* by Elizabeth Cothen Low. Westport, CT: Libraries Unlimited. Copyright © 2009.

Shoo Fly (Traditional, PreS/K–5)

Shoo fly don't both-er me; Shoo fly don't both-er me; Shoo fly don't both-er me; I be-long to some body, I feel, I feel, I feel, I feel like a morn-ing star, I feel, I feel, I feel, I feel like a morn-ing star. Shoo fly don't both-er me; Shoo fly don't both-er me; Shoo fly don't both-er me; For I belong to some-bod-y.

Poetry

Hurt No Living Thing

See "Multiple Animals" chapter, Poetry section.

Kindness to Animals

See "Multiple Animals" chapter, Poetry section.

"Will You Walk into My Parlour?"

See "Spiders" chapter, Poetry section.

JELLYFISH

Fingerplays and Action Rhymes

Three Jellyfish (Traditional, PreS/K–5)

Three jellyfish, three jellyfish, (Show three fingers.)
Three jellyfish, sitting on a rock. (Rest three fingers of right hand on left fist.)
One fell off! (Have one finger fly off rock and dive into imaginary water.)
Ooooooo . . . Splash!>
Two jellyfish, two jellyfish, (Show two fingers.)
Two jellyfish, sitting on a rock . . . (Repeat refrain as in previous verse.)

One jellyfish, one jellyfish, (Show one finger.)
One jellyfish, sitting on a rock . . . (Repeat refrain as in first verse.)

No jellyfish, no jellyfish,
No jellyfish, sitting on a rock.
One jumped up! . . . Hooray! (Have one finger jump back onto left fist.)

One jellyfish, one jellyfish,
One jellyfish, sitting on a rock.
Another jumped up! . . . Hooray! (Have another finger jump back onto left fist.)

Two jellyfish, two jellyfish,
Two jellyfish, sitting on a rock . . . (Repeat refrain as in previous verse.)

Three jellyfish, three jellyfish,
Three jellyfish, sitting on a rock.
One fell off! . . . Ooooooo . . . Splash! (Have finger fly off rock and dive into imaginary water.)

Poetry

Kindness to Animals

See "Multiple Animals" chapter, Poetry section.

KANGAROOS

Fingerplays and Action Rhymes

Jump, Jump, Jump, Goes the Big Kangaroo (Traditional, PreS/K–5)

Jump, jump, jump, (Stand up and jump.)
Goes the big kangaroo.
I thought there was one, (Hold up one finger.)
But I see there are two. (Hold up two fingers.)

The mother takes her young one
Along in a pouch, (Touch tummy.)
Where he can nap like a child
On a couch.
Jump, jump, jump. (Stand up and jump.)
Jump, jump, jump.

Nursery Rhymes

The Panther (Traditional)

See "Multiple Animals" chapter, Nursery Rhymes section.

LIONS

Fingerplays and Action Rhymes

Frogs Jump

See "Multiple Animals" chapter, Fingerplays and Action Rhymes section.

Red Lion (Traditional, Game, PreS/K–5)

Red Lion, Red Lion,
Come out of your den.
Whoever you catch
Can be one of your men. (Whoever is the red lion chases the rest of the children.)

Nursery Rhymes

The Lion and the Unicorn (Traditional, PreS/K–5)

The lion and the unicorn
Were fighting for the crown;
The lion beat the unicorn
All around the town.

Some gave them white bread,
And some gave them brown;
Some gave them plum cake
And drummed them out of town.

A Man of Words and Not of Deeds

See "Multiple Animals" chapter, Nursery Rhymes section.

Poetry

The Lion (Hilaire Belloc, K–5/6+)

The Lion, the Lion, he dwells in the waste,
He has a big head and a very small waist;
But his shoulders are stark, and his jaws they are grim,
And a good little child will not play with him.

Of Baiting the Lion (Owen Seaman, 6+)

Remembering his taste for blood
You'd better bait him with a cow;
Persuade the brute to chew the cud
Her tail suspended from a bough;
It thrills the lion through and through
To hear the milky creature moo.

Having arranged this simple ruse,
Yourself you climb a neighboring tree;
See to it that the spot you choose
Commands the coming tragedy;
Take up a smallish Maxim gun,
A search-light, whisky, and a bun.

It's safer, too, to have your bike
Standing immediately below,
In case your piece should fail to strike,
Or deal an ineffective blow;
The Lion moves with perfect grace,
But cannot go the scorcher's pace.

Keep open ear for subtle signs;
Thus, when the cow profusely moans,
That means to say, the Lion dines.
The crunching sound, of course, is bones;
Silence resumes her ancient reign—
This shows the cow is out of pain.

But when a fat and torpid hum
Escapes the eater's unctuous* nose,
Turn up the light and let it come
Full on his innocent repose;*
Then pour your shot between his eyes,
And go on pouring till he dies.

Play, even so, discretion's part;
Descend with stealth; bring on your gun;
Then lay your hand above his heart
To see if he is really done;
Don't skin him till you know he's dead
Or you may perish in his stead!

Years hence, at home, when talk is tall,
You'll set the gun-room wide agape,*
Describing how with just a small
Pea-rifle, going after ape
You met a Lion unaware,
And felled him flying through the air.

* Unctuous: Greasy
* Repose: Rest
* Agape: Amazed

Sage Counsel

See "Multiple Animals" chapter, Poetry section.

From *The Big Book of Animal Rhymes, Fingerplays, and Songs* by Elizabeth Cothen Low.
Westport, CT: Libraries Unlimited. Copyright © 2009.

LIZARDS

Songs

Over in the Meadow

See "Multiple Animals" chapter, Songs section.

Poetry

When Fishes Set Umbrellas Up

See "Multiple Animals" chapter, Poetry section.

LLAMAS

Poetry

The Llama (Hilaire Belloc, 6+)

The Llama is a woolly sort of fleecy hairy goat,
With an indolent* expression and an undulating* throat
Like an unsuccessful literary man.
And I know the place he lives in (or at least—I think I do)
It is Equador, Brazil or Chili—possibly Peru;
You must find it in the Atlas if you can.

* Indolent: Lazy
* Undulating: Moving in waves

LOBSTERS AND OTHER SHELLFISH

Nursery Rhymes

The Crawdad Song (Traditional, African American, PreS/K–5)

You get a line and I'll get a pole, honey,
You get a line and I'll get a pole, babe.
You get a line and I'll get a pole,
And we'll go fishing in crawdad hole.

A Gaping Wide-Mouthed Waddling Frog

See "Multiple Animals" chapter, Nursery Rhymes section.

Lanky Lawrence Lost His Lass and Lobster (Traditional, Tongue Twister, K–5/6+)

Lanky Lawrence lost his lass and lobster;
Did Lanky Lawrence lose his lass and lobster?
If Lanky Lawrence lost his lass and lobster,
Where are the lass and lobster Lanky Lawrence lost?

Lobsters! Live Lobsters!—All Alive, Lobsters! (Traditional, K–5/6+)

Lobsters, alive ho! Live lobsters! And dead,
Who've changed their jet armour to beautiful red,
And yet of no delicate flavour despoiled—
Lobsters alive ho! Live lobsters, and boiled!

Poetry

Kindness to Animals

See "Multiple Animals" chapter, Poetry section.

The Monkey's Glue

See "Multiple Animals" chapter, Poetry section

MAMMOTHS

Poetry

The Frozen Mammoth (Hilaire Belloc, 6+)

This creature, though rare, is still found in the East
Of the Northern Siberian Zone.
It is known to the whole of that group
That the carcass will furnish an excellent soup,
Though the cooking it offers one drawback at least
(Of a serious nature I own):
If the skin be but punctured before it is boiled,
Your confection is wholly and utterly spoiled.
And hence (on account of the size of the beast)
The dainty is nearly unknown.

MICE, RATS, AND MUSKRATS

Fingerplays and Action Rhymes

Five Little Mice Came Out to Play (Traditional, PreS/K–5)

Five little mice came out to play (Hold up all five fingers.)
Gathering crumbs along the way.
Out came pussycat sleek and fat (Bend fingers so that they look like claws.)
Four little mice went scampering back. (Hold up four fingers.)

Four little mice came out to play . . . (Repeat refrain. Hold up four fingers.)
Three little mice came out to play . . . (Repeat refrain. Hold up three fingers.)
Two little mice came out to play . . . (Repeat refrain. Hold up two fingers.)

One little mouse came out to play. (Hold up one finger.)
Gathering crumbs along the way.
Out came pussycat sleek and fat (Bend fingers so that they look like claws.)
No little mice went scampering back. (Shrug shoulders.)

Five Little Mice on the Pantry Floor (Emilie Poulsson, PreS/K–5)

Five little mice on the pantry floor, (Hold up five fingers.)
Seeking for bread-crumbs or something more.
Five little mice on the shelf up high, (Place left hand flat and palm down. Wiggle right fingers on top of it.)
Feasting so daintily on a pie. (Interlock fingers of both hands so that they form a circle.)

But the big round eyes of the wise old cat (Place thumbs and fingers of each hand together, so that they form two smaller circles. Place over eyes.)
See what the five little mice are at.

Quickly she jumps!—but the mice run away, (Have left hand pounce on right hand.)
And hide in their snug little holes all day. (Hide fingers behind back.)

"Feasting in pantries may be very nice;
But home is the best!" say the five little mice.

Frogs Jump

See "Multiple Animals" chapter, Fingerplay and Action Rhymes section.

Little Mousie (Traditional, B/T/PreS)

See the little mousie (Place first two fingers and thumb together.)
Creeping up the stair. (Have fingers travel up arm.)
Looking for a warm nest
There, oh, there. (Place fingers in inner part of your elbow.)

Mouse in a Hole (Traditional, B/T/PreS/K–5)

A mouse lived in a little hole, (Place fingers of left hand together in right fist.)
Lived softly in a little hole,
When all was quiet, as quiet as can be . . . (Whisper this part.)
Out popped she! (Have left thumb pop out.)

'Round and 'Round the Haystack (Traditional, B/T)

'Round and 'round the haystack, (Circle baby's wrist with finger.)
Went the little mouse,
One step, (Have finger climb up arm.)
Two steps,
In his little house. (Tickle baby under armpit.)

Where Are the Baby Mice? (Traditional, B/T/PreS)

Where are the baby mice? (Hide right fist behind back.)
Squeak, squeak, squeak.
I cannot see them peek, peek, peek. (Have fist peep out from behind back.)
Here they come out of their hole in the wall. (Bring fist around front.)
One, two, three, four, five, and that is all. (Slowly open fingers one by one.)

Nursery Rhymes

Birds of a Feather Flock Together

See "Multiple Animals" chapter, Nursery Rhymes section.

"Bow-Wow," Says the Dog

See "Multiple Animals" chapter, Nursery Rhymes section

Debajo del botón (Traditional, Spanish, B/T/PreS/K–5)

Debajo del botón, tón, tón,
que encontró Martín, tín, tín,
había un ratón, tón, tón.
Ay, qué chiquitín, tín, tín.

Translation: Underneath the Button

Underneath the button,
Found by Martín,
Was a mouse,
So tiny.

Dame Wiggins of Lee and Her Seven Wonderful Cats.

See "Cats" chapter, Nursery Rhyme section.

The Giant Jim, Great Giant Grim (Traditional, PreS/K–5/6+)

The giant Jim, great giant grim
Wears a hat without a brim,
Weighs a ton, and wears a blouse,
And trembles when he meets a mouse.

From *The Big Book of Animal Rhymes, Fingerplays, and Songs* by Elizabeth Cothen Low.
Westport, CT: Libraries Unlimited. Copyright © 2009.

A Grey-Hound Invited a Green-Finch to Tea

See "Multiple Animals" chapter, Nursery Rhymes section.

Jerry Hall (Traditional, PreS/K–5)

Jerry Hall,
He is so small,
A rat could eat him,
Hat and all.

Hickory, Dickory, Dock

See Songs section in this chapter.

Hoddley, Poddley, Puddle and Fogs

See "Pets" subsection of "Multiple Animals" chapter, Nursery Rhymes section.

I Saw a Ship a-Sailing

See "Multiple Animals" chapter, Nursery Rhymes section.

The Little Priest of Felton (Traditional, K–5)

The little priest of Felton,
The little priest of Felton,
He killed a mouse within his house,
And ne'er a one to help him.

Little Tim Sprat (Traditional, PreS/K–5)

Little Tim Sprat
Had a pet rat,
In a tin cage with a wheel.
Said little Tim Sprat,
Each day to his rat:
"If hungry, my dear, you must squeal."

Little Tom Tittlemouse (Traditional, PreS/K–5)

Little Tom Tittlemouse
Lived in a bell-house;
The bell-house broke,
And Tommy Tittlemouse woke.

Little Tommy Titmouse

See "Multiple Animals" chapter, Nursery Rhymes section.

Little Tommy Tittlemouse, Lived in a Little House (Traditional, PreS/K–5)

Little Tommy Tittlemouse
Lived in a little house;
He caught fishes
In other men's ditches.

My Father He Died

See "Multiple Animals" chapter, Nursery Rhymes section.

Pretty John Watts (Traditional, PreS/K–5)

Pretty John Watts,
We are troubled with rats,
Will you drive them out of the house?
We have mice, too, in plenty,
That feast in the pantry;
But let them stay,
And nibble away;
What harm is a little brown mouse?

Puss Came Dancing

See "Multiple Animals" chapter, Nursery Rhymes section.

Six Little Mice (Traditional, PreS/K–5)

Six little mice sat down to spin;
Pussy passed by and she peeped in.
"What are you doing, my little men?"
"Weaving coats for gentlemen."
"Shall I come in and cut off your threads?"
"No, no, Mistress Pussy, you'd bite off our heads."
"Oh, no, I'll not; I'll help you to spin."
"That may be so, but you can't come in."

There Was an Old Woman (Traditional, K–5/6+)

There was an old woman
Lived under a hill,
She put a mouse in a bag,
And sent it to the mill:
The miller did swear
By the point of his knife,
He never took toll
Of a mouse in his life.

There Was a Rat, for Want of Stairs (Traditional, PreS/K–5)

There was a rat, for want of stairs,
Went down a rope to say his prayers.

This Is the House That Jack Built

See "Farm Animals" subsection of "Multiple Animals" chapter, Nursery Rhymes section.

Three Blind Mice

See Songs section in this chapter.

Three Young Rats with Black Felt Hats

See "Multiple Animals" chapter, Nursery Rhymes section.

When I Was a Little Boy (Traditional, K–5/6+)

When I was a little boy
I lived by myself,
And all the bread and cheese I got
I laid up on a shelf.

The rats and the mice
They made such a strife,
I had to go to London town
To buy me a wife.

The streets were so broad
And the lanes were so narrow,
I was forced to bring my wife home
In a wheelbarrow.

The wheelbarrow broke
And gave my wife a fall,
The deuce* take
Wheelbarrow, wife, and all.

* Deuce: Devil

Songs

Ain't It Great to Be Crazy?

See "Multiple Animals" chapter, Songs section.

Farmer in the Dell

See "Farm Animals" subsection of "Multiple Animals" chapter, Songs section.

Hickory, Dickory, Dock (Traditional, B/T/PreS/K–5)

(Also known as **Dickory, Dickory, Dock** or **Dickery, Dickery, Dock**)

Hick - o - ry, dick - o - ry dock; The mouse ran up the clock; The

clock struck "one," The mouse ran down; Hick - o - ry, dick - o - ry

dock.

Verse 1:　(Includes Instructions):
　　　　Hickory, dickory, dock. (Swing arm in front of you like pendulum)
　　　　The mouse ran up the clock, (Run fingers up arm.)
　　　　The clock struck one, (Clap hands over head once.)
　　　　The mouse ran down, (Have fingers run down arm.)
　　　　Hickory, dickory, dock. (Swing arm in front of you like pendulum)

Over in the Meadow

See "Multiple Animals" chapter, Songs section.

There Was a Crooked Man

See "Cats" chapter, Songs section.

Three Blind Mice (Traditional, B/T/PreS/K–5)

Three blind mice, See how they run! They all ran aft-er the farm-er's wife; She cut off their tails with a carv-ing knife; Did ev-er you hear such a tale in your life, A-bout three blind mice.

Three Little Mice (Traditional, K–5/6+)

Three lit-tle mice crept out to see, what they could find to have for tea. For they were dain-ty sau-cy mice, and liked to nib-ble some-thing nice, But Pus-sy's eyes so big and bright, soon sent them scam-per-ing off in a fright.

Verse 2:   Three Tabby Cats went forth to mouse,
And said, "Let's have a gay carouse."*
For they were active handsome cats,
And famed for catching mice and rats.
But savage dogs, disposed to bite,
These cats declined to encounter in fight.

* Carouse: Drunken party

Poetry

The City Mouse (Christina Rossetti, K–5/6+)

The city mouse lives in a house;—
The garden mouse lives in a bower,
He's friendly with the frogs and toads,
And sees the pretty plants in flower.
The city mouse eats bread and cheese;—
The garden mouse eats what he can;
We will not grudge him seeds and stalks,
Poor little timid furry man.

A City Plum Is Not a Plum

See "Multiple Animals" chapter, Poetry section.

Elf and Dormouse (Oliver Herford, K–5/6+)

Under a toadstool
Crept a wee Elf,
Out of the rain
To shelter himself.

Under the toadstool,
Sound asleep,
Sat a big Dormouse
All in a heap.

Trembled the wee Elf
Frightened, and yet
Fearing to fly away
Lest he get wet.

To the next shelter
Maybe a mile
Sudden the wee Elf
Smiled a wee smile.

Tugged till the toadstool
Toppled in two
Holding it over him
Gayly he flew.

Soon he was safe home,
Dry as could be.
Soon woke the Dormouse
"Good gracious me!

Where is my toadstool!"
Loud he lamented,
And that's how umbrellas
First were invented.

If a Mouse Could Fly

See "Multiple Animals" chapter, Poetry section.

The Moon

See "Multiple Animals" chapter, Poetry section.

There Was an Old Man Who Supposed (Edward Lear, K–5/6+)

There was an Old Man who supposed
That the street door was partially closed;
But some very large Rats
Ate his coats and his hats,
While that futile Old Gentleman dozed.

Two Rats (Laura E. Richards, K–5/6+)

He was a rat, and she was a rat
And down in one hole they did dwell,
And both were as black as a witch's cat
And they loved one another well.

He had a tail, and she had a tail
Both long and curling and fine;
And each said, "Yours is the finest tail
In the world—excepting mine."

He smelled the cheese, and she smelled the cheese,
And they both pronounced it good;
And both remarked it would greatly add
To the charms of their daily food.

So he ventured out, and she ventured out,
And I saw them go with pain.
But what befell them I never can tell,
For they never came back again.

MICROBES

Poetry

The Microbe (Hilaire Belloc, 6+)

The Microbe is so very small
You cannot make him out at all,
But many sanguine* people hope
To see him through a microscope.
His jointed tongue that lies beneath
A hundred curious rows of teeth;
His seven tufted tails with lots
Of lovely pink and purple spots,
On each of which a pattern stands,
Composed of forty separate bands;
His eyebrows of a tender green;
All these have never yet been seen—
But Scientists, who ought to know,
Assure us that they must be so. . . .
Oh! let us never, never doubt
What nobody is sure about!

* Sanguine: Optimistic

From *The Big Book of Animal Rhymes, Fingerplays, and Songs* by Elizabeth Cothen Low.
Westport, CT: Libraries Unlimited. Copyright © 2009.

MONGOOSE

Nursery Rhyme

The Panther

See "Multiple Animals" chapter, Nursery Rhymes section.

MONKEYS

Fingerplays and Action Rhymes

Five Little Monkeys (Traditional, B/T/PreS)

(Also known as **Three Little Monkeys Jumping on the Bed**)

Five little monkeys (Show five fingers.)
Jumping on the bed, (Have fingers "jump" up and down.)
One fell off (Show one finger.)
And bumped his head. (Rub head with hands.)
Mama called the doctor (Pretend to hold phone.)
And the doctor said,
"No more monkeys
Jumping on the bed." (Shake index finger on one hand and place other hand on hip.)

Second Verse: Four little monkeys… (Repeat refrain as in previous verse. Show four fingers.)
Third Verse: Three little monkeys… (Repeat refrain as in first verse. Show three fingers.)
Fourth Verse: Two little monkeys… (Repeat refrain as in first verse. Show two fingers.)
Fifth Verse: One little monkey… (Repeat refrain as in first verse. Show one finger.)

Five Little Monkeys Swinging from a Tree

See "Multiple Animals" chapter, Fingerplays and Action Rhymes section.

I Am a Gold Lock (Traditional, Call and Response, PreS/K–5)

1. "I am a gold lock." (Adult calls out this line.)
2. "I am a gold key." (Children instructed to say this line.)

1. "I am a silver lock."
2. "I am a silver key."

1. "I am a brass lock."
2. "I am a brass key."

1. "I am a lead lock."
2. "I am a lead key."

1. "I am a monk lock."
2. "I am a monk key!"

I Went Up One Pair of Stairs (Traditional, Call and Response, PreS/K–5)

1. "I went up one pair of stairs." (Adult calls out this line.)
2. "Just like me." (Children instructed to say this line.)

1. "I went up two pairs of stairs."
2. "Just like me."

1. I went into a room."
2. "Just like me."

From *The Big Book of Animal Rhymes, Fingerplays, and Songs* by Elizabeth Cothen Low.
Westport, CT: Libraries Unlimited. Copyright © 2009.

1. "I looked out of a window."
2. "Just like me."

1. "And there I saw a monkey."
2. "Just like me."

A Little Monkey Likes to Do Just the Same as You and You (Traditional, B/T/PreS/K–5)

A little monkey likes to do,
Just the same as you and you. (Point to children.)

When you sit up very tall,
The monkey sits up very tall. (Mime each action.)

When you pretend to throw a ball,
The monkey pretends to throw a ball.

When reach up to the sky,
The monkey reaches up to the sky.

When you clap your hands,
The monkey claps her hands.

When you fold them in your lap,
The monkey folds them in her lap.

Suggestion: Have a monkey puppet imitate each action or have children play monkey role.

Monkey See, Monkey Do (Traditional, B/T/PreS/K–5)

Oh, when you clap, clap, clap your hands.
The monkey clap, clap, claps his hands. (Mime each action.)

Chorus: Monkey see, monkey do.
The monkey does the same as you.

And when you stamp, stamp, stamp your feet.
The monkey stamp, stamp, stamps his feet.

Chorus

And when you jump, jump, jump up high,
The monkey jump, jump, jumps up high.

Chorus

And when you make a funny face.
The monkey makes a funny face.

Chorus

From *The Big Book of Animal Rhymes, Fingerplays, and Songs* by Elizabeth Cothen Low.
Westport, CT: Libraries Unlimited. Copyright © 2009.

And when you turn yourself around,
The monkey turns himself around.

Nursery Rhymes

A Gaping Wide-Mouthed Waddling Frog

See "Multiple Animals" chapter, Nursery Rhymes section.

The Little Black Dog

See "Multiple Animals" chapter, Nursery Rhymes section.

Matthew Mendlegs Missed a Mangled Monkey (Traditional, Tongue Twister, K–5/6+)

Matthew Mendlegs missed a mangled monkey;
Did Matthew Mendlegs miss a mangled monkey?
If Matthew Mendlegs missed a mangled monkey,
Where's the mangled monkey, Matthew Mendlegs missed?

The Monkey's Wedding (Traditional, 6+)

The monkey married the Baboon's sister,
Smacked his lips and then he kissed her,
He kissed so hard he raised a blister.
She set up a yell.
The bridesmaid stuck on some court plaster,
It stuck so fast it couldn't stick faster,
Surely 't was a sad disaster,
But it soon got well.

What do you think the bride was dressed in?
White gauze veil and a green glass breast-pin,
Red kid shoes—she was quite interesting,
She was quite a belle.
The bridegroom swell'd with a blue shirt collar,
Black silk stock that cost a dollar,
Large false whiskers the fashion to follow;
He cut a monstrous swell.

What do you think they had for supper?
Black-eyed peas and bread and butter,
Ducks in the duck-house all in a flutter,
Pickled oysters too.
Chestnuts raw and boil'd and roasted,
Apples sliced and onions toasted,
Music in the corner posted,
Waiting for the cue.

What do you think was the tune they danced to?
"The drunken Sailor"—sometimes "Jim Crow,"
Tails in the way—and some got pinched, too,

'Cause they were too long.
What do you think they had for a fiddle?
An old Banjo with a hole in the middle,
A Tambourine made out of a riddle,
And that's the end of my song.

* Swell: Fashionable image

There Was a Monkey Climbed a Tree

See "Multiple Animals" chapter, Nursery Rhymes section.

Songs

Animal Fair

See "Multiple Animals" chapter, Songs section.

Pop! Goes the Weasel

See "Multiple Animals" chapter, Songs section.

Poetry

Big Baboon (Hilaire Belloc, 6+)

The Big Baboon is found upon
The plains of Cariboo;
He goes about with nothing on,
(A shocking thing to do.)

But if he dressed respectable
And let his whiskers grow,
How like this Big Baboon would be
To Mister So-and-so!

The Chimpanzee (Oliver Herford, 6+)

Children, behold the Chimpanzee:
He sits on the ancestral tree
From which we sprang in ages gone.
I'm glad we sprang: had we held on,
We might, for aught that I can say,
Be horrid Chimpanzees today.

Kindness to Animals

See "Multiple Animals" chapter, Poetry section.

The Marmozet (Hilaire Belloc, 6+)

The species Man and Marmozet*
Are intimately linked;
The Marmozet survives as yet,
But Men are all extinct.

* Marmozet: A small South American monkey; also spelled marmoset

The Monkey's Glue

See "Multiple Animals" chapter, Poetry section.

MOOSE

Songs

Down by the Bay

See "Multiple Animals" chapter, Songs section.

MULTIPLE ANIMALS

Fingerplays and Action Rhymes

Can You Hop Like a Rabbit? (Traditional, PreS/K–5)

Can you hop like a rabbit? (Put hands next to ears and hop up and down.)
Can you jump like a frog? (Crouch and leap up.)
Can you fly like a bird? (Flap arms up and down.)
Can you run like a dog? (Run in place and move hands back and forth as if "dog paddling.")
Can you walk like a duck? (Put hands on hips and waddle back and forth.)
Can you swim like a fish? (Have arm move in wave motion.)
And be still, like a good child— (Fold holds and stay still.)
As still as this?

Creeping, Creeping, Creeping (Traditional, B/T/PreS)

Creeping, creeping, creeping
Comes a little cat. (Have index and middle finger "walk" up arm.)
But the bunny with his long ears
Hops, like that! (Hold up index and middle finger in "V" shape, and hop them down arm.)

Five Little Monkeys Swinging from a Tree (Traditional, PreS/K–5)

(Also known as Five Little Monkeys Sitting in a Tree)

Five little monkeys swinging from a tree, (Hold up three fingers and swing them back and forth.)
Teasing Mr. Crocodile, "You can't catch me!" (Place hands on either side of face with thumbs touching cheeks and fingers spread out as if taunting crocodile.)
Along came Mr. Crocodile, quiet as can be, and (Move hand in gentle swimming motion)
Snapped that monkey right outta that tree. (Clap forcefully.)

Second Verse: Four little monkeys . . . (Repeat refrain as in previous verse. Show four fingers.)
Third Verse: Three little monkeys . . . (Repeat refrain as in first verse. Show three fingers.)
Fourth Verse: Two little monkeys . . . (Repeat refrain as in first verse. Show two fingers.)
Fifth Verse: One little monkey . . . (Repeat refrain as in first verse. Show one finger.)

Frogs Jump (Traditional, PreS/K–5)

Frogs jump. (Stand up and mime actions.)
Caterpillars hump.

Worms wiggle.
Bugs jiggle.

Rabbits hop.
Horses clop.

Snakes slide.
Sea-gulls glide.

Mice creep.
Deer leap.

Puppies bounce.
Kittens pounce.

Lions stalk—
But I walk!

Here Is a Nest for the Robin (Traditional, PreS/K–5)

(Also known as This Is a Nest for Mr. Bluebird)

Here is a nest for the robin; (Cup hands together.)
Here is a hive for the bee; (Place fists side by side.)
Here is a hole for the bunny; (Form circle with both hands.)
And here is a house for me. (Fingertips form a "roof" over head.)

A Little Boy's Walk (Emilie Poulsson, PreS/K–5)

A little boy went walking
One lovely summer's day:
He saw a little rabbit (Hold up index and middle finger in a "V" shape.)
That quickly ran away; (Hide hand behind hand.)

He saw a shining river
Go winding in and out,
And little fishes in it (Place palms together and bend wrists back and forth.)
Were swimming all about;

And slowly, slowly turning,
The great wheel of the mill; (Make two fists and roll them around one another.)
And then the tall church steeple,
The little church so still; (Interlock all fingers, except index fingers which stand up straight.)

The bridge above the water; (Interlock fingers and point thumbs downwards.)
And when he stopped to rest,
He saw among the bushes
A wee ground-sparrow's nest. (Cup hands together.)

And as he watched the birdies (Place thumbs together and wiggle fingers above head.)
Above the tree-tops fly,
He saw the clouds a-sailing (Look up and point at the ceiling.)
Across the sunny sky.

He saw the insects playing; (Wiggle fingers on the ground.)
The flowers that summer brings; (Open hands wide.)
He said, "I'll go tell mamma!
I've seen so many things!"

From *The Big Book of Animal Rhymes, Fingerplays, and Songs* by Elizabeth Cothen Low.
Westport, CT: Libraries Unlimited. Copyright © 2009.

Wee Wiggie (Traditional, B/T/PreS)

Wee Wiggie, (Tug on little toe or pinky.)
Poke Piggie, (Tug on fourth toe or ring finger.)
Tom Whistle, (Tug on middle toe or finger.)
John Gristle, (Tug on second toe or index finger.)
And Old Big Gobble, Gobble, Gobble! (Tug on big toe or thumb.)

Nursery Rhymes

Animal Fair

See Songs section in this chapter.

As I Walked over the Hill One Day (Traditional, PreS/K–5)

As I walked over the hill one day,
I listened and heard a mother-sheep say,
"In all the green world there is nothing so sweet,
As my little lamb, with his nimble feet;
With his eye so bright,
And his wool so white,
Oh, he is my darling, my heart's delight!"
And the mother-sheep and her little one
Side by side lay down in the sun.

I went to the kitchen and what did I see,
But the old gray cat with her kittens three!
I heard her whispering soft: said she,
"My kittens, with tails so cunningly curled,
Are the prettiest things that can be in the world.
The bird on the tree,
And the old ewe, she,
May love their babies exceedingly;
But I love my kittens there,
Under the rocking-chair.
I love my kittens with all my might,
I love them at morning, noon, and night.
Now I'll take up my kitties, the kitties I love,
And we'll lie down together, beneath the warm stove."

I went to the yard and saw the old hen
Go clucking about with her chickens ten;
She clucked and she scratched and she bustled away,
And what do you think I heard the hen say?
I heard her say, "The sun never did shine
On anything like to these chickens of mine;
You may hunt the full moon, and the stars, if you please,
But you never will find such chickens as these.
My dear, downy darlings, my sweet little things,
Come, nestle now cozily under my wings."
So the hen said,

And the chickens all sped
As fast as they could to their nice feather bed.

Birds of a Feather Flock Together (Traditional, PreS/K–5)

Birds of a feather flock together,
And so will pigs and swine;
Rats and mice will have their choice,
And so will I have mine.

"Bow-Wow," Says the Dog (Traditional, PreS/K–5)

(Also known as The Dog Says, "Bow-Wow")

"Bow-wow," says the dog.
"Mew, mew," says the cat.
"Grunt, grunt," says the hog,
And "Squeak," goes the rat.

"Tu-whu," says the owl.
"Caw, caw," says the crow.
"Quack, quack," goes the duck,
And "Moo," says the cow,
And what cuckoos say you know.

The Cock's on the Housetop (Traditional, PreS/K–5)

The cock's on the housetop,
Blowing his horn;
The bull's in the barn
A-threshing the corn;

The maids in the meadow
Are making the hay;
The ducks in the river
Are swimming away.

Daniel and Dick Rode the Horse to the Fair (Traditional, K–5/6+)

Daniel and Dick rode the horse to the fair,
But they would not let Jane to their party belong;
So crept in a snail-shell, and said she'd ride there,
And begged four black beetles to draw her along.

And when the black beetles were harnessed so gay,
They made four nice ponies as ever were seen;
They nodded their heads and they trotted away,
And the folk at the fair all thought Jane was the queen.

A Dog and a Cock (Traditional, K–5/6+)

A dog and a cock,
A journey once took,
They traveled along till 'twas late;

The dog he made free
In the hollow of a tree,
And the cock on the boughs of it sat.

The cock nothing knowing,
In the morn fell a crowing,
Upon which comes a fox to the tree;
"Says he, I declare,
Your voice is above,
All the creatures I ever did see.

Oh! would you come down
I the favorite might own,"
Said the cock, there's a porter below;
"If you will go in,
I promise I'll come down."
So he went, and was worried for it too.

Fishes Swim in Water Clear (Traditional, PreS/K–5)

Fishes swim in water clear,
Birds fly up into the air,
Serpents creep along the ground,
Boys and girls run round and round.

The Friendly Beasts (Traditional, K–5/6+)

Jesus our Brother, kind and good,
Was humbly born in a stable rude,
The friendly beasts around Him stood,
Jesus our Brother, kind and good.

"I," said the donkey, shaggy and brown,
"I carried His mother up hill and down,
I carried her safely to Bethlehem town.
I," said the donkey, shaggy and brown.

"I," said the cow all white and red,
"I gave Him my manger for His bed,
I gave Him my hay to pillow His head.
I," said the cow all white and red.

"I," said the sheep with curly horn,
"I gave Him my wool for His blanket warm.
He wore my coat on Christmas morn.
I," said the sheep with curly horn.

"I," said the dove from the rafters high,
"I cooed Him to sleep that He should not cry,
We cooed Him to sleep, my mate and I.
I," said the dove from the rafters high.

"I," said the camel, yellow and black,
"Over the desert, on my back,
I brought Him a gift in the Wise Men's pack,
I," said the camel, yellow and black.

Thus ev'ry beast by some good spell,
In the stable dark was glad to tell
Of the gift he gave Emmanuel.
The gift he gave Emmanuel.

A Gaping Wide-Mouthed Waddling Frog (Traditional, K–5/6+)

Twelve huntsmen with horn and hounds,
Hunting over other men's grounds;
Eleven ships sailing over the main,
Some bound for France and some for Spain:
I wish them all safe back again;
Ten comets in the sky,
Some low and some high;
Nine peacocks in the air,
I wonder how they all came there,
I do not know and I do not care;
Eight joiners᛫ in joiner's hall,
Working with their tools and all;
Seven lobsters in a dish,
As fresh as any heart could wish;
Six beetles against the wall,
Close by an old woman's apple stall;
Five puppies by our dog Ball,
Who daily for their breakfast call;
Four horses stuck in a bog,
Three monkeys tied to a clog,᛫
Two pudding ends would choke a dog,
With a gaping, wide-mouthed, waddling frog.

* Joiners: Carpenters
* Clog: Heavy block of wood

A Gentleman of Wales (Traditional, PreS/K–5)

Little John Morgan,
A gentleman of Wales,
Came riding on a nanny-goat
And selling of pigs' tails.

Chicky, cuckoo, my little duck,
See-saw, sickna downy;
Gallop a trot, gallop a trot,
And hey for Dublin towny!

From *The Big Book of Animal Rhymes, Fingerplays, and Songs* by Elizabeth Cothen Low.
Westport, CT: Libraries Unlimited. Copyright © 2009.

A Grey-Hound Invited a Green-Finch to Tea (Traditional, K–5/6+)

A grey-hound invited a green-finch to tea,
And they were as merry as merry could be;
But just as their tea they were going to begin.
A little brown mouse and a red-breast came in;
And asked if the terrible news they had heard,
That a great large white cat had destroyed the black-bird;
A blue-bottle fly who did chance to be near,
Protested it pleased her the tidings to hear;
For blackbird had ate up her father and mother,
Her uncle and aunt, and her sister and brother.
So here ends my song, which you see does display
The colours of green, and of red, and of grey,
Of brown, and of white, and of black, and of blue!
Could I have contrived, I'd have put yellow too.

I Saw a Ship a-Sailing (Traditional, PreS/K–5/6+)

I saw a ship a-sailing,
A-sailing on the sea,
And oh, but it was all laden,
With pretty things for thee.

There were comfits* in the cabin,
And apples in the hold;
The sails were made of silk,
And the masts were made of gold.

The four-and-twenty sailors,
That stood between the decks,
Were four-and-twenty white mice
With chains about their necks.

The captain was a duck
With a packet on his back,
And when the ship began to move,
The captain said, "Quack! Quack!"

* Comfits: A fruit or nut with sugar coating

I Went to the Toad (Traditional, K–5/6+)

I went to the toad that lies under the wall,
I charmed him out, and he came at my call;
I scratched out the eyes of owl before,
I tore the bat's wing; what would you have more?

In Fir Tar Is (Traditional, K–5/6+)

In fir tar is,
In oak none is.
In mud eel is,

In clay none is.
Goat eat ivy,
Mare eat oats.

Suggestion: Said fast, this rhyme is supposed to sound like it is in a foreign language.

In the Month of February (Traditional, PreS/K–5)

In the month of February,
When green leaves begin to spring,
Little lambs do skip like fairies,
Birds do couple, build, and sing.

The Little Black Dog (Traditional, K–5/6+)

This little black dog ran round the house,
And set the bull a-roaring,
And drove the monkey in the boat,
Who set the oars a-rowing,
And scared the cock upon the rock,
Who cracked his throat with crowing.

Little Piggy Wiggy (Traditional, K–5/6+)

Come hither, little piggy wiggy,
Come and learn your letters,
And you shall have a knife and fork
To eat with, like your betters.

No, no! the little pig replied,
My trough will do as well,
I'd rather eat my victuals there,
Than go and learn to spell;
With a tingle, tangle, titmouse!
Robin knows great A,
And B, and C, and D, and E,
F, G, H, I, J, K.

Come hither, little pussy cat,
If you'll your grammar study,
I'll give you silver clogs to wear,
Whenever the gutter's muddy.
No! whilst I grammar learn, says puss,
Your house will in a trice
Be overrun, from top to bottom,
With the rats and mice;
With a tingle, tangle, titmouse!
Robin knows great A,
And B, and C, and D, and E,
F, G, H, I, J, K.

Come hither, little puppy dog,
I'll give you a new collar,

From *The Big Book of Animal Rhymes, Fingerplays, and Songs* by Elizabeth Cothen Low.
Westport, CT: Libraries Unlimited. Copyright © 2009.

If you will learn to read your book,
And be a clever scholar.
No, no! replied the puppy dog,
I've other fish to fry,
For I must learn to guard your house,
And bark when thieves come nigh;
With a tingle, tangle, titmouse!
Robin knows great A,
And B, and C, and D, and E,
F, G, H, I, J, K.

Come hither, good little boy,
And learn your alphabet,
And you a pair of boots and spurs,
Like your papa's shall get.
O yes! I'll learn my alphabet,
And when I well can read,
Perhaps papa will give me too,
A pretty long-tailed steed;
With a tingle, tangle, titmouse!
Robin knows great A,
And B, and C, and D, and E,
F, G, H, I, J, K.

* Victuals: Food
* Trice: Instant

Little Tommy Titmouse (Traditional, K–5)

Little Tommy Titmouse sat on Jenny's knee,
He sung tweedledum, and she sung tweedledee!
Tweedle, tweedle, tweedle, both sung through their nose,
The dog he joined the concert with three great loud bow wows;
The cat jumped up with wonder, and frightened ran away,
Believing it was thunder, she dared no longer stay!

A Man of Words and Not of Deeds (Traditional, 6+)

A man of words and not of deeds,
Is like a garden full of weeds;
And when the weeds begin to grow,
It's like a garden full of snow;
And when the snow begins to fall,
It's like a bird upon the wall;
And when the bird away does fly,
It's like an eagle in the sky;
And when the sky begins to roar,
It's like a lion at door;
And when the door begins to crack,
It's like a stick across your back;
And when your back begins to smart,
It's like a penknife in your heart;

And when your heart begins to bleed,
You're dead, and dead, and dead, indeed.

The Moon Is Up (Traditional, 6+)

The moon is up, the moon is up!
The larks begin to fly,
And, like a drowsy buttercup,
Dark Phoebus˙ skims the sky,
The elephant, with cheerful voice,
Sings blithely˙ on the spray;
The bats and beetles all rejoice,
Then let me, too, be gay.

I would I were a porcupine,
And wore a peacock's tail;
To-morrow, if the moon but shine,
Perchance I'll be a whale.
Then let me, like the cauliflower,
Be merry while I may,
And, ere there comes a sunny hour
To cloud my heart, be gay!

* Phoebus: Sun (Apollo)
* Blithely: Merrily

My Father He Died (Traditional, 6+)

My father he died, but I can't tell you how,
He left me six horses to drive in my plough:

Refrain: With a whim, wang, wabble oh!
Jack's sing saddle oh,
Blossy boys, bubble oh,
Under the broom.

I sold my six horses and I bought me a cow;
I'd fain have made a fortune, but didn't know how:

Refrain

I sold my cow and bought me a calf;
I'd fain have made a fortune, but I lost the best half:

Refrain

I sold my calf and bought me a cat;
A pretty thing she was, in my corner sat:

Refrain

I sold my cat and bought me a mouse;
He carried fire in his tail, and burnt down my house.

Refrain

Oliver Oglethorpe Ogled an Owl and Oyster (Traditional, Tongue Twister, K–5/6+)

Oliver Oglethorpe ogled an owl and oyster;
Did Oliver Oglethorpe ogle an owl and oyster?
If Oliver Oglethorpe ogled an owl and oyster,
Where are the owl and oyster Oliver Oglethorpe ogled?

One Old Oxford Ox (Traditional, Tongue Twister, K–5/6+)

One old Oxford ox opening oysters;
Two tee-totums' totally tired of trying to trot to Tadbury;
Three tall tigers tippling tenpenny tea;
Four fat friars fanning fainting flies;
Five frippery Frenchmen foolishly fishing for flies;
Six sportsmen shooting snipe;'
Seven Severn salmon swallowing shrimp;
Eight Englishmen eagerly examining Europe;
Nine nimble noblemen nibbling nonpareils;'
Ten tickers tinkling upon ten tin tinderboxes with ten tenpenny tacks;
Eleven elephants elegantly equipt;
Twelve typographical topographers typically translating types.

* Tee-totums: Tops
* Snipe: A kind of bird that lives in a marsh
* Nonpareils: A kind of chocolate dessert

Over the Hills and Far Away (Traditional, K–5/6+)

Tom, he was a piper's son,
He learnt to play when he was young,
And all the tune that he could play
Was, "Over the hills and far away."
Over the hills and a great way off,
The wind shall blow my top-knot off.

Tom with his pipe made such a noise,
That he pleased both the girls and boys;
And they all stopped to hear him play,
"Over the hills and far away."

Tom with his pipe did play with such skill,
That those who heard him could never keep still;
Whenever they heard they began to dance,
Even pigs on their hind legs would after him prance.

As Dolly was milking her cow one day,
Tom took his pipe and began for to play;
So Doll and the cow danced "The Cheshire Round,"
Till the pail was broken and the milk ran on the ground.

He met old Dame Trot with a basket of eggs,
He used his pipe and she used her legs;

From *The Big Book of Animal Rhymes, Fingerplays, and Songs* by Elizabeth Cothen Low. Westport, CT: Libraries Unlimited. Copyright © 2009.

She danced about till the eggs were all broke,
She began to fret, but he laughed at the joke.

Tom saw a cross fellow was beating an ass,
Heavy laden with pots, pans, dishes, and glass;
He took out his pipe and he played them a tune,
And the poor donkey's load was lightened full soon.

The Panther (Traditional, 6+)

Be kind to the panther! for when thou wert young,
In thy country far over the sea,
'Twas a panther ate up thy papa and mamma,
And had several mouthfuls of thee!

Be kind to the badger! for who shall decide
The depths of his badgerly soul?
And think of the tapir when flashes the lamp
O'er the fast and the free-flowing bowl.

Be kind to the camel! nor let word of thine
Ever put up his bactrian˙ back;
And cherish the she-kangaroo with her bag,
Nor venture to give her the sack.

Be kind to the ostrich! for how canst thou hope
To have such a stomach as it?
And when the proud day of your bridal shall come,
Do give the poor birdie a bit.

Be kind to the walrus! nor ever forget
To have it on Tuesday to tea;
But butter the crumpets on only one side,
Save such as are eaten by thee.

Be kind to the bison! and let the jackal
In the light of thy love have a share;
And coax the ichneumon˙ to grow a new tail,
And have lots of larks in its lair.

Be kind to the bustard! that genial bird,
And humor its wishes and ways;
And when the poor elephant suffers from bile,
Then tenderly lace up his stays!

* Bactrian: A type of camel from the Middle East
* Ichneumon: Mongoose

Polly Piper Plucked a Pigeon (Traditional, K–5/6+)

Polly Piper plucked a pigeon,
Charley Chester chocked a cat;

Willy Wimble winged a widgeon,*
Well, good Sir, and what of that?

Polly Piper's papa praised her,
Charley's cousin cracked his crown;*
Willy's wife said, Will amazed her,
Now, good Sir, you're wiser grown.

* Widgeon: Kind of duck
* Crown: Top of the head

Puss Came Dancing (Traditional, PreS/K–5)

(Also known as A Cat Came Fiddling out of a Barn)

Puss came dancing out of a barn
With a pair of bagpipes under her arm;
She could sing nothing, but, Fiddle cum fee,
The mouse has married the humble-bee.
Pipe, cat! Dance, mouse!
We'll have a wedding at our good house.

Robin and Richard Were Two Pretty Men (Traditional, K–5/6+)

Robin and Richard were two pretty men;
They laid in bed till the clock struck ten;
Then up starts Robin, and looks at the sky,
"Oh, brother Richard, the sun's very high:

The bull's in the barn threshing the corn,
The cock's on the dunghill blowing his horn.
The cat's at the fire frying of fish,
The dog's in the pantry, breading his dish."

Simple Simon

See Songs section in this subsection.

There Was a Monkey Climbed a Tree (Traditional, K–5/6+)

There was a monkey climbed a tree,
When he fell down, then down fell he.

There was a crow sat on a stone,
When he was gone, then there was none.

There was an old wife did eat an apple,
When she ate two, she ate a couple.

There was a horse going to the mill,
When he went on, he stood not still.

There was a butcher cut his thumb,
When it did bleed, then blood did come.

There was a lackey ran a race,
When he ran fast, he ran apace.

There was a cobbler clouting shoon,
When they were mended, they were done.

There was a chandler making candle,
When he them strip, he did them handle.

There was a navy went to Spain,
When it returned, it came again.

* Shoon: Shoes

'Tis Midnight (Traditional, K–5/6+)

'Tis midnight, and the setting sun
Is slowly rising in the west;
The rapid rivers slowly run,
The frog is on his downy nest.
The pensive goat and sportive cow,
Hilarious, leap from bough to bough.

Three Young Rats with Black Felt Hats (Traditional, K–5/6+)

Three young rats with black felt hats,
Three young ducks with white straw flats,

Three young dogs with curling tails,
Three young cats with demi-veils,

Went out to walk with two young pigs
In satin vests and sorrel* wigs;

But suddenly it chanced to rain
And so they all went home again.

* Sorrel: Light brownish-red

Uprising See the Fitful Lark (Traditional, 6+)

Uprising see the fitful lark
Unfold his pinion* to the stream;
The pensive watch-dog's mellow bark
O'ershades yon cottage like a dream:
The playful duck and warbling bee
Hop gayly on, from tree to tree!

How calmly could my spirit rest
Beneath yon primrose bell so blue,
And watch those airy oxen drest
In every tint of pearling hue!
As on they hurl the gladsome plough,
While fairy zephyrs˙ deck each brow!

* Pinion: Wing
* Zephyrs: Breezes

What Are Little Boys Made Of?

See Songs section in this subsection.

Why Is Pussy in Bed? (Traditional, 6+)

"Why is Pussy in bed, pray?"
"She's sick," says the fly,
"And I fear she will die!
That's why she's in bed!"

"Pray, what's her disorder?"
"She's got a locked jaw,"
Says the little jackdaw,
"And that's her disorder."

"Who makes her gruel?"
"I," says the horse,
"For I am her nurse,
And I make her gruel!"

"Pray who is her doctor?"
"Quack! Quack!" says the duck,
"I that task undertook,
And I am her doctor."

"Who pays the fee?"
"I," says the bitch,
"Because I am rich;
So I pay the fee."

"Who thinks she'll recover?"
"I," says the deer,
"For I did last year!
So I think she'll recover."

Songs

Ain't It Great to Be Crazy? (Traditional, PreS/K–5/6+)

A horse and a flea and three blind mice,
Sat on a curbstone shooting dice.
The horse he slipped and fell on the flea.
"Whoops," said the flea, "There's a horse on me."

Chorus:

Boom, Boom, Ain't it great to be cra - zy? Boom, Boom, Ain't it great to be

cra - zy? Gid - dy and fool - ish the whole day through, Boom,

Boom, Ain't it great to be cra - zy?

Verse 2: Way down south where bananas grow,
A flea stepped on an elephants toe.
The elephant cried, with tears in his eyes,
"Why don't you pick on someone your size?"

Repeat Chorus

Verse 3: Way up north where there's ice and snow.
There lived a penguin and his name was Joe.
He got so tired of black and white,
He wore pink slacks to the dance last night!

Repeat Chorus

Verse 4: Eli, Eli, he sells socks
A dollar a pair and a nickel a box.
The more you wear 'em the shorter they get.
And you put 'em in the water and they don't get wet!

Repeat Chorus

From *The Big Book of Animal Rhymes, Fingerplays, and Songs* by Elizabeth Cothen Low.
Westport, CT: Libraries Unlimited. Copyright © 2009.

Animal Fair (Traditional, K–5/6+)

I went to the a-ni-mal fair; The birds and the beasts were there. The

big ba-boon by the light of the moon was comb-ing his au-burn hair. You

should have seen the monk! He sat on the e-le-phant's trunk. The

e-le-phant sneezed and fell to his knees. And what be-came of the monk!

Spoken: The monk, The monk, The monk?

Down by the Bay (Traditional, PreS/K–5/6+)

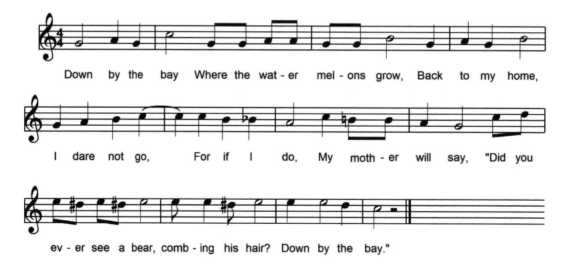

Down by the bay Where the wat-er mel-ons grow, Back to my home,

I dare not go, For if I do, My moth-er will say, "Did you

ev-er see a bear, comb-ing his hair? Down by the bay."

Verse 2:   Down by the bay where the watermelon grow
Back to my home I dare not go.
For if I do my mother will say,
"Did you ever see a whale with a polka dot tail?"
Down by the bay.

Verse 3:   . . . "Did you ever see a moose kissing a goose?" . . .

Verse 4:   . . . "Did you ever see a bee with a sunburned knee?" . . .

Suggestion: Have children make up additional rhymes.

Home on the Range (Brewster M. Higley, K–5/6+)

Oh, give me a home where the buff-a-lo roam, and the deer and the
an-te-lope play, Where sel-dom is heard a dis-cou-rag-ing word, And the
sky is not cloudy all day.

Chorus:

Home, Home on the range, where the deer and the an-te-lope play. Where
sel-dom is heard a dis-cou-rag-ing word, And the sky is not cloud-y all
day.

Verse 2:   How often at night when the heavens are bright
With the light of the glittering stars,
Have I stood there amazed and asked as I gazed,
If their glory exceeds that of ours.

Repeat Chorus

Verse 3:   Where the air is so pure, the zephyrs so free
The breezes so balmy and light.
That I would not exchange my home on the range
For all of the cities so bright.

Hush, Little Baby, Don't Say a Word (Traditional, B/T/PreS)

Hush, lit-tle ba-by, don't say a word. Pa-pa's gon-na buy you a

mock-ing bird. If that mock-ing bird don't sing, Pa-pa's gon-na buy you a

dia-mond ring.

Verse 3:   If that ring just turns to brass,
Papa's gonna buy you a looking glass.

Verse 4:   If that looking glass gets broke,
Papa's gonna buy you a billy goat.

Verse 5:   If that billy goat don't pull,
Papa's gonna find you a cart and bull.

Verse 6:   If that cart and bull turn over,
Papa's gonna buy you a dog named Rover.

Verse 7:   If that dog named Rover don't bark,
Papa's gonna buy you a horse and cart.

Verse 8:   If that horse and cart fall down,
You'll still be the sweetest little baby in town.

I Know an Old Lady Who Swallowed a Fly (Traditional, PreS/K–5/6+)

(Also known as There Was an Old Lady/Woman)

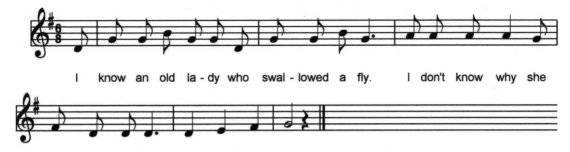

I know an old la-dy who swal-lowed a fly. I don't know why she

swal-lowed the fly. Per-haps she'll die.

Verse 2: I know an old lady who swallowed a spider
That wiggled and jiggled and tickled inside her.
She swallowed the spider to catch the fly,
But I don't know why she swallowed the fly,
Perhaps she'll die.

Verse 3: I know an old lady who swallowed a bird,
How absurd! She swallowed a bird.
She swallowed the bird to catch the spider,
That wiggled and jiggled and tickled inside her.
She swallowed the spider to catch the fly,
But I don't know why she swallowed the fly,
Perhaps she'll die.

Verse 4: I know an old lady who swallowed a cat.
Think of that! She swallowed a cat.
She swallowed the cat to catch the bird . . .

Verse 5: I know an old lady who swallowed a dog,
What a hog! She swallowed a dog!
She swallowed the dog to catch the cat . . .

Verse 6: I know an old lady who swallowed a cow,
I don't know how she swallowed a cow.
She swallowed the cow to catch the dog . . .

Verse 7: I know an old lady who swallowed a horse,
She's dead, of course!

From *The Big Book of Animal Rhymes, Fingerplays, and Songs* by Elizabeth Cothen Low.
Westport, CT: Libraries Unlimited. Copyright © 2009.

Over in the Meadow (Lyrics by Olive A. Wadsworth, PreS/K–5)

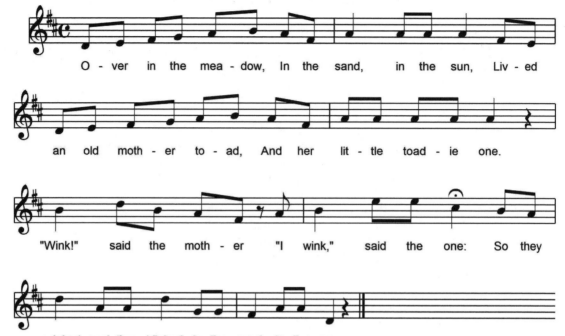

O - ver in the mea - dow, In the sand, in the sun, Liv - ed

an old moth - er to - ad, And her lit - tle toad - ie one.

"Wink!" said the moth - er "I wink," said the one: So they

winked and they blinked in the sand, in the sun.

Verse 2:   Over in the meadow,
           Where the stream runs blue
           Lived an old mother fish
           And her little fishes two
           "Swim!" said the mother;
           "We swim!" said the two,
           So they swam and they leaped
           Where the stream runs blue.

Verse 3:   Over in the meadow,
           In a hole in a tree,
           Lived an old mother bluebird
           And her little birdies three.
           "Sing!" said the mother,
           "We sing!" said the three,
           So they sang and were glad
           In a hole in the tree.

Verse 4:   Over in the meadow,
           In the reeds on the shore,
           Lived an old mother muskrat
           And her little ratties four,
           "Dive!" said the mother,
           "We dive!" said the four,
           So they dived and they burrowed
           In the reeds on the shore.

Verse 5: Over in the meadow,
        In a snug beehive,
        Lived a mother honey bee
        And her little bees five,
        "Buzz!" said the mother;
        "We buzz!" said the five,
        So they buzzed and they hummed
        In the snug beehive.

Verse 6: Over in the meadow,
        In a nest built of sticks,
        Lived a black mother crow
        And her little crows six.
        "Caw!" said the mother;
        "We caw!" said the six,
        So they cawed and they called
        In their nest built of sticks.

Verse 7: Over in the meadow,
        Where the grass is so even,
        Lived a gay mother cricket
        And her little crickets seven.
        "Chirp!" said the mother,
        "We chirp!" said the seven,
        So they chirped cheery notes
        In the grass soft and even.

Verse 8: Over in the meadow,
        By the old mossy gate,
        Lived a brown mother lizard
        And her little lizards eight.
        "Bask!" said the mother,
        "We bask!" said the eight,
        So they basked in the sun
        On the old mossy gate.

Verse 9: Over in the meadow,
        Where the quiet pool shine,
        Lived an green mother frog
        And her little froggies nine.
        "Croak!" said the mother;
        "We croak!" said the nine,
        So they croaked and they splashed
        Where the quiet pools shine.

Verse 10: Over in the meadow,
        In a sly little den,
        Lived a grey mother spider,
        And her little spiders ten.
        "Spin!" said the spider;

From *The Big Book of Animal Rhymes, Fingerplays, and Songs* by Elizabeth Cothen Low.
Westport, CT: Libraries Unlimited. Copyright © 2009.

"We spin!" said the ten,
So they spun lacy webs in
Their sly little den.

Verse 11: Over in the meadow,
In the soft summer even,
Lived a mother firefly
And her little flies eleven.
"Glow," said the mother;
"We glow," said the eleven—
So they glowed like stars
In the soft summer even.

Verse 12: Over in the meadow,
Where the men dig and delve
Lived a wise mother ant,
And her little ants twelve.
"Toil," said the mother;
"We toil," said the twelve—
So they toiled and were wise
Where the men dig and delve.

Pop! Goes the Weasel (Traditional, PreS/K–5)

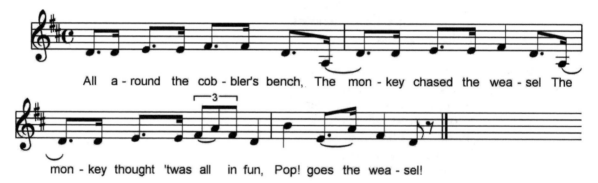

All a-round the cob-bler's bench, The mon-key chased the wea-sel The mon-key thought 'twas all in fun, Pop! goes the wea-sel!

Simple Simon (Traditional, K–5/6+)

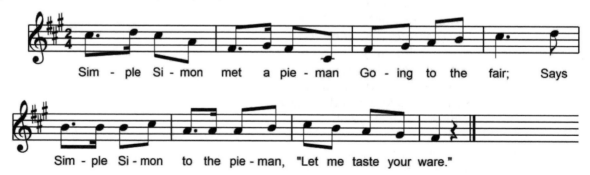

Sim-ple Si-mon met a pie-man Go-ing to the fair; Says Sim-ple Si-mon to the pie-man, "Let me taste your ware."

Verse 2: Said the pieman unto Simon,
   "Show me first your penny."
   Said Simple Simon to the pieman,
   "Indeed I have not any."

Verse 3: He went to catch a dickey bird
   And thought he could not fail,
   Because he's got a little salt
   To put upon its tail.

Verse 4: He went to shoot a wild duck,
   But the wild duck flew away;
   Says Simon, I can't hit him,
   Because he will not stay.

Verse 5: He went to try if cherries ripe
   Did grow upon a thistle;
   He pricked his finger very much
   Which made poor Simon whistle.

Verse 6: Simple Simon went a-fishing,
   For to catch a whale;
   But all the water he had got
   Was in his mother's pail.

Verse 7: Simple Simon went a-hunting
   For to catch a hare;
   He rode a goat about the streets
   But couldn't find one there.

Verse 8: He went to ride a spotted cow
   That had a little calf;
   She threw him down upon the ground,
   Which made the people laugh.

Verse 9: Once Simon made great snowball,
   And brought it in to roast;
   He laid it down before the fire,
   And soon the ball was lost.

Verse 10: He went for water in a sieve,
   But soon it all ran through;
   And now poor Simple Simon
   Bids you all adieu.

From *The Big Book of Animal Rhymes, Fingerplays, and Songs* by Elizabeth Cothen Low.
Westport, CT: Libraries Unlimited. Copyright © 2009.

Skip to My Lou (Traditional, B/T/PreS/K–5)

Lost   my   part - ner,   What'll   I   do?   Lost   my   part - ner,   What'll   I   do?

Lost   my   part - ner,   What'll   I   do?   Skip   to   my   lou   my   dar - ling.

Chorus:

Skip,   skip,   skip to my Lou,   Skip,   skip,   skip to my Lou,   Skip,   skip,   skip to my Lou,

Skip   to   my   Lou   my   dar - ling.

Verse 2:   I'll get another one, prettier than you,
I'll get another one, prettier than you,
I'll get another one, prettier than you,
Skip to my Lou, my darling.

Chorus

Verse 3:   Fly's in the buttermilk,
Shoo, fly, shoo,
Fly's in the buttermilk,
Shoo, fly, shoo,
Fly's in the buttermilk,
Shoo, fly, shoo,
Skip to my Lou, my darling.

Chorus

Verse 4:   Can't get a red bird,
Jay bird'll do.
Can't get a red bird,
Jay bird'll do.
Can't get a red bird,
Jay bird'll do.
Skip to my Lou, my darling.

Chorus

Verse 5:   Cat's in the cream jar,
    Ooh, ooh, ooh,
    Cat's in the cream jar,
    Ooh, ooh, ooh,
    Cat's in the cream jar,
    Ooh, ooh, ooh,
    Skip to my Lou, my darling.

    Chorus

Verse 6:   Pig in the parlor,
    What'll we do?
    Pig in the parlor,
    What'll we do?
    Pig in the parlor,
    What'll we do?
    Skip to my Lou, my darling.

The Twelve Days of Christmas (Traditional, PreS/K–5/6+)

On the first day of Christ-mas, my true love gave to me, a

par-tridge in a pear tree.

Verse 2:   On the second day of Christmas
    My true love sent to me,
    Two turtledoves, and
    A partridge in a pear tree.

Verse 3:   On the third day of Christmas
    My true love sent to me
    Three French hens . . . (Continue with other gifts: two turtle doves and a partridge in a pear tree.)

Verse 4:   On the fourth day of Christmas
    My true love sent to me
    Four calling birds . . . (Continue with other gifts.)

Verse 5:   On the fifth day of Christmas
    My true love sent to me
    Five gold rings . . . (Continue with other gifts.)

Verse 6:   On the sixth day of Christmas
    My true love sent to me
    Six geese a-laying . . . (Continue with other gifts.)

From *The Big Book of Animal Rhymes, Fingerplays, and Songs* by Elizabeth Cothen Low.
Westport, CT: Libraries Unlimited. Copyright © 2009.

Verse 7: On the seventh day of Christmas
My true love sent to me
Seven swans a-swimming . . . (Continue with other gifts.)

Verse 8: On the eighth day of Christmas
My true love sent to me
Eight maids a-milking . . . (Continue with other gifts.)

Verse 9: On the ninth day of Christmas
My true love sent to me
Nine drummers drumming . . . (Continue with other gifts.)

Verse 10: On the tenth day of Christmas
My true love sent to me
Ten pipers piping . . . (Continue with other gifts.)

Verse 11: On the eleventh day of Christmas
My true love sent to me
Eleven ladies dancing . . . (Continue with other gifts.)

Verse 12: On the twelfth day of Christmas
My true love sent to me
Twelve lords a-leaping . . . (Continue with other gifts.)

What Are Little Boys Made Of? (Traditional, PreS/K–5)

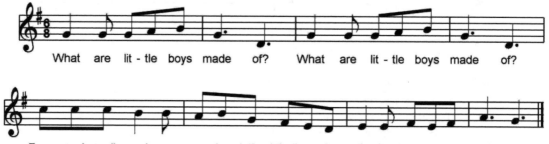

What are lit-tle boys made of? What are lit-tle boys made of?

Frogs and snails and pup -py dog tails, That's what lit-tle boys a-re made of.

Verse 2: What are little girls made of?
What are little girls made of?
Sugar and spice
And all that's nice,
That's what little girls are made of.

Poetry

A City Plum Is Not a Plum (Christina Rossetti, 6+)

A city plum is not a plum;
A dumb-bell is no bell, though dumb;
A party rat is not a rat;
A sailor's cat is not a cat;

A soldier's frog is not a frog;
A captain's log is not a log.

Kindness to Animals (J. Ashby-Sterry, 6+)

Speak gently to the herring and kindly to the calf,
Be blithesome˙ with the bunny, at barnacles don't laugh!
Give nuts unto the monkey, and buns unto the bear,
Ne'er hint at currant jelly if you chance to see a hare!
Oh, little girls, pray hide your combs when tortoises draw nigh,
And never in the hearing of a pigeon whisper Pie!
But give the stranded jelly-fish a shove into the sea,—
Be always kind to animals wherever you may be!

Oh, make not game of sparrows, nor faces at the ram,
And ne'er allude to mint sauce when calling on a lamb.
Don't beard the thoughtful oyster, don't dare the cod to crimp,
Don't cheat the pike, or ever try to pot the playful shrimp.
Tread lightly on the turning worm, don't bruise the butterfly,
Don't ridicule the wry-neck,˙ nor sneer at salmon-fry;
Oh, ne'er delight to make dogs fight, nor bantams˙ disagree,—
Be always kind to animals wherever you may be!

Be lenient with lobsters, and ever kind to crabs,
And be not disrespectful to cuttle-fish or dabs;˙
Chase not the Cochin-China, chaff not the ox obese,
And babble not of feather-beds in company with geese.
Be tender with the tadpole, and let the limpet˙ thrive,
Be merciful to mussels, don't skin your eels alive;
When talking to a turtle don't mention calipee˙—
Be always kind to animals wherever you may be.

* Blithesome: Merry
* Wryneck: Kind of woodpecker
* Bantams: Small fowl
* Dabs: Flounders
* Limpet: Kind of mussel
* Calipee: Edible part of turtle's body beneath lower shell

Hurt No Living Thing (Christina Rossetti, K–5/6+)

Hurt no living thing,
Ladybird nor butterfly,
Nor moth with dusty wing,
Nor cricket chirping cheerily,
Nor grasshopper, so light of leap,
Nor dancing gnat,
Nor beetle fat,
Nor harmless worms that creep.

If a Mouse Could Fly (Christina Rossetti, K–5/6+)

If a mouse could fly,
Or if a crow could swim,

From The Big Book of Animal Rhymes, Fingerplays, and Songs by Elizabeth Cothen Low.
Westport, CT: Libraries Unlimited. Copyright © 2009.

Or if a sprat could walk and talk,
I'd like to be like him.
If a mouse could fly,
He might fly away;
Or if a crow could swim,
It might turn him grey;
Or if a sprat˙ could walk and talk,
What would he find to say?

* Sprat: A kind of small fish

The Monkey's Glue (Goldwin Goldsmith, 6+)

When the monkey in his madness
Took the glue to mend his voice,
'Twas the crawfish showed his sadness
That the bluebird could rejoice.

Then the perspicacious˙ parrot
Sought to save the suicide
By administering carrot,
But the monkey merely died.

So the crawfish and the parrot
Sauntered slowly toward the sea,
While the bluebird stole the carrot
And returned the glue to me.

* Perspicacious: Clever

The Moon (Robert Louis Stevenson, 6+)

The moon has a face like the clock in the hall;
She shines on thieves on the garden wall,
On streets and fields and harbour quays,
And birdies asleep in the forks of the trees.

The squalling cat and the squeaking mouse,
The howling dog by the door of the house,
The bat that lies in bed at noon,
All love to be out by the light of the moon.

But all of the things that belong to the day
Cuddle to sleep to be out of her way;
And flowers and children close their eyes
Till up in the morning the sun shall arise.

The Owl and the Pussycat (Edward Lear, 6+)

The owl and the pussycat went to sea
In a beautiful pea-green boat
They took some honey and plenty of money
Wrapped up in a five-pound note.

The owl looked up the stars above
And sang to a small guitar,
"O, lovely pussy, o pussy my love,
What a beautiful pussy you are, you are
What a beautiful pussy you are!"

Pussy said to the owl, "You elegant fowl,
How charmingly sweet you sing.
O, let us be married, too long we have tarried,
But what shall we do for a ring?"

They sailed away for a year and a day
To the land where Bongtree grows.
And there in a wood a Piggywig stood
With a ring at the end of his nose, his nose.

"Dear Pig, are you willing to sell for one shilling
Your ring?" Said the Piggy, "I will."
So they took it away and were married next day
By the turkey who lives on the hill.

They dined on mince and slices of quince
Which they ate with a runcible spoon;
And hand in hand on the edge of the sand
They danced by the light of the moon, the moon,
They danced by the light of the moon.

The Peacock Has a Score of Eyes (Christina Rossetti, 6+)

The peacock has a score of eyes,
With which he cannot see;
The cod-fish has a silent sound,
However that may be;
No dandelions tell the time,
Although they turn to clocks;
Cat's-cradle˙ does not hold the cat,
Nor foxglove˙ fit the fox.

* Cat's cradle: A game that involves wrapping string between hands in a special pattern
* Foxglove: A variety of herb

Sage Counsel (A. T. Quiller-Couch, 6+)

The lion is the beast to fight,
He leaps along the plain,
And if you run with all your might,
He runs with all his mane.
I'm glad I'm not a Hottentot,
But if I were, with outward cal-lum
I'd either faint upon the spot
Or hie me up a leafy pal-lum.

From *The Big Book of Animal Rhymes, Fingerplays, and Songs* by Elizabeth Cothen Low.
Westport, CT: Libraries Unlimited. Copyright © 2009.

The chamois is the beast to hunt;
He's fleeter than the wind,
And when the chamois is in front,
The hunter is behind.
The Tyrolese make famous cheese
And hunt the chamois o'er the chaz-zums;
I'd choose the former if you please,
For precipices give me spaz-zums.

The polar bear will make a rug
Almost as white as snow;
But if he gets you in his hug,
He rarely lets you go.
And Polar ice looks very nice,
With all the colors of a pris-sum;
But, if you'll follow my advice,
Stay home and learn your catechissum.

* Chamois: Kind of European antelope, lives in the mountains
* Catechissum (Catechisms): Religious teachings

Swift and Sure the Swallow (Christina Rossetti, K–5/6+)

Swift and sure the swallow,
Slow and sure the snail:
Slow and sure may miss his way,
Swift and sure may fail.

Winter Night (Mary F. Butts, K–5/6+)

Blow, wind, blow!
Drift the flying snow!
Send it twirling, whirling overhead!
There's a bedroom in a tree
Where, snug as snug can be,
The squirrel nests in his cozy bed.

Shriek, wind, shriek!
Make the branches creak!
Battle with the boughs till break o' day!
In a snow-cave warm and tight,
Through the icy winter night
The rabbit sleeps the peaceful hours away.

Call, wind, call!
In entry and in hall!
Straight from off the mountain white and wild!
Soft purrs the pussy-cat,
On her little fluffy mat,
And beside her nestles close her furry child.

Scold, wind, scold!
So bitter and so bold!
Shake the windows with your tap, tap, tap!
With half-shut dreamy eyes
The drowsy baby lies
Cuddled closely in his mother's lap.

What Does the Donkey Bray About? (Christina Rossetti, K–5/6+)

What does the donkey bray about?
What does the pig grunt through his snout?
What does the goose mean by a hiss?
Oh, Nurse, if you can tell me this,
I'll give you such a kiss.
The cockatoo calls "cockatoo,"
The magpie chatters "how d'ye do?"
The jackdaw bids me "go away,"
Cuckoo cries "cuckoo" half the day:
What do the others say?

When Fishes Set Umbrellas Up (Christina Rossetti, K–5/6+)

When fishes set umbrellas up
If the rain-drops run,
Lizards will want their parasols
To shade them from the sun.

When the Cows Come Home the Milk Is Coming (Christina Rossetti, K–5/6+)

When the cows come home the milk is coming,
Honey's made while the bees are humming;
Duck and drake on the rushy* lake,
And the deer live safe in the breezy brake;
And timid, funny, brisk little bunny,
Winks his nose and sits all sunny.

* Rushy: Covered with rushes, a type of marsh plant

Farm Animals

Nursery Rhymes

As I Was Going to Banbury (Traditional, K–5/6+)

As I was going to Banbury,
Upon a summer's day,
My dame had butter, eggs, and fruit,
And I had corn and hay.
Joe drove the ox, and Tom the swine,
Dick took the foal and mare;
I sold them all—then home to dine,
From famous Banbury fair.

Hey, Diddle Diddle

See Songs section in this subsection.

Higglety, Pigglety, Pop! (Traditional, PreS/K–5)

Higglety, pigglety, pop!
The dog has eaten the mop;
The pig's in a hurry,
The cat's in a flurry,
Higglety, pigglety, pop!

High Diddle Doubt (Traditional, PreS/K–5)

(Also known as **Rowsty Dowt, My Fire's All Out**)

High diddle doubt, my candle's out,
My little maid is not at home;
Saddle my hog and bridle my dog,
And fetch my little maid home.

Hush-a-Bye (Traditional, 6+)

Hush-a-bye a baa-lamb,
Hush-a-bye a milk cow,
You shall have a little stick
To beat the naughty bow-wow.

Little Boy Blue

See Song section in this subsection.

Sukey, You Shall Be My Wife (Traditional, K–5/6+)

Sukey, you shall be my wife
And I will tell you why:
I have got a little pig,
And you have got a sty;
I have got a dun cow,
And you can make good cheese;
Sukey, will you marry me?
Say Yes, if you please.

This Is the House that Jack Built (Traditional, PreS/K–5/6+)

This is the house that Jack built.

This is the malt
That lay in the house that Jack built.

This is the rat,
That ate the malt
That lay in the house that Jack built.

This is the cat,
That killed the rat,
That ate the malt
That lay in the house that Jack built.

This is the dog,
That worried the cat,
That killed the rat,
That ate the malt
That lay in the house that Jack built.

This is the cow with the crumpled horn,
That tossed the dog,
That worried the cat,
That killed the rat,
That ate the malt
That lay in the house that Jack built.

This is the maiden all forlorn,
That milked the cow with the crumpled horn,
That tossed the dog,
That worried the cat,
That killed the rat,
That ate the malt
That lay in the house that Jack built.

This is the man all tattered and torn,
That kissed the maiden all forlorn,
That milked the cow with the crumpled horn,
That tossed the dog,
That worried the cat,
That killed the rat,
That ate the malt
That lay in the house that Jack built.

This is the priest all shaven and shorn,
That married the man all tattered and torn,
That kissed the maiden all forlorn,
That milked the cow with the crumpled horn,
That tossed the dog,
That worried the cat,
That killed the rat,
That ate the malt
That lay in the house that Jack built.

This is the cock that crowed in the morn,
That waked the priest all shaven and shorn,
That married the man all tattered and torn,
That kissed the maiden all forlorn,
That milked the cow with the crumpled horn,
That tossed the dog,

That worried the cat,
That killed the rat,
That ate the malt
That lay in the house that Jack built.

This is the farmer sowing his corn,
That kept the cock that crowed in the morn,
That waked the priest all shaven and shorn,
That married the man all tattered and torn,
That kissed the maiden all forlorn,
That milked the cow with the crumpled horn,
That tossed the dog,
That worried the cat,
That killed the rat,
That ate the malt
That lay in the house that Jack built.

What an Odd Dame (Traditional, K–5/6+)

What an odd dame Mother Bulletout's grown!
She dresses her ducks and her drakes in cocked hats,
Her hens wear hoop petticoats made of whalebone!
And she puts little breeches on all her Tom cats!

Whistle, Daughter, Whistle (Traditional, K–5/6+)

"Whistle, daughter, whistle,
And I'll give you a sheep."
"Mother, I'm asleep."

"Whistle, daughter, whistle,
And you shall have a cow."
"Mother, I don't know how."

"Whistle, daughter, whistle,
And I'll give you a man.
"Mother, now I can!" (Loud whistle.)

Songs

Farmer in the Dell (Traditional, PreS/K–5)

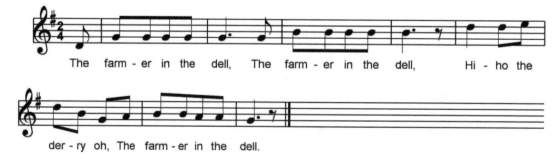

The farm-er in the dell, The farm-er in the dell, Hi - ho the
der - ry oh, The farm-er in the dell.

From *The Big Book of Animal Rhymes, Fingerplays, and Songs* by Elizabeth Cothen Low.
Westport, CT: Libraries Unlimited. Copyright © 2009.

Verse 2:   The farmer takes a wife,
           The farmer takes a wife,
           Hi-ho the derry-oh,
           The farmer takes a wife.

Verse 3:   The wife takes a child . . . (Repeat refrain as in previous verse.)
Verse 4:   The child takes a nurse . . . (Repeat refrain as in previous verse.)
Verse 5:   The nurse takes a dog . . . (Repeat refrain as in previous verse.)
Verse 6:   The dog takes a cat . . . (Repeat refrain as in previous verse.)
Verse 7:   The cat takes a mouse . . . (Repeat refrain as in previous verse.)
Verse 8:   The mouse takes the cheese . . . (Repeat refrain as in previous verse.)
Verse 9:   The cheese stands alone . . . (Repeat refrain as in previous verse.)

Fiddle-I-Fee (Traditional, PreS/K–5)

I had a cat and the cat pleased me, I fed my cat und-er yon-der tree, Cat said, Fid-dle-I-Fee.

Verse 2:   I had a hen and the hen pleased me,
           I fed my hen under yonder tree.
           Hen goes chimmy-chuck, chimmy-chuck.
           Cat goes Fiddle-I-Fee.

Verse 3:   I had a duck and the duck pleased me,
           I fed my duck under yonder tree.
           Duck goes quack, quack . . . (Continue with other animals: hen and cat.)

Verse 4:   I had a goose and the goose pleased me . . .
           Goose goes swishy, swashy . . .. (Continue with other animals.)

Verse 5:   I had a sheep and the sheep pleased me . . .
           Sheep goes baa, baa . . . (Continue with other animals.)

Verse 6:   I had a pig and the pig pleased me . . .
           Pig goes griffy, gruffy . . . (Continue with other animals.)

Verse 7:   I had a cow and the cow pleased me . . .
           Cow goes moo, moo . . . (Continue with other animals.)

Verse 8:   I had a horse and the horse pleased me . . .
           Horse goes neigh, neigh . . . (Continue with other animals.)

Verse 9:   I had a dog and the dog pleased me . . .
           Dog goes bow-wow, bow-wow . . . (Continue with other animals.)

From *The Big Book of Animal Rhymes, Fingerplays, and Songs* by Elizabeth Cothen Low.
Westport, CT: Libraries Unlimited. Copyright © 2009.

Hey, Diddle Diddle (Traditional, B/T/PreS/K–5)

Hey, did - dle, did - dle, the cat and the fid - dle, The cow jumped ov - er the

moon; The lit - tle dog laugh - ed to see such sport, And the

dish ran away with the spoon.

Little Boy Blue (Traditional, B/T/PreS/K–5)

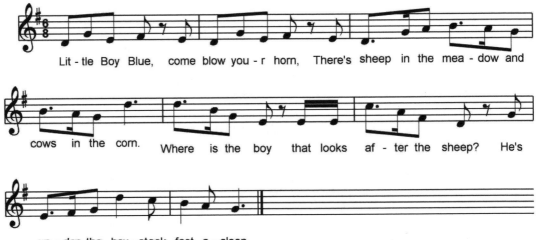

Lit - tle Boy Blue, come blow you - r horn, There's sheep in the mea - dow and

cows in the corn. Where is the boy that looks af - ter the sheep? He's

un - der the hay - stack fast a - sleep.

Additional Lines:
Will you wake him?
No, not I,
For if I do,
He's sure to cry.

From *The Big Book of Animal Rhymes, Fingerplays, and Songs* by Elizabeth Cothen Low.
Westport, CT: Libraries Unlimited. Copyright © 2009.

Old MacDonald (Traditional, B/T/PreS/K–5)

Old Mac-Don-ald had a farm, E - I - E - I - O, and on that farm he had a cow,

E - I - E - I - O, With a moo, moo, here and a moo, moo, there,

here a moo, there a moo, e-very-where a moo, moo, Old Mac-Don-ald had a farm,

E - I - E - I - O.

Verse 2: Old MacDonald had a farm,
E-I-E-I-O,
And on this farm he had a sheep . . .
E-I-E-I-O,
With a baa, baa, here,
And a baa, baa, there,
Here a baa, there a baa,
Everywhere a baa, baa.
A moo, moo here,
And a moo, moo there,
Here a moo, there a moo,
Everywhere a moo, moo.
Old MacDonald had a farm,
E-I-E-I-O!

Verse 3: And on this farm he had a cat,
E-I-E-I-O,
With a meow, meow, here . . .

Verse 4: And on this farm he had a horse,
E-I-E-I-O,
With a neigh, neigh, here . . .

Suggestion: Continue with more animal sounds, such "maa" for a goat, "woof" for a dog, "oink" for a pig, etc.

From *The Big Book of Animal Rhymes, Fingerplays, and Songs* by Elizabeth Cothen Low.
Westport, CT: Libraries Unlimited. Copyright © 2009.

Mythical and Imaginary Creatures

Nursery Rhymes

Davy Doldrum (Traditional, Tongue Twister, K–5/6+)

Davy Doldrum dreamed he drove a dragon.
Did Davy Doldrum dream he drove a dragon?
If Davy Doldrum dreamed he drove a dragon,
Where's the dragon Davy Doldrum dreamed be drove?

The Lion and the Unicorn

See "Lions" chapter, Nursery Rhymes section.

When that Seint George Hadde Slyne Ye Draggon (Traditional, 6+)

When that Seint George hadde sleyne ye draggon,
He sate him down furinst a flaggon;
And, wit ye well,
Within a spell
He had a bien plaisaunt jag on.

* Flaggon (Flagon): Kind of vessel
* Jag: Inebriated feeling

Poetry

The Bloated Biggaboon (H. Cholmondeley-Pennell, 6+)

The bloated Biggaboon
Was so haughty, he would not repose
In a house, or a hall, or ces choses,
But he slept his high sleep in his clothes—
'Neath the moon.
The bloated Biggaboon
Pour'd contempt upon waistcoat and skirt,
Holding swallow-tails even as dirt—
So he puff'd himself out in his shirt,
Like a b'loon.

* Ces choses: These things

Jabberwocky (Lewis Carroll, Nonsense Verse, 6+)

'Twas brillig, and the slithy toves
Did gyre and gimble in the wabe;
All mimsy were the borogoves,
And the mome raths outgrabe.

"Beware the Jabberwock, my son!
The jaws that bite, the claws that catch!
Beware the Jubjub bird, and shun
The frumious Bandersnatch!"

From *The Big Book of Animal Rhymes, Fingerplays, and Songs* by Elizabeth Cothen Low.
Westport, CT: Libraries Unlimited. Copyright © 2009.

He took his vorpal sword in hand:
Long time the manxome foe he sought.
So rested he by the Tumtum tree,
And stood awhile in thought.

And as in uffish thought he stood,
The Jabberwock with eyes of flame,
Came whiffling through the tulgey wood,
And burbled as it came!

One, two! One, two! And through, and through
The vorpal blade went snicker-snack!
He left it dead, and with its head
He went galumphing back.

"And hast thou slain the Jabberwock?
Come to my arms, my beamish boy!
Oh, frabjous day! Callooh! Callay!"
He chortled in his joy.

'Twas brillig, and the slithy toves
Did gyre and gimble in the wabe;
All mimsy were the borogoves
And the mome raths outgrabe.

The Sea-Serpent (Planche, 6+)

All bones but yours will rattle when I say
I'm the sea-serpent from America.
Mayhap you've heard that I've been round the world;
I guess I'm round it now, Mister, twice curled.
Of all the monsters through the deep that splash,
I'm "number one" to all immortal smash.
When I lie down and would my length unroll,
There ar'n't half room enough 'twixt pole and pole.
In short, I grow so long that I've a notion
I must be measured soon for a new ocean.

Pets

Fingerplays and Action Rhymes

One Little, Two Little, Three Little Kittens (Traditional, PreS/K–5)

One little, two little, three little kittens (Show three fingers.)
Were napping in the sun. (Fold hands on side of head to signify sleep.)
One little, two little, three little puppies (Show three fingers.)
Said, "Let's have some fun."

Up to the kittens the puppies went creeping (Creep fingers on ground out towards the children.)
As quiet as could be. (Put finger to lip and make shushing sound.)
One little, two little, three little kittens (Show three fingers.)
Went scampering up a tree! (Wriggle fingers in the air.)

Nursery Rhymes

Dingle Dingle Doosey (Traditional, PreS/K–5)

Dingle dingle doosey,
The cat's in the well,
The dog's away to Bellingen
To buy the bairn* a bell.

* Bairn: Child

Hoddley, Poddley, Puddle and Fogs (Traditional, PreS/K–5)

Hoddley, poddley,
Puddle and fogs,
Cats are to marry
The poodle dogs;
Cats in blue jackets
And dogs in red hats,
What will become
Of the mice and the rats?

There Was a Man, and His Name Was Dob (Traditional, K–5/6+)

There was a man, and his name was Dob,
And he had a wife, and her name was Mob,
And he had a dog, and he called it Cob,
And she had a cat called Chitterabob.

"Cob!," calls Dob,
"Chitterabob!," calls Mob,
Cob was Dob's dog,
Chitterabob Mob's cat.

Songs

Poor Dog Bright (Traditional, PreS/K–5)

Poor dog Bright, Ran off with all his might, Be -cause the cat was

chas - ing him, Poor dog Bright.

Verse 2: Poor cat Fright,
Ran off with all her might,
Because the dog was after her,
Poor cat Fright.

Poetry

The Dog Lies in His Kennel (Christina Rossetti, B/T/PreS/K–5)

The dog lies in his kennel,
And Puss purrs on the rug,
And baby perches on my knee
For me to love and hug.
Pat the dog and stroke the cat,
Each in its degree;
And cuddle and kiss my baby,
And baby kiss me.

Pussy Has a Whiskered Face (Christina Rossetti, PreS/K–5)

Pussy has a whiskered face,
Kitty has such pretty ways;
Doggie scampers when I call,
And has a heart to love us all.

OWLS

Fingerplays and Action Rhymes

There Was a Little Boy Went into a Barn (Traditional, PreS/K–5)

There was a little boy went into a barn,
And lay down on some hay; (Lay index finger on face-up palm.)
An owl came out and flew about, (Place thumbs together and wiggle fingers in air.)
And the little boy ran away. (Hold up index finger and hide it behind back.)

A Wise Old Owl Sat in an Oak (Traditional, PreS/K–5)

A wise old owl sat in an oak,
The more he heard the less he spoke; (Cup hand around ear, then place index finger on mouth.)
The less he spoke the more he heard. (Place index finger on mouth, then cup hand around ear.)
Why aren't we all like that wise old bird?

Nursery Rhymes

The Brown Owl Sits in the Ivy Bush (Traditional, PreS/K–5)

The brown owl sits in the ivy-bush,
And she looketh wondrous wise,
With a horny beak beneath her cowl,
And a pair of large round eyes.

"Bow-Wow," says the Dog

See "Multiple Animals" chapter, Nursery Rhymes section

I Went to the Toad

See "Multiple Animals" chapter, Nursery Rhymes section

Of All the Gay Birds That Ever I Did See (Traditional, PreS/K–5)

Of all the gay birds that ever I did see,
The owl is the fairest by far to me,
For all day long she sits on a tree,
And when the night comes away flies she.

Oliver Oglethorpe Ogled an Owl and Oyster

See "Multiple Animals" chapter, Nursery Rhymes section.

An Owl Sat Alone on the Branch of a Tree (Traditional, PreS/K–5)

An owl sat alone on the branch of a tree
And he was quiet as quiet could be.
'Twas night and his eyes were open like this
And he looked all around; not a thing did he miss

Some brownies climbed up the trunk of the tree
And sat on a branch as quiet as he
Said the wise old owl, "To-Whoo, To-Whoo."
Up jumped the brownies and away they all flew.

Tecolotito morado (Traditional, Spanish, K–5/6+)

Tecolotito morado,
Pájaro madrugador.
Me prestaras tus alitas,
Para ir a ver a mi amor.

Tacurú cua, cua, cua,
Pobrecito tecolotito,
Ya se cansa de llorar.

Si yo fuero tecolote,
No me lanzaría a volar.
Me quedara en mi nidito
Y acabándome de criar.

Translation: Little Purple Owlet

Little purple owlet,
Singing as dawn shines above,
Won't you lend me your swift wings
That I may fly to my love?

Tecuru kwa, kwa, kwa,
Poor little owlet,
It is tired from crying so.

If I were a little owlet,
I would never steal away;
Till my wings were strong and steady,
Safe within my nest I'd stay.

There Was an Old Woman Named Towl (Traditional, K–5/6+)

There was an old woman named Towl,
Who went to sea with her owl;
But the owl was seasick,
And screamed for physic,
Which sadly annoyed Mistress Towl.

* Physic: Medicine

Three Owlets (Traditional, K–5/6+)

Three little owlets
In a hollow tree,
Cuddled up together
Close as could be.

When the moon came out
And the dew lay wet,
Mother flew about
To see what she could get.

She caught a little mouse,
So velvety and soft,
She caught some little sparrows,
And then she flew aloft

To the three little owlets
In a hollow tree,
Cuddled up together
Close as could be.

"Tu-whoo," said the old owl,
"Isn't this good cheer!"
"Tu-whit," said the owlets,
"Thank you, mother dear."
Tu-whit, tu-whit, tu-whit,
Tu-whoo!

There Was an Owl Who Lived in an Oak (Traditional, K–5/6+)

(Also known as **In an Oak There Lived an Owl**)

There was an owl lived in an oak,
Wisky, wasky, weedle;
And every word he ever spoke
Was, Fiddle, faddle, feedle.

A gunner chanced to come that way,
Wisky, wasky, weedle;
Says he, I'll shoot you, silly bird.
Fiddle, faddle, feedle.

Poetry

The Owl and the Pussycat

See "Multiple Animals" chapter, Poetry section.

There Was an Old Man with a Beard

See "Birds" chapter, Poetry section.

A White Hen Sitting

See "Chickens" chapter, Poetry section.

OYSTERS

Nursery Rhymes

Oliver Oglethorpe Ogled an Owl and Oyster

See "Multiple Animals" chapter, Nursery Rhymes section.

One Old Oxford Ox

See "Multiple Animals" chapter, Nursery Rhymes section.

Poetry

Kindness to Animals

See "Multiple Animals" chapter, Poetry section.

PANTHERS

Nursery Rhymes

The Panther

See "Multiple Animals" chapter, Nursery Rhymes section.

PARROTS

Nursery Rhymes

El perico (Traditional, Spanish, K–5/6+)

Señora, su periquito
Me quiere llevar al rio,
Y yo le digo que no,
Porque me muero de frio.

Pica, pica, pica, perico,
Pica, pica, pica la arena,
Pica, pica, pica, perico,
Pica, pica, pica a tu hermana.

Quisiera ser periquito,
Para andar siempre en el aire,
Y allí decirte secretos
Sin que los oyera nadie.

Vuela, vuela, vuela, perico,
Vete á la tierra caliente;
Huye, huye, huye, perico,
Huye, húyete de la gente.

Translation: The Parrot

Ma'am, your little parrot,
Wants to take me to the river;
But I told him that I could not,
I'd die from the cold,

Pick, pick, pick, parrot,
Pick, pick, pick, at the sand,
Pick, pick, pick, parrot,
Pick, pick, pick, at your sister.
I should like to be a little parrot,
In the air shifting and veering,
There to tell you all my secrets
Without anybody's hearing.

Fly off, fly off, fly off, parrot,
Seek the hotter lands of the tropics;
Flee then, flee then, flee then, parrot,
Flee then, flee then from everybody.

Little Poll Parrot (Traditional, PreS/K–5)

Little Poll Parrot
Sat in his garret*
Eating his toast and tea;
A little brown mouse
Jumped into the house
And stole it all away.

* Garret: Attic

There Was an Old Woman of Gloucester (Traditional, K–5/6+)

There was an old woman of Gloucester,
Whose parrot two guineas it cost her,
But its tongue never ceasing,
Was vastly displeasing,
To the talkative woman of Gloucester.

Poetry

I Have a Poll Parrot (Christina Rossetti, K–5/6+)

I have a Poll parrot,
And Poll is my doll,
And my nurse is Polly,
And my sister Poll.
"Polly!" cried Polly,
"Don't tear Polly dolly"—
While soft-hearted Poll
Trembled for the doll.

From *The Big Book of Animal Rhymes, Fingerplays, and Songs* by Elizabeth Cothen Low.
Westport, CT: Libraries Unlimited. Copyright © 2009.

PEACOCKS

Nursery Rhymes

Cock Robin and Jenny Wren

See "Birds" chapter, Nursery Rhymes section.

A Gaping Wide-Mouthed Waddling Frog

See "Multiple Animals" chapter, Nursery Rhymes section.

El pavo real (Traditional, Spanish, K–5/6+)

Ya se cayo el arbolito
Donde dormía el pavo real.
Y ahora dormirá en el suelo
Como cualquier animal.
¡Ha, ha, ha, ha!

Translation: The Royal Peacock

Now that the tree has fallen,
Where the peacock slept the night through,
On the hard ground he must slumber
As other animals do.
Ha, ha, ha, ha!

The Moon Is Up

See "Multiple Animals" chapter, Nursery Rhymes section.

When the Peacock Loudly Calls (Traditional Saying, K–5/6+)

When the peacock loudly calls,
Then look out for rain and squalls.

* Squalls: Strong winds

Poetry

The Peacock Has a Score of Eyes

See "Multiple Animals" chapter, Poetry section.

PENGUINS

Songs

Ain't It Great to Be Crazy?

See "Multiple Animals" chapter, Songs section.

PIGS

Fingerplays and Action Rhymes

The First Little Pig Danced a Merry, Merry Jig (Traditional, B/T/PreS)

The first little pig (Show thumb.)
Danced a merry, merry jig.
The second little pig ate candy (Hold up index finger as well.)
The third little pig (Add middle finger.)
Wore a blue and yellow wig.
The fourth little pig was a dandy. (Add ring finger.)
The fifth little pig (Point to pinky finger.)
Never grew very big,
So they called him
Tiny Little Andy.

"Let Us Go to the Wood" (Traditional, B/T)

(Also known as "Let's Go to the Wood")

"Let us go to the wood," says this little pig. (Wriggle right wrist.)
"What to do there?" says that little pig. (Wriggle left wrist.)
"To look for our mother," says this little pig. (Wriggle right ankle.)
"What to do with her?" says that little pig. (Wriggle left ankle.)
"To kiss her and kiss her." (Kiss baby and tickle her.)

The Pettitoes Are Little Feet (Traditional, PreS/K–5)

The pettitoes are little feet,
And the little feet not big. (Place hands close together to signify a small distance.)
Great feet belong to the grunting hog, (Hold hands further apart and grunt.)
And the pettitoes to the little pig. (Place hands together and say, wee, wee.)

The Pigs (Emilie Poulsson, PreS/K–5)

Piggie Wig and Piggie Wee, (Hold up left thumb, then hold up right thumb.)
Hungry pigs as pigs could be,
For their dinner had to wait
Down behind the barnyard gate. (Touch fingertips of both hands together for gate.)

Piggie Wig and Piggie Wee
Climbed the barnyard gate to see,
Peeping through the gate so high, (Keeping fingertips together, slip thumbs through index and
     middle fingers.)
But no dinner could they spy.

Piggie Wig and Piggie Wee
Got down sad as pigs could be;
But the gate soon opened wide (Have hands swing away from each other outwards.)
And they scampered forth outside.

Piggie Wig and Piggie Wee,
What was their delight to see
Dinner ready not far off
Such a full and tempting trough! (Cup hands.)

Piggie Wig and Piggie Wee,
Greedy pigs as pigs could be,
For their dinner ran pell-mell; (Have thumbs run forward.)
In the trough both piggies fell. (Point thumbs downwards.)

* Pell-mell: Hastily in a disorganized manner

This Little Pig Went to the Barn (Traditional, B/T/PreS)

This little pig went to the barn, (Tug on thumb or big toe.)
This ate all the corn, (Tug on second toe or index finger.)
This said she would tell, (Tug on third toe or middle finger.)
This said he wasn't well, (Tug on fourth toe or ring finger.)
This went weke, weke, weke, (Tug on little toe or pinky and tickle baby.)
Over the door sill.

This Little Pig Went to Market (Traditional, B/T/PreS)

(Also known as This Little Piggy or This Little Piggie)

This little pig went to market, (Tug on thumb or big toe.)
This little pig stayed at home, (Tug on second toe or index finger.)
This little pig had roast beef, (Tug on third toe or middle finger.)
This little pig had none, (Tug on fourth toe or ring finger.)
And this little pig cried, Wee-wee-wee (Tug on little toe or pinky and tickle baby.)
All the way home.

Two Mother Pigs Lived in a Pen (Traditional, B/T/PreS)

Two mother pigs lived in a pen, (Hold up both thumbs.)
Each had four babies and that made ten. (Show all ten fingers.)
These four babies were black as night, (Hold up four fingers on right hand.)
There four babies were black and white. (Show four fingers on left hand.)
But all eight babies loved to play
And they rolled and rolled in the mud all day. (Close fists and roll hands over one another.)

Wee Wiggie

See "Multiple Animals" chapter, Fingerplay and Action Rhymes section.

Nursery Rhymes

As I Was Going to Banbury

See "Farm Animals" subsection of "Multiple Animals" chapter, Nursery Rhymes section.

Barber, Barber, Shave a Pig (Traditional, PreS/K–5)

Barber, barber, shave a pig,
How many hairs will make a wig?
"Four and twenty, that's enough."
Give the barber a pinch of snuff.

Birds of a Feather Flock Together

See "Multiple Animals" chapter, Nursery Rhymes section.

"Bow-Wow," Says the Dog

See "Multiple Animals" chapter, Nursery Rhymes section.

Christmas Comes but Once a Year (Traditional, PreS/K–5)

Christmas comes but once a year
And when it comes it brings good cheer,
A pocket full of money,
And a cellar full of beer,
And a good fat pig to last you all the year.

Come Dance a Jig (Traditional, PreS/K–5)

Come dance a jig
To my Granny's pig,
With a raudy, rowdy, dowdy;
Come dance a jig
To my Granny's pig,
And pussy-cat shall crowdy.

Dickery, Dickery, Dare (Traditional, PreS/K–5)

Dickery, dickery, dare,
The pig flew up in the air;
The man in brown
Soon brought him down,
Dickery, dickery, dare.

Elsie Marley Has Grown So Fine (Traditional, PreS/K–5)

Elsie Marley's grown so fine,
She won't get up to serve the swine,
But lies in bed till eight or nine.
And surely she does take her time.

Grandfa' Grig (Traditional, K–5)

Grandfa' Grig
Had a pig,
In a field of clover;
Piggy died,
Grandfa' cried,
And all the fun was over.

A Gentleman of Wales

See "Multiple Animals" chapter, Nursery Rhymes section.

Higglety, Pigglety, Pop!

See "Farm Animals" subsection of "Multiple Animals" chapter, Nursery Rhymes section.

High Diddle Doubt

See "Farm Animals" subsection of "Multiple Animals" chapter, Nursery Rhymes section.

Little Betty Winckle (Traditional, K–5/6+)

(Also known as **Little Betty Pringle**)

Little Betty Winckle she had a pig,
It was a little pig, not very big;
When he was alive he lived in the clover.
But now he's dead and that's all over.
Johnny Winckle he sat down and cried,
Betty Winckle she lay down and died:
So there was an end of one, two, three,
Johnny Winckle he,
Betty Winckle she,
And Piggy Wiggy.

Little Piggy Wiggy

See "Multiple Animals" chapter, Nursery Rhymes section.

A Long-Tailed Pig (Traditional, PreS/K–5)

A long-tailed pig, or a short-tailed pig,
Or a pig without any tail;
A sow pig, or a boar pig,
Or a pig with a curly tail.

Little Jack Sprat (Traditional, PreS/K–5)

Little Jack Sprat's pig,
He was not very little,
Nor yet very big;
He was not very lean,
He was not very fat,
"It's a good pig to grunt,"
Said little Jack Sprat.

A Little Pig Found a Fifty-Dollar Note (Traditional, K–5/6+)

A little pig found a fifty-dollar note,
And purchased a hat and a very fine coat,
With trousers, and stockings, and shoes;
Cravat, and shirt-collar, and gold-headed cane;
Then proud as could be, did he march up the lane;
Says he, "I shall hear all the news."

*Cravat: Scarf

Over the Hills and Far Away

See "Multiple Animals" chapter, Nursery Rhymes section.

Piggy on the Railway (Traditional, K–5/6+)

Piggy on the railway,
Picking up stones;
Along came an engine
And broke poor Piggy's bones.

"Oh!" said the Piggy,
"That's not fair."
"Oh!" said the engine driver,
"I don't care!"

Sukey, You Shall Be My Wife

See "Farm Animals" subsection of "Multiple Animals" chapter, Nursery Rhymes section.

There Was a Lady Loved a Swine (Traditional, K–5/6+)

"There was a lady loved a swine,
Honey," quoth she,
"Pig-hog wilt thou be mine?"
"Hoogh," quoth he.

"I'll build thee a silver sty,
Honey," quoth she,
"And in it thou shalt lie."
"Hoogh," quoth he.

"Pinned with a silver pin,
Honey," quoth she,
"That thou may go out and in."
"Hoogh," quoth he.

"Wilt thou have me now,
Honey?" quoth she.
"Speak or my heart will break."
"Hoogh," quoth he.

Tom, Tom, The Piper's Son

See Songs section in this chapter.

To Market, to Market

See Songs section in this chapter.

Three Young Rats with Black Felt Hats

See "Multiple Animals" chapter, Nursery Rhymes section.

Upon My Word of Honor (Traditional, PreS/K–5)

(Also known as **As I Went to Bonner**)

Upon my word of honor,
As I went to Bonner,
I met a pig,
Without a wig,
Upon my word and honor.

Whose Little Pigs Are These, These, These (Traditional, PreS/K–5)

Whose little pigs are these, these, these?
Whose little pigs are these?
They are Roger the Cook's,
I know by their looks—
I found them among my peas.

Songs

Down by the Bay

See "Multiple Animals" chapter, Songs section.

Fiddle-I-Fee

See "Farm Animals" subsection of "Multiple Animals" chapter, Songs section.

Skip to My Lou

See "Multiple Animals" chapter, Songs section.

Three Little Piggies (Traditional, K–5/6+)

A jol-ly old sow once lived in a sty, and three lit-tle pig-gies had she, And she wad-dled a-bout say-ing "Umph, Umph, Umph" while the lit-tle ones said, "Wee, Wee," And she wad-dled a-bout say-ing "Umph, Umph, Umph" while the lit-tle ones said, "Wee, Wee!"

Verse 2: "My dear little brothers," said one of the pigs,
"My dear little piggies," said he,
"Let us all for the future say, 'Umph, umph, umph,'
'Tis so childish to say, 'Wee, wee;"
"Let us all for the future say,
'Umph, umph, umph,'
'Tis so childish to say, 'Wee, wee;"

Verse 3: Then these little piggies grew skinny and lean,
And lean they might very well be.
For they all tried to go "Umph! Umph!"
And they wouldn't say, "Wee, wee, wee."

Verse 4: So after a time these little pigs died,
They all of felo de se;
From trying too hard to "Umph! Umph! Umph!"
When they only could say "Wee! Wee!"

Verse 5: A moral there is to this little song,
A moral that's easy to see;
Don't try while yet young to say "Umph! Umph! Umph!"
For you only can say "Wee! Wee!"

Tom, Tom, The Piper's Son (Traditional, PreS/K–5)

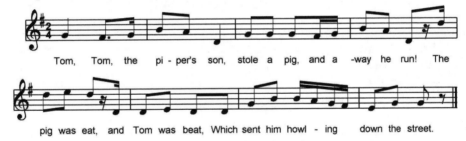

Tom, Tom, the pi-per's son, stole a pig, and a-way he run! The

pig was eat, and Tom was beat, Which sent him howl-ing down the street.

To Market, to Market (Traditional, B/T/PreS/K–5)

To mar-ket, to mar-ket, to buy a fat pig; Home a-gain, home a-gain,

jig-ge-ty-jig; To mar-ket, to mar-ket, to buy a fat hog;

Home a-gain, home a-gain, jig-ge-ty jog.

Extra Lines: To market, to market to buy a plum bun,
Home again, home again, market is done.

Poetry

If a Pig Wore a Wig (Christina Rossetti, 6+)

If a pig wore a wig,
What could we say?
Treat him as a gentleman,
And say "Good day."
If his tail chanced to fail,
What could we do? —
Send him to the tailoress
To get one new.

Precocious Piggy (Thomas Hood, K–5/6+)

"Where are you going to, you little pig?"
"I'm leaving my Mother, I'm growing so big!"
"So big, young pig,
So young, so big!
What, leaving your Mother, you foolish young pig!"

"Where are you going to, you little pig?"
"I've got a new spade, and I'm going to dig."
"To dig, little pig?
A little pig dig!
Well, I never saw a pig with a spade that could dig!"

"Where are you going to, you little pig?"
"Why, I'm going to have a nice ride in a gig!"
"In a gig, little pig!
What, a pig in a gig!
Well, I never saw a pig ride in a gig!"

"Where are you going to, you little pig?"
"Well, I'm going to the ball to dance a fine jig!"
"A jig, little pig!
A pig dance a jig!
Well, I never before saw a pig dance a jig!"
"Where are you going to, you little pig?"
"I'm going to the fair to run a fine rig."
"A rig, little pig!
A pig run a rig!
Well, I never before saw a pig run a rig!"

"Where are you going to, you little pig?"
"I 'm going to the barber's to buy me a wig!"
"A wig, little pig!
A pig in a wig!
Why, whoever before saw a pig in a wig!"

What Does the Donkey Bray About?

See "Multiple Animals" chapter, Poetry section.

PLATYPUS

Poetry

The Platypus (Oliver Herford, 6+)

My child, the Duck-billed Platypus
A sad example sets for us:
From him we learn how Indecision
Of character provokes Derision.

This vacillating Thing, you see,
Could not decide which he would be,
Fish, Flesh or Fowl, and chose all three.
The scientists were sorely vexed
To classify him; so perplexed
Their brains, that they, with Rage at bay,
Call him a horrid name one day,—
A name that baffles, frights and shocks us,
Ornithorhynchus Paradoxus.

From *The Big Book of Animal Rhymes, Fingerplays, and Songs* by Elizabeth Cothen Low.
Westport, CT: Libraries Unlimited. Copyright © 2009.

PORCUPINES

Nursery Rhymes

The Moon Is Up

See "Multiple Animals" chapter, Nursery Rhymes section.

Poetry

The Porcupine (Hilaire Belloc, 6+)

What! Would you slap the Porcupine?
Unhappy child—desist!
Alas! That any friend of mine
Should turn Tupto-philist.˙
To strike the meanest and the least
Of creatures is a sin.
How much more bad to beat a beast
With prickles on its skin.

* Tupto-philist: Made up word meaning "one that loves to strike"

RABBITS AND HARES

Fingerplays and Action Rhymes

Can You Hop Like a Rabbit?

See "Multiple Animals" chapter, Fingerplays and Action Rhymes section.

Creeping, Creeping, Creeping

See "Multiple Animals" chapter, Fingerplays and Action Rhymes section.

Easter Bunny's Ears Are Floppy (Traditional, B/T/PreS)

Easter Bunny's ears are floppy. (Bend fingers downward and place on ears.)
Easter Bunny's feet are hoppy. (Touch feet and hop.)
His fur is soft and his nose is fluffy, (Rub arms and nose.)
Tail is short and powder-puffy. (Place fist on lower back for tail.)

Frogs Jump

See "Multiple Animals" chapter, Fingerplays and Action Rhymes section.

Here is a Bunny (Traditional, B/T/PreS/K–5)

Here is a bunny (Hold up two bent fingers on right hand.)
With ears so funny. (Wiggle fingers back and forth.)
Here is her hole (Form circle with fingers on left hand.)
In the ground.
When a noise she hears, (Straighten out fingers on right hand into "V" shape.)
She pricks up her ears,
And jumps hops in her hole
In the ground. (Have fingers on right hand jump into circle.)

Here Is a Nest for the Robin

See "Multiple Animals" chapter, Fingerplays and Action Rhymes section.

A Little Boy's Walk

See "Multiple Animals" chapter, Fingerplays and Action Rhymes section

Little Peter Rabbit (Traditional, PreS/K–5)

Little Peter Rabbit (Make rabbit ears with hands.)
Had a fly upon his ear, (Point to ear.)
Little Peter Rabbit had a fly upon his ear,
Little Peter Rabbit had a fly upon his ear,
And he flicked it (Pretend to flick ear.)
'Til he flew away. (Wiggle fingers in the air.)

From *The Big Book of Animal Rhymes, Fingerplays, and Songs* by Elizabeth Cothen Low.
Westport, CT: Libraries Unlimited. Copyright © 2009.

Little Rabbit Foo Foo (Traditional, PreS/K–5/6+)

(Also known as Little Bunny Foo Foo)

Little Rabbit Foo Foo,
Hopping thru the forest, (Make V shape with index and middle fingers and "hop" fingers up and
    down.)
Scooping up the field mice (Cup right hand and pretend to scoop something up.)
And boppin' 'em on the head. (Lightly slap top of right fist with left palm.)
Down came the good fairy
And she said:
"Little Rabbit Foo Foo,
I don't want to see you (Wave index finger in the air.)
Scooping up the field mice (Cup right hand and pretend to scoop something up.)
And boppin' 'em on the head." (Lightly slap top of right fist with left palm.)
"I'll give you three chances, (Hold up three fingers.)
And if you don't behave
I'll turn you into a goon!"

Verse 2:   The next day:
            Little Rabbit Foo Foo… (Repeat refrain as in previous verse except with "two chances.")

Verse 3:   The next day:
            Little Rabbit Foo Foo… (Repeat refrain as in previous verse except with "one more
        chance.")

Verse 4:   The next day:
            Little Rabbit Foo Foo,
            Hopping thru the forest, (Make V shape with index and middle fingers and "hop"
        fingers
                    up and down.)
            Scooping up the field mice (Cup right hand and pretend to scoop something up.)
            And boppin' 'em on the head. (Lightly slap top of right fist with left palm.)
            Down came the good fairy
            And she said:
            "I gave you three chances and you didn't listen.
            Now I'm going to turn you into a goon!
                    POOF!" (Close fists tightly, then release all ten fingers.)
The moral of the story is: HARE TODAY, GOON TOMORROW!

"My Little Bunnies Now Must Go to Bed" (Traditional, B/T/PreS)

(Also known as "Come My Bunnies, It's Time for Bed" and Bunnies' Bedtime)

"My little bunnies now must go to bed," (Rest head on folded hands.)
The little mother rabbit said.
"But I will count them first to see,
If they have all come back to me.
One bunny, two bunnies, three bunnies dear, (Count to five on fingers.)
Four bunnies, five bunnies—yes, all are here.
They are the prettiest things alive,
"My bunnies one, two, three, four, five." (Count again.)

Once I Saw a Bunny (Traditional, PreS/K–5)

Once I saw a bunny (Form "V" shape with index and middle fingers of right hand.)
And a green cabbage head. (Form fist with left hand.)
"I think I'll have some cabbage,"
The little bunny said.
So she nibbled and she nibbled, (Have thumb and first two fingers of the right hand form mouth to
    nibble on left fist.)
And she pricked her ears to say, (Form "V" shape with right hand again.)
"Now I think it's time
I should be hopping on my way." (Have right hand hop away.)

One, Two, Three, Four, Five, Once I Caught a Hare Alive (Traditional, PreS/K–5)

One, two, three, four, five, (Count out fingers on one hand.)
Once I caught a hare alive. (Close fist.)
Six, seven, eight, nine, ten, (Count out fingers on other hand.)
Then I let her go again. (Open both hands.)

There Was a Little Bunny Who Lived in the Wood (Traditional, B/T/PreS/K–5)

There was a little bunny who lived in the wood,
He wiggled his ears as a good bunny should. (Place hands on head and wiggle.)
He hopped by a squirrel, (Hop for next several verses.)
He hopped by a tree.
He hopped by a duck,
And he hopped by me.
He stared at the squirrel. (Stop and stare.)
He stared at the tree.
He stared at the duck.
But he made faces at me! (Make a funny face.)

Nursery Rhymes

Bye, Baby Bunting

See Songs section.

In a Cabin in the Woods (Traditional, PreS/K–5)

Little cabin in the wood,
Little man by the window stood,
Little rabbit hopping by,
Knocking at the door.
"Help me! Help me, sir!" he said,
Or the hunter will shoot me dead
Little rabbit come inside
Safely you'll abide.

The Rabbits (Traditional, K–5)

Between the hill and the brook, ook, ook,
Two rabbits sat in the sun, O!

And then they ate the green, green grass,
Till all the grass was gone, O!
And when they had eaten enough, nough, nough,
They sat down to have a talk, O!
When there came a man with a gun, un, un,
And fired at them over the walk, O!

But when they found they were sound, ound, ound,
Nor hurt by the gun, un, un, O!
They picked themselves up from the ground, ound, ound,
And scampered away like fun, O!

Whoop, Whoop, and Hollow

See "Multiple Animals" chapter, Nursery Rhymes section.

Songs

Bye, Ba

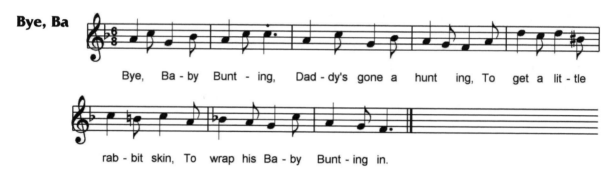

Bye, Ba-by Bunt-ing, Dad-dy's gone a hunt-ing, To get a lit-tle

rab-bit skin, To wrap his Ba-by Bunt-ing in.

Simple Simon

See "Multiple Animals" chapter, Songs section.

Poetry

Kindness to Animals

See "Multiple Animals" chapter, Poetry section.

The Story of the Wild Huntsman (Heinrich Hoffman, 6+)

This is the Wild Huntsman that shoots the hares;
With the grass-green coat he always wears;
With game-bag, powder-horn and gun,
He's going out to have some fun.
He finds it hard without a pair
Of spectacles, to shoot the hare.

He put his spectacles upon his nose, and said,
"Now I will shoot the hares and kill them dead."
The hare sits snug in leaves and grass,

And laughs to see the green man pass.
Now as the sun grew very hot,
And he a heavy gun had got,
He lay down underneath a tree
And went to sleep as you may see.
And, while he slept like any top,
The little hare came, hop, hop, hop,—
Took gun and spectacles, and then
Softly on tiptoe went off again.

The green man wakes, and sees her place
The spectacles upon her face.
She pointed the gun at the hunter's heart,
Who jumped up at once with a start.
He cries, and screams, and runs away.
"Help me, good people, help! I pray."
At last he stumbled at the well,
Head over ears, and in he fell.
The hare stopped short, took aim, and hark!
Bang went the gun!—she missed her mark!

The poor man's wife was drinking up
Her coffee in her coffee-cup;
The gun shot cup and saucer through;
"Oh dear!" cried she, "what shall I do?"
Hiding close by the cottage there,
Was the hare's own child, the little hare.
When he heard the shot he quickly arose,
And while he stood upon his toes,
The coffee fell and burned his nose;
"Oh dear," he cried, "what burns me so?"
And held up the spoon with his little toe.

When the Cows Come Home the Milk Is Coming

See "Multiple Animals" chapter, Poetry section.

Winter Night

See "Multiple Animals" chap

RHINOCEROSES

Poetry

The Rhinoceros (Hilaire Belloc, 6+)

Rhinoceros, your hide looks all undone,
You do not take my fancy in the least:
You have a horn where other brutes have none:
Rhinoceros, you are an ugly beast.

SCORPIONS

Poetry

The Scorpion (Hilaire Belloc, K–5/6+)

The Scorpion is as black as soot,
He dearly loves to bite;
He is a most unpleasant brute
To find in bed, at night.

SEA HORSES

Poetry

The Horses of the Sea (Christina Rossetti, K–5/6+)

The horses of the sea
Rear a foaming crest,
But the horses of the land
Serve us the best.
The horses of the land
Munch corn and clover,
While the foaming sea-horses
Toss and turn over.

SHEEP

Fingerplays and Action Rhymes

The Lambs (Emilie Poulsson, K–5)

This is the meadow where all the long day (Hold arms out and interlock fingers, making a large
circle.)
Ten little frolicsome lambs are at play.
These are the measures the good farmer brings (Cup hands individually.)
Salt in, or cornmeal, and other good things.

This is the lambkins' own big water-trough; (Form cup with both hands.)
Drink little lambkins, and then scamper off!
This is the rack where in winter they feed; (Place palms back to back, stretch and interlock fingers.)
Hay makes a very good dinner indeed.

These are the big shears to shear the old sheep; (Stretch out index and middle fingers. Open and
shut like a pair of scissors.)
Dear little lambkins their soft wool may keep.
Here, with its big double doors shut so tight, (Interlock and fold down fingers of both hands.)
This is the barn where they all sleep at night.

Nursery Rhymes

As I Walked over the Hill One Day

See "Multiple Animals" chapter, Nursery Rhymes section.

Baa, Baa, Black Sheep

See Songs section in this chapter.

Bobbin-a-Bobbin (Traditional, K–5/6+)

Bobbin-a-Bobbin bent his bow,
And shot at a woodcock and killed a yowe:*
The yowe cried ba, and he ran away,
But never came back 'till midsummer day.

* Yowe: Ewe

Dame Wiggins of Lee and Her Seven Wonderful Cats

See "Cats" chapter, Nursery Rhymes section.

God's Care (Traditional, PreS/K–5)

In the pleasant sunny meadows,
Where the buttercups are seen,
And the daisies' little shadows
Lie along the level green,

From *The Big Book of Animal Rhymes, Fingerplays, and Songs* by Elizabeth Cothen Low.
Westport, CT: Libraries Unlimited. Copyright © 2009.

Flocks of quiet sheep are feeding,
Little lambs are playing near,
And the watchful shepherd leading
Keeps them safe from harm and fear.

Like the lambs we little children
Have a shepherd kind and good;
It is God who watches o'er us,
Gives us life and daily food.

The Friendly Beasts

See "Multiple Animals" chapter, Nursery Rhymes section.

In the Month of February

See "Multiple Animals" chapter, Nursery Rhymes section.

Hush-a-Bye

See "Farm Animals" subsection of "Multiple Animals" chapter, Nursery Rhymes section.

Lambs to Sell! Young Lambs to Sell! (Traditional, PreS/K–5)

"Lambs to sell! Young lambs to sell!
A flock of young lambs, each so pretty and small,
This man in his basket can carry them all,
Save one on his finger, his business to tell,
While merrily singing, 'Young lambs to sell.' "

Little Bo-Peep Has Lost Her Sheep

See Songs section in this chapter.

Old Woman, Old Woman (Traditional, PreS/K–5)

Old woman, old woman,
Shall we go a-shearing?
Speak a little louder, sir,
I'm very thick of hearing.

Old woman, old woman,
Shall I love you dearly?
Thank you very kindly, sir,
Now I hear you very clearly.

A Red Sky at Night (Traditional, Saying, K–5/6+)

A red sky at night is a shepherd's delight;
A red sky in the morning is a shepherd's warning.

Sleep, Baby, Sleep

See Songs section in this chapter.

From *The Big Book of Animal Rhymes, Fingerplays, and Songs* by Elizabeth Cothen Low.
Westport, CT: Libraries Unlimited. Copyright © 2009.

Whistle, Daughter, Whistle

See "Farm Animals" subsection of "Multiple Animals" chapter, Nursery Rhymes section.

A Whistling Girl and a Flock of Sheep (Traditional, Saying, PreS/K–5)

A whistling girl and a flock of sheep
Are two good things for a farmer to keep.

White Sheep (Traditional, Riddle, K–5/6+)

White sheep, white sheep,
On a blue hill,
When the wind stops,
You all stand still.

When the wind blows,
You walk away slow.
White sheep, white sheep,
Where do you go?

Answer: Clouds

Young Lambs to Sell! (Traditional, PreS/K–5)

"Young lambs to sell!
Young lambs to sell!
If I'd as much money as I could tell,
I never would cry—Young lambs to sell."

Songs

Baa, Baa, Black Sheep (Traditional, B/T/PreS/K–5)

"Baa! Baa! Black sheep, have you an-y wool?" "Yes, sir, yes, sir, three bags full, One for my mas-ter, and one for my dame, And one for the lit-tle boy that lives in the lane." "Baa! Baa! Black sheep, have you an-y wool? Yes, sir, yes, sir, three bags full."

From The Big Book of Animal Rhymes, Fingerplays, and Songs by Elizabeth Cothen Low.
Westport, CT: Libraries Unlimited. Copyright © 2009.

Fiddle-I-Fee

See "Farm Animals" subsection of "Multiple Animals" chapter, Songs section.

Little Bo-Peep Has Lost Her Sheep (Traditional, PreS/K–5)

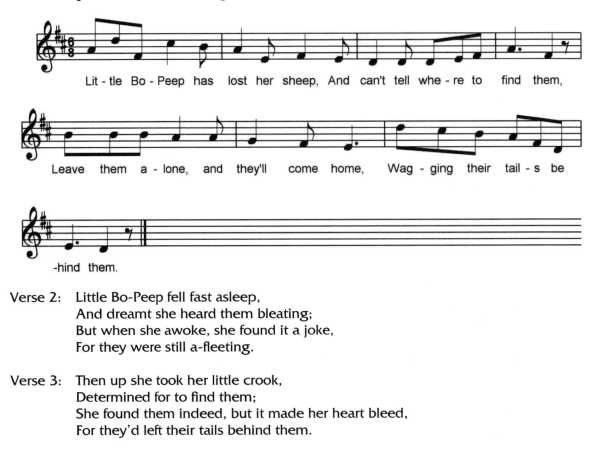

Lit-tle Bo-Peep has lost her sheep, And can't tell whe-re to find them,

Leave them a-lone, and they'll come home, Wag-ging their tail-s be

-hind them.

Verse 2:   Little Bo-Peep fell fast asleep,
          And dreamt she heard them bleating;
          But when she awoke, she found it a joke,
          For they were still a-fleeting.

Verse 3:   Then up she took her little crook,
          Determined for to find them;
          She found them indeed, but it made her heart bleed,
          For they'd left their tails behind them.

Verse 4:   It happened one day, as Bo-Peep did stray
          Into a meadow hard by,
          There she espied their tails side by side,
          All hung on a tree to dry.

Verse 5:   She heaved a sigh, and wiped her eye,
          And over the hillocks went rambling,
          And tried what she could, as a shepherdess should,
          To tack again each to its lambkin.

Little Boy Blue

See "Farm Animals" subsection of "Multiple Animals" chapter, Songs section.

Mary Had a Little Lamb (Sarah J. Hale, PreS/K–5)

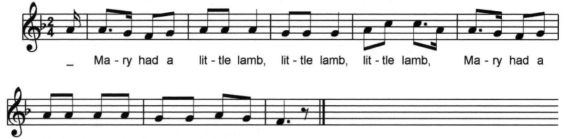

Ma - ry had a lit - tle lamb, lit - tle lamb, lit - tle lamb, Ma - ry had a

lit - tle lamb, Its fleece was white as snow.

Verse 2: And everywhere that Mary went,
Mary went, Mary went.
Everywhere that Mary went,
The lamb was sure to go.

Verse 3: It followed her to school one day,
School one day, school one day.
It followed her to school one day,
Which was against the rules.

Verse 4: It made the children laugh and play,
Laugh and play, laugh and play.
It made the children laugh and play,
To see a lamb at school.

Verse 5: And so the teacher turned it out,
Turned it out, turned it out.
And so the teacher turned it out
But still it lingered near.

Verse 6: And waited patiently about,
Patiently about, patiently about.
And it waited patiently about,
'Till Mary did appear.

Verse 7: "Why does the lamb love Mary so?
Love Mary so, Mary so."
"Why does the lamb love Mary so?"
The eager children cry;

Verse 8: "Why Mary loves the lamb, you know,
Lamb you know, Lamb you know."
"Why Mary loves the lamb, you know,"
The teacher did reply.

Old MacDonald

See "Farm Animals" subsection of "Multiple Animals" chapter, Songs section.

The Sheep (Traditional, K–5/6+)

(Also known as **The Sheep and the Boy**)

La - zy sheep, pray tell me why, In the pleas - ant fields you lie,

Eat - ing grass and dais - ies white, From the morn - ing till the night.

Ev - ery - thing can som - thing do, But what kind of use are you?

Verse 2: Nay, my little master, nay,
Do not serve me so, I pray,
Don't you see the wool that grows
On my back to make you clothes?
Cold, and very cold you'd get,
If I did not give you it.

Verse 3: Sure it seems a pleasant thing
To nip the daises in the spring,
But many chilly nights I pass
On the cold and dewy grass,
Or pick a scanty dinner where
All the common's brown and bare.

Verse 4: Then the farmer comes at last,
When the merry spring is past,
And cuts my wholly coat away
To warm you on a wintry day,
Little master, this is why
In the grassy fields I lie.

Sleep, Baby, Sleep (Traditional, B/T/PreS)

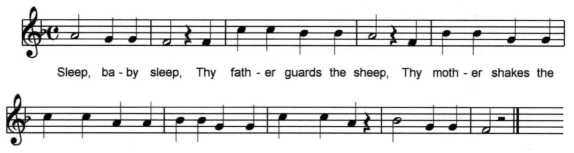

Sleep, ba - by sleep, Thy fath - er guards the sheep, Thy moth - er shakes the

dream - land tree, And from it fall sweet dreams for thee, Sleep, ba - by sleep.

Verse 2: Sleep, baby, sleep,
          Our cottage vale is deep;
          The little lamb is on the green,
          With woolly fleece so soft and clean,
          Sleep, baby, sleep.

Verse 3: Sleep, baby, sleep,
          Down where the woodbines creep;
          Be always like the lamb so mild,
          A kind and sweet and gentle child,
          Sleep, baby, sleep.

Poetry

A Frisky Lamb (Christina Rossetti, PreS/K–5)

A frisky lamb
And a frisky child
Playing their pranks
In a cowslip meadow:
The sky all blue
And the air all mild
And the fields all sun
And the lanes half shadow.

Kindness to Animals

See "Multiple Animals" chapter, Poetry section.

Mary Had a Little Lamb

See Songs section in this chapter.

A Motherless Soft Lambkin (Christina Rossetti, K–5/6+)

A motherless soft lambkin
Along upon a hill;
No mother's fleece to shelter him
And wrap him from the cold:—
I'll run to him and comfort him,

From *The Big Book of Animal Rhymes, Fingerplays, and Songs* by Elizabeth Cothen Low.
Westport, CT: Libraries Unlimited. Copyright © 2009.

I'll fetch him, that I will;
I'll care for him and feed him
Until he's strong and bold.

On the Grassy Banks (Christina Rossetti, PreS/K–5/6+)

On the grassy banks
Lambkins at their pranks;
Woolly sisters, woolly brothers
Jumping off their feet
While their woolly mothers
Watch by them and bleat.

The Welsh Mutton (Hilaire Belloc, K–5/6+)

The Cambrian Welsh or Mountain Sheep
Is of the Ovine race,
His conversation is not deep
But then—observe his face!

SKUNKS

Nursery Rhymes

I Stuck My Head in a Little Skunk's Hole (Traditional, PreS/K–5)

I stuck my head in a little skunk's hole,
And the little skunk said,
"Well, bless my soul!
Take it out! Take it out!
Take it out! Remove it!"

Oh, I didn't take it out,
And the little skunk said,
"If you don't take it out
You'll wish you had.
Take it out! Take it out!"
Pheew! I removed it!

SNAILS

Fingerplays and Action Rhymes

The Snail Is So Slow (Traditional, B/T/PreS/K–5)

The snail is so slow, the snail is so slow. (Have fist very slowly move up arm.)
He creeps and creeps along.
The snail is so-o-o s-l-o-w.

Snail, Snail, Put Out Your Horns (Traditional, B/T/PreS/K–5)

Snail, snail, put out your horns, (Make a fist, then have index and little finger pop out for horns.)
And I'll give you bread and barley corns.

Slowly, Slowly, Very Slowly (Traditional, B/T/PreS)

Slowly, slowly, very slowly, (Let fingers slowly crawl up arm, speak very slowly.)
Creeps the garden snail.
Slowly, slowly, very slowly,
Up the wooden rail.

Quickly, quickly, very quickly, (Speak quickly in a high-pitched voice.)
Runs the little mouse. (Have fingers run in a circular movement on tummy.)
Quickly, quickly very quickly,
'Round about the house.

Nursery Rhymes

Daniel and Dick Rode the Horse to the Fair

See "Multiple Animals" chapter, Nursery Rhymes section.

Four and Twenty Tailors (Traditional, K–5/6+)

Four and twenty tailors
Went to kill a snail;
The best man among them
Durst not touch her tail.
She put out her horns
Like a little Kyloe* cow;
Run, tailors, run,
Or she'll kill you all e'en now.

* Kyloe: A variety of Scottish cow

Snail, Snail, Come Out of Your Hole (Traditional, K–5/6+)

Snail, snail, come out of your hole,
Or else I will beat you as black as coal.

What Are Little Boys Made Of?

See "Multiple Animals" chapter, Nursery Rhymes section.

Songs

Six Little Snails (Traditional, PreS/K–5)

Six lit - tle snails liv'd in a tree, Joh - ny threw a big stone, down came three.

Poetry

Swift and Sure the Swallow

See "Multiple Animals" chapter, Poetry section.

SNAKES

Fingerplays and Action Rhymes

Frogs Jump
See "Multiple Animals" chapter, Fingerplays and Action Rhymes section.

Nursery Rhymes

Fishes Swim in Water Clear
See "Multiple Animals" chapter, Fingerplays and Action Rhymes section.

Poetry

The Python (Hilaire Belloc, 6+)

A Python I should not advise,—
It needs a doctor for its eyes,
And has the measles yearly,

However, if you feel inclined
To get one (to improve your mind,
And not from fashion merely),
Allow no music near its cage;

And when if flies into a rage
Chastise it, most severely.

I had an Aunt in Yucatan
Who bought a Python from a man
And kept it for a pet.
She died, because she never knew
These simple little rules and few;—

The Snake is living yet.

The Viper (Hilaire Belloc, 6+)

Yet another great truth I record in my verse,
That some Vipers are venomous, some the reverse;
A fact you may prove if you try;

By procuring two Vipers, and letting them bite;
With the first you are only the worse for a fright,
But after the second you die.

SPIDERS

Fingerplays and Action Rhymes

The Eentsy, Weentsy Spider

See Song section in this chapter.

Nursery Rhymes

If You Wish to Live and Thrive (Traditional, Saying, K–5/6+)

If you wish to live and thrive,
Let a spider run alive.

Little Miss Muffet

See Song section in this chapter.

"Spider, Spider! What Do You Spin?" (Traditional, 6+)

"Spider, spider! What do you spin?"
"Mainsails for a man of war!"*
"Spider, spider! 'Tis too thin:
Tell me truly what is it for?"

"Why, good fly!" the spider said,
" 'Tis for curtains for the king,
When he sleeps in his state-bed!"
"Spider! 'Tis too slight a thing!"

"Slight! Oh no! Your eyes deceive!"
Said the spider to the fly;
"Strong and firm, and tight I weave!
Come, examine! Touch and try."

"Cunning spider! 'Twill not do,
Of your arts I am aware;
Grannum cautioned me of you,
And told me why you spread you snare."

*Man of war: Warship

From *The Big Book of Animal Rhymes, Fingerplays, and Songs* by Elizabeth Cothen Low.
Westport, CT: Libraries Unlimited. Copyright © 2009.

Songs

The Eentsy, Weentsy Spider (Traditional, B/T/PreS/K–5)

(Also known as **The Itsy Bitsy Spider, The Eency Weency Spider, The Incy Wincy Spider, The Incey Wincey Spider,** and **The Eensy, Weensy Spider**)

The een-sty ween-tsy spi-der went up the wat-er spout. Down came the

rain and washed the spi-der out. Out came the sun and dried up all the

rain, The een-sty ween-tsy spid-er went up the spout a-gain.

Verse 1 (Instructions): The eentsy weentsy spider (Place left index finger and right thumb together; then bring right index finger and left thumb together.)
Went up the water spout. (Alternate this pattern moving upwards.)
Down came the rain (Wiggle fingers on both hands and move downward.)
And washed the spider out. (Cross hands and then sweep them outwards to sides of body.)
 Out came the sun (Form circle over head with arms.)
And dried up all the rain;
And the eency weency spider (Repeat previous motion.)
Went up the spout again.

I Know an Old Lady Who Swallowed a Fly

See "Multiple Animals" chapter, Songs section.

Little Miss Muffet (Traditional, B/T/PreS/K–5)

Lit-tle Miss Muf-fet sat on a tuf-fet, eat-ing her curds and whey; A

-long came a spi-der who sat down be-side her and frigh-tened Miss Muf-fet a

-way.

Over in the Meadow

See "Multiple Animals" chapter, Songs section.

Poetry

"Will You Walk into My Parlour?" (Mary Howitt, 6+)

"Will you walk into my parlour?" said the Spider to the Fly.
" 'Tis the prettiest little parlour that ever you did spy;
The way into my parlour is up a winding stair,
And I have many curious things to show you when you're there."
"Oh, no, no," said the little Fly, "to ask me is in vain;
For who goes up your winding stair can ne'er come down again."
"I'm sure you must be weary, dear! with soaring up so high,
Will you rest upon my little bed?" said the Spider to the Fly;
"There are pretty curtains drawn around, the sheets are fine and thin,
And if you like to rest awhile, I'll snugly tuck you in:"
"Oh, no, no!" said the little Fly, "For I have heard it said,
They never, never wake again who sleep upon your bed."

The Spider turned him round about and went into his den,
For well he knew the silly Fly would soon come back again;
So he wove a subtle web in a little corner sly,
And he set his table ready to dine upon the Fly:
Then he came out to his door again and merrily did sing,
"Come hither, hither, pretty Fly with pearl and silver wing."

Alas! Alas! How very soon this silly little Fly,
Hearing all these flattering speeches came quickly buzzing by;
With gauzy wing she hung aloft, then near and nearer drew,
Thinking only of her crested head and gold and purple hue:
Thinking only of her brilliant wings, poor silly thing, at last
Up jumped the wicked Spider and fiercely held her fast!

He dragged her up his winding stair into his dismal den,
Within his little parlour, but she ne'er came out again!
And now all you young maidens who may this story hear,
To idle flattering speeches, I pray you, ne'er give ear:
Unto an evil counselor close heart and ear and eye,
And learn a lesson from the tale of the Spider and the Fly.

SQUIRRELS

Fingerplays and Action Rhymes

Five Little Squirrels (Traditional, K–5)

One, two, three, four, five, (Count to five on fingers.)
Five little squirrels sitting in a tree;
Said this little squirrel, "What do I see?" (Hold up fingers one by one.)
Said this little squirrel, "I see a gun."
Said this little squirrel, "Uh-oh! Let's run."
Said this little squirrel, "Let's hide in the shade."
Said this little squirrel, "I'm not afraid."
Then Bang! Went the gun
And they scrambled away. (Hide fingers behind back.)

Gray Squirrel (Traditional, PreS/K–5)

(Also known as **Squirrel, Squirrel**)

Gray squirrel, gray squirrel,
Swish your bushy tail. (Wave hand behind back.)
Gray squirrel, gray squirrel,
Swish your bushy tail.
Wrinkle up your little nose, (Lightly push on nose with index finger.)
Hold a nut between your toes. (Hold up toes.)
Gray squirrel, gray squirrel,
Swish your bushy tail. (Wave hand behind back.)

This Is the Squirrel (Traditional, PreS/K–5)

This is the squirrel
With eyes so bright, (Point to eyes.)
Hunting for nuts
With all his might. (Pretend to dig in ground.)
This is the hole (Touch thumb and index finger of right hand together, leaving a hole in the middle.)
Where day by day,
Nut after nut
He stores away. (Use left hand to pretend to place nuts in "hole.")
When winter comes
With its cold and storm,
He'll sleep curled up, (Hug arms and curl up body.)
All snug and warm.

This Little Squirrel (Traditional, B/T/PreS/K–5)

This little squirrel said, "Let's run and play." (Tug on fingers one by one.)
This little squirrel said, "Let's hunt nuts today."
This little squirrel said, "Yes, nuts are good."

This little squirrel said, "They're our best food."
　　　This little squirrel said, "Come climb this tree, (Have index and middle finger run up arm.)
And crack these nuts, one, two, three." (Count out one, two, three using other hand.)

The Squirrel (Emilie Poulsson, K–5, 6+)

"Little squirrel, living there
In the hollow tree, (Touch thumb and index finger of right hand together, leaving a hole in the middle.
　　　Place left thumb in middle of hole.)
I've a pretty cage for you; (Interlock fingers of both hands, forming an arch.)
Come and live with me!

You may turn the little wheel, (Roll hands around one another to simulate turning of a wheel.)
That will be great fun!
Slowly round, or very fast (Roll hands slowly, then faster.)
If you faster run.

Little squirrel, I will bring
In my basket here (Cup both hands together.)
Every day a feast of nuts!
Come, then, squirrel dear."

But the little squirrel said
From his hollow tree:
"Oh! No, no! I'd rather far (Shake head.)
Live here and be free!"

So my cage is empty yet,
And the wheel is still;
But my little basket here (Cup both hands together.)
Oft with nuts I fill.

If you like, I'll crack the nuts, (Lightly pound left fist with right fist.)
Some for you and me, (Point to children, then to self.)
For the squirrel has enough
In his hollow tree.

Whisky, Frisky, Hoppity Hop (Traditional PreS/K–5)

Whisky, frisky,
Hippity hop,
Up he goes
To the tree-top! (Raise hands high in the air.)

Whirly, twirly,
Round and round,
Down he scampers
To the ground. (Put hands on the ground.)

Furly, curly,
What a tail!
Tall as a feather,
Broad as a sail! (Wave hand behind back to mimic tail.)

Where's his supper?
In the shell;
Snappy, crackity, (Lightly pound left fist with right fist.)
Out it fell! (Look on ground to see where nut went.)

Songs

Squirrel Loves a Pleasant Chase (Traditional, PreS/K–5)

The squir-rel loves a pleas-ant chase, Tra, la, la, la, la, la, To

out your hands and we will see, Which of the two will quick-er be! Tra

la, la, la, la, la, Tra, la, la, la, la, la.

Poetry

Winter Night

See "Multiple Animals" chapter, Poetry section.

SWANS

Nursery Rhymes

Swan Swam Over the Sea (Traditional, Tongue Twister, K–5/6+)

Swan swam over the sea,
Swim, swan, swim;
Swan swam back again,
Well swum swan!

Songs

The Twelve Days of Christmas

See "Multiple Animals" chapter, Songs section.

TAPIRS

Nursery Rhymes

The Panther

See "Multiple Animals" chapter, Nursery Rhymes section.

TIGERS

Fingerplays and Action Rhymes

Eeny, Meeny, Miney, Mo (Traditional, Counting-Out Rhyme, PreS/K–5)

(Also known as **Eenie, meenie, minie, mo** and **Eena, Meena, Mina, Mo**)

Eeny, meeny, miney, mo. (With each word, point to a different child, until you reach the last "mo.")
Catch a tiger by the toe.
If he hollers, let him go.
Eeny, meeny, miney, mo.

Nursery Rhymes

One Old Oxford Ox

See "Multiple Animals" chapter, Nursery Rhymes section.

The Tiger (Traditional, K–5/6+)

There was a young lady of Niger,
Who smiled as she rode on a tiger;
They returned from the ride
With the lady inside
And the smile on the face of the tiger.

Poetry

The Tiger (Hilaire Belloc, K–5/6+)

The Tiger on the other hand
Is kittenish and mild.
He makes a pretty playfellow
For any little child;
And mothers of large families
(who claim to common sense)
Will find a Tiger well repay
The trouble and expense.

This poem follows Belloc's "The Lion," found in the "Lions" chapter Poetry section.

TURKEYS

Fingerplays and Action Rhymes

Five Fat Turkeys Are We (Traditional, PreS/K–5)

Five fat turkeys are we. (Hold up right five fingers.)
We slept all night in a tree. (Hold up left hand with fingers pointing to the sky. Touch left fingertips to bottom of wrist.)
When the cook came around
We couldn't be found. (Shrug shoulders.)
So that's why we're here, you see. (Hold up right five fingers again.)

Turkey Is a Funny Bird (Traditional, PreS/K–5)

The turkey is a funny bird, (Spread out five fingers on hand with thumb extended.)
His head goes wobble, wobble, (Move thumb back and forth.)
And he knows just one word:
Gobble, gobble, gobble. (Bring thumb and fingers of right hand together in "talking" motion.)

Wee Wiggie

See "Multiple Animals" chapter, Fingerplays and Action Rhymes section

Nursery Rhymes

I Met a Turkey Gobbler (Traditional, PreS/K–5)

I met a turkey gobbler
When I went out to play.
"Mr. Turkey Gobbler,
How are you today?"
"Gobble, gobble, gobble,
That I cannot say.
Don't ask me such a question
On Thanksgiving Day."

Old Goody Gadabout (Traditional, 6+)

Old Goody Gadabout,
She fed her turkey-poult,*
With a whole quart of fine ale;
And then did debate,
Why it could not walk straight,
And sighed that all creatures were frail.

* Poult: Young poultry

Songs

Turkey in the Straw (Traditional, K–5/6+)

As, I was a-go-ing down the road, with a tir-ed team an-d a

heav-y load, I cracked my whip and the lead-er sprung, I

says, "Day - day," to the wa-gon tongue. Turk-ey in the straw,

tur-key in the hay, Tur-key in the straw, tur-key in the hay,

Roll them up and twist them up a high tuck-a-haw, And

twist them up a tune cal-led Tur-key in the Straw.

TURTLES

Fingerplays and Action Rhymes

There Was a Little Turtle (Vachel Lindsay, PreS/K–5)

There was a little turtle. (Hold arm so that right palm is facing ceiling. Place other palm on top of right one and have it face downward. Cup both hands.)

He lived in a box. (Have right thumb touch left index finger, and have left thumb touch right index finger to form box, extend fingers.)

He swam in a puddle. (Make swimming motion with hand.)

He climbed on the rocks. (Have index and middle fingers make climbing motion—bend fingers at knuckles and wiggle up and down.)

He snapped at a mosquito. (Make the fingers and thumb of your hand pretend to bite at something.)

He snapped at a flea. (Repeat last action for "flea," "minnow," and "me.")

He snapped at a minnow.

He snapped at me.

He caught the mosquito. (Clap hands. Repeat action for next two.)

He caught the flea.

He caught the minnow.

But he didn't catch me! (Shake head, wave index finger, and smile.)

This Is My Turtle (Traditional, PreS/K–5)

(Also known as Here Is My Turtle)

This is my turtle, (Hold left fist out with palm facing downward and left thumb tucked in.)
He lives in a shell.
He likes his home very well. (Nod head up and down.)
He pokes his head out (Pop thumb out of fist.)
When he wants to eat.
And pulls it back in (Bring thumb back into fist.)
When he wants to sleep.

Poetry

Kindness to Animals

See "Multiple Animals" chapter, Poetry section.

WALRUSES

Nursery Rhymes

The Panther
See "Multiple Animals" chapter, Nursery Rhymes section.

WEASELS

Songs

Pop! Goes the Weasel

See "Multiple Animals" chapter, Songs section.

WHALES

Nursery Rhymes

The Moon Is Up

See "Multiple Animals" chapter, Nursery Rhymes section.

Songs

Down by the Bay

See "Multiple Animals" chapter, Songs section.

Simple Simon

See "Multiple Animals" chapter, Songs section.

Poetry

The Whale (Hilaire Belloc, 6+)

The whale that wanders round the Pole
Is not a table fish
You cannot bake or boil him whole,
Nor serve him in a dish;But you may cut his blubber up
And melt it down for oil.
And so replace the colza bean
(A product of the soil.)
These facts should all be noted down
And ruminated on,
By every boy in Oxford town
Who wants to be a Don.*

*Don: A professor or fellow at an English university

 WOLVES

Nursery Rhymes

'Tis Sweet to Roam (Traditional, K–5/6+)

'Tis sweet to roam when morning's light
Resounds across the deep;
And the crystal song of the woodbine* bright
Hushes the rocks to sleep,
And the blood-red moon in the blaze of noon
Is bathed in a crumbling dew,
And the wolf rings out with a glittering shout,
To-whit, to-whit, to-whoo!

* Woodbine: A kind of vine

WOODCHUCKS

Also known as Groundhogs

Nursery Rhymes

How Much Wood Would a Woodchuck Chuck (Traditional, Tongue Twister, K–5/6+)

How much wood would a woodchuck chuck
If a woodchuck could chuck wood?
He would chuck as much wood
As a woodchuck could chuck
If a woodchuck could chuck wood.

 WORMS

Fingerplays and Action Rhymes

Five Little Robins Lived in a Tree

See "Birds" chapter, Fingerplays and Action Rhymes section.

Frogs Jump

See "Multiple Animals" chapter, Fingerplays and Action Rhymes section.

When a Robin Cocks His Head

See "Birds" chapter, Fingerplays and Action Rhymes section.

Nursery Rhymes

Nobody Likes Me (Traditional, PreS/K–5)

Nobody likes me,
Everybody hates me,
Guess I'll go eat worms,
Long, thin, slimy ones,
Short, fat, juicy ones,
Itsy bitsy, fuzzy, wuzzy worms.

Down goes the first one,
Down goes the second one,
Oh, how they wiggle and squirm,
Up comes the first one,
Up comes the second one,
Oh, how they wiggle and squirm.

Poetry

Hurt No Living Thing

See "Multiple Animals" chapter, Poetry section.

Kindness to Animals

See "Multiple Animals" chapter, Poetry section.

From *The Big Book of Animal Rhymes, Fingerplays, and Songs* by Elizabeth Cothen Low.
Westport, CT: Libraries Unlimited. Copyright © 2009.

YAKS

Poetry

The Yak (Hilaire Belloc, K–5/6+)

As a friend to the children,
Commend me the yak;
You will find it exactly the thing:
It will carry and fetch,
You can ride on its back,
Or lead it about with a string.

The Tartar who dwells in the plains of Tibet
(A desolate region of snow),
Has for centuries made it a pet,
And surely the Tartar should know!

Then tell your papa where the yak can be got,
And if he is awfully rich,
He will buy you the creature—
Or else he will not:
(I cannot be positive which.)

ZEBRAS

Nursery Rhymes

When The Monkey Saw the Zebra (Traditional, K–5/6+)

When the monkey saw the zebra,
He began to switch his tail,
"Well, I never!" was his comment,
"It's a horse that's been to jail;
It's a horse that's been to jail;
Well, I never!" was his comment,
"It's a horse that's been to jail!"

BIBLIOGRAPHY

Web Sites

Dictionary.com: http://dictionary.reference.com/

Digital Tradition Folk Music Database—Yet Another Digital Tradition Page: http://sniff.numachi.com

The Free Dictionary: http://www.thefreedictionary.com/

Lester S. Levy Collection of Sheet Music, Special Collections at the Sheridan Libraries of The John Hopkins University: http://levysheetmusic.mse.jhu.edu

Historic American Sheet Music, Duke University Libraries Digital Collection: http://library.duke.edu/digitalcollections/hasm/

Merriam-Webster Online: http://www.merriam-webster.com/

Music for the Nation, American Sheet Music, Library of Congress: http://memory.loc.gov

NIEHS Kid's Pages, National Institutes of Environmental Health Sciences: http://kids.niehs.nih.gov/music.htm

Songs for Teaching: http://songsforteaching.com

Sheet Music Digital: www.sheetmusicdigital.com

Books

Ada, Alma Flor, and F. Isabel Campoy. *Mama Goose: A Latino Nursery Treasury, Un Tesoro de Rimas Infantiles.* New York: Hyperion Books for Children, 2004.

Anonymous. n.d. *Mother Goose's Melody or Sonnets for the Cradle.* Hockliffe Collection, 2001. Available at: http://www.cts.dmu.ac.uk/AnaServer?hockliffe+0+start.anv.

Anonymous. 1820? *Nursery Rhymes.* Hockliffe Collection, 2001. http://www.cts.dmu.ac.uk/AnaServer?hockliffe+0+start.anv.

Anonymous. 1850. *Old Mother Goose.* Hockliffe Collection, 2001. Available at: http://www.cts.dmu.ac.uk/AnaServer?hockliffe+0+start.anv.

Anonymous. *The Only True Mother Goose Melodies.* Project Gutenberg, 2004. http://www.gutenberg.org/etext/4901.

Anonymous. 1807. *Original Ditties for the Nursery: So Wonderfully Contrived That They May Be Either Sung or Said, by Nurse or Baby.* Hockliffe Collection, 2001. Available at: http://www.cts.dmu.ac.uk/AnaServer?hockliffe+0+start.anv.

Arnold, Sarah Louise. 1914. *Manual for Teachers: To Accompany The See and Say Series: Book Two.* Google Books, 2007. Available at: http://books.google.com/books?id=wtoAAAAAYAAJ.

Bancroft, Jessie Hubbell. *Games for the Playground, Home, School and Gymnasium.* New York: Macmillan, 1909.

Baring-Gould, William, and Stuart Ceil Baring-Gould. *The Annotated Mother Goose: Nursery Rhymes Old and New.* New York: Bramhall House, 1962.

Beall, Pamela Conn, and Susan Hagen Nipp. *Wee Sing for Baby.* New York: Price Stern Sloan, 1996.

Beall, Pamela Conn, and Susan Hagen Nipp. *Wee Sing Bible Songs.* Los Angeles: Price Stern Sloan, 1986.

Beall, Pamela Conn, and Susan Hagen Nipp. *Wee Sing: Children's Songs and Fingerplays.* New York: Price Stern Sloan, 2005.

Beall, Pamela Conn, and Susan Hagen Nipp. *Wee Sing for Christmas.* Los Angeles: Price Stern Sloan, 1984.

Beall, Pamela Conn and Susan Hagen Nipp. *Wee Sing Nursery Rhymes & Lullabies.* Los Angeles: Price Stern Sloan, 1985.

Beall, Pamela Conn, and Susan Hagen Nipp. *Wee Sing Silly Songs.* Los Angeles: Price Stern Sloan, 1982.

Beall, Pamela Conn, and Susan Hagen Nipp. *Wee Sing: Animals, Animals, Animals.* New York: Price Stern Sloan, 2002.

Beall, Pamela Conn, and Susan Hagen Nipp. *Wee Sing: Games, Games, Games.* New York: Price Stern Sloan, 2002.

Belloc, Hilaire. 1896. *The Bad Child's Book of Beasts.* Baldwin Online Children's Literature Project, 200-2008. http://www.mainlesson.com/display.php?author=belloc&book=beasts&story=_contents.

Belloc, Hilaire. 1897. *More Beasts for Worse Children.* Baldwin Online Children's Literature Project, 200-2008. http://www.mainlesson.com/display.php?author=belloc&book=more&story=_contents.

Blake, Quentin, illust. *Penguin Book of Nonsense Verse.* New York: Penguin Books, 1994.

Booth, David. *Poetry Goes to School: From Mother Goose to Shel Silverstein.* Markham, Ontario: Pembroke Publishers, 2004.

Botsford, Florence Hudson, ed. *Folk Songs of Many Peoples: With English Version by American Poets.* Vol. 2. New York: The Womans Press, 1922.

Braun, Win, and Carl Bruan. *Readers Theatre for Young Children.* Winnipeg, Canada: Portage & Main Press, 2000.

Brewster, Paul G. *Children's Games and Rhymes.* Vol. 1. Manchester, NH: Ayer Publishing, 1976.

Briggs, Diane. *101 Fingerplays, Stories, and Songs to Use with Finger Puppets.* Chicago: American Library Association, 1999.

Briggs, Diane. *Preschool Favorites: 35 Storytimes Kids Love.* Chicago: ALA Editions, 2007.

Brown, Florence Warren, and Neva L. Boyd. *Old English and American Games for School and Playground.* Chicago: H.T. FitzSimons Company, 1915.

Brown, Marc. *Finger Rhymes.* New York: Dutton Children's Books, 1980.

Brown, Marc. *Hand Rhymes.* New York: Dutton Children's Books, 1985.

Charner, Kathy. *The Giant Encyclopedia of Science Activities for Children 3 to 6.* Beltsville, MD: Gryphon House, 1998.

Cheviot, Andrew. 1896. *Proverbs, Proverbial Expressions, and Popular Rhymes of Scotland*. Google Books, 2005. http://books.google.com/books?id=XsC6Dy8A2d4C.

Chorao, Kay. *Knock at the Door and Other Baby Action Rhymes*. New York: Dutton Children's Books, 1999.

Cole, Joanna. *Anna Banana: 101 Jump-Rope Rhymes*. New York: Beech Tree Paperback Book, 1989.

Cole, Joanna, and Stephanie Calmenson. *The Eentsy, Weentsy Spider: Fingerplays and Action Rhymes*. New York: William Morrow and Company, 1991.

Cole, Joanna, and Stephanie Calmenson. *Pat-a-Cake and Other Play Rhymes*. New York: Morrow Junior Books, 1992.

Colgin, Mary Lou. *One Potato, Two Potato, Three Potato, Four: 165 Chants for Children*. Beltsville, MD: Gryphon House, 1982.

Cooper, Kay. *Too Many Rabbits: and Other Fingerplays about Animals, Nature, Weather, and the Universe*. New York: Scholastic, 1995.

Cooper, Kay. *The Neal-Schuman Index to Finger-Plays*. New York: Neal-Schuman Publishers, 1993.

Corbett, Pie. *The Playtime Treasury: A Collection of Playground Rhymes, Games, and Action Songs*. New York: Doubleday, 1989.

Cromwell, Liz, Dixie Hibner, and John R. Faitel. *Finger Frolics: Revised*. rev. ed. Livonia, MI: Partner Press, 1983.

Curry, Charles Madison. 1921. *Children's Literature: A Textbook of Sources for Teachers and Teacher*. Google Books, 2007. http://books.google.com/books?id=_nJAAAAAIAAJ.

Daniel, Mark. *A Child's Treasury of Animal Verse*. New York: Dial Books for Young Readers, 1989.

Defty, Jeff. *Creative Fingerplays & Action Rhymes: An Index and Guide to Their Use*. Phoenix, AZ: Oryx Press, 1992.

Delamar, Gloria T. *Children's Counting-Out Rhymes, Fingerplays, Jump-Rope and Bounce-Ball Chants and Other Rhythms, A Comprehensive English-Language Reference*. Jefferson, NC: McFarland, 1983.

dePaola, Tomie, illustrator. *Tomie dePaola's Mother Goose*. New York: G.P. Putnam's Sons, 1985.

Ehrmann, Mary B. *Little Songs for Little Folks*. Cincinnati, OH: The Willis Music Co., 1911.

Elliot, J. W. *National Nursery Rhymes and Nursery Songs*. London: Novello and Company, 1870.

Engelbreit, Mary. *Mary Engelbreit's Mother Goose: One Hundred Best Loved Verses*. New York: HarperCollins, 2005.

Feldman, Jean R. *Transition Time: Let's Do Something Different!*. Beltsville, MD: Gryphon House, 1995.

Feldman, Jean R. *Transition Tips and Tricks for Teachers: Prepare Young Children for Changes*. Beltsville, MD: Gryphon House, 2000.

Follen, Eliza, and Lee Cabot. 1856. *Little Songs*. Google Books, 2007. http://books.google.com/books?id=g40DAAAAYAAJ.

Foster, John. *Fire Words: A Book of Wordplay Poems*. Oxford, UK: Oxford University Press, 2000.

Fowke, Edith. *Sally Go Round the Sun: Three Hundred Children's Songs, Rhymes and Games*. Garden City, NY: Doubleday, 1969.

Fox, Dan. *Children's Songbook: Over 130 All-Time Favorites to Play, Listen, and Sing.* Pleasantville, NY: The Reader's Digest Association, 2005.

Fox, Dan. *A Treasury of Children's Songs: Forty Favorites to Sing and Play.* New York: Henry Holt and Metropolitan Museum of Art, 2003.

Fox, Dan. *A Treasury of Christmas Songs: Twenty-Five Favorites to Sing and Play.* New York: Henry Holt, 2004.

Fuld, James J. *The Book of World-Famous Music: Classical, Popular and Folk.* 4th ed. Mineola, NY: Dover, 1995.

Glazer, Tom. *Do Your Ears Hang Low?: Fifty More Musical Fingerplays.* Garden City, NY: Doubleday, 1980.

Glazer, Tom. *Eye Winker, Tom Tinker, Chin Chopper: Fifty Musical Fingerplays.* Garden City, NY: Doubleday, 1973.

Glazer, Tom. *Mother Goose Songbook.* New York: Doubleday, 1990.

Grayson, Marion. *Let's Do Fingerplays.* Fairfield, CT: Robert B. Luce, 1962.

The Great Big Book of Children's Songs. Milkwaukee, WI: Hal Leonard Co., 1995.

Greenaway, Kate. *Kate Greenaway's Mother Goose.* San Marino, CA: Huntington Library Press, 2006.

Greenwald, Celia. *Children's Games with Words.* New York: The Empire Music Co., 1907.

Griego, Margot C., Betsy L. Bucks, Sharon S. Gilbert, and Laurel H. Kimball. *Tortillitas Para Mama and Other Nursery Rhymes, Spanish and English.* New York: Henry Holt, 1981.

Halliwell, James Orchard. 1886. *Nursery Rhymes of England.* Google Books, 2007. http://books.google.com/books?id=0jcDAAAAYAAJ.

Hansen, Charles, and Cynthia Stilley, eds. *Ring a Ring O'Roses: Finger Plays for Preschool Children.* 10th ed. Flint, MI: Flint Public Library, 1996.

Hart, Jane. *Singing Bee: A Collection of Favorite Children's Songs.* New York: Lothrop, Lee, & Shepard Books, 1982.

Hefley, James C. *Way Back in the" "Korn" Fields.* Garland, TX: Hannibal Books, 1994.

Herr, Judy, and Yvonne Libby-Larson. *Creative Resources for the Early Childhood Classroom.* Vol. 3. Clifton Park, NY: Thomson Delmar Learning, 2000.

Herr, Judy, and Yvonne Libby-Larson. *Creative Resources for the Early Childhood Classroom.* Vol. 4. Clifton Park, NY: Thomson Delmar Learning, 2000.

Ireson, Barbara, ed. *Barnes Book of Nursery Verse.* New York: A.S. Barnes and Co., 1960.

Krull, Kathleen. *Gonna Sing My Head Off!: American Folk Songs for Children.* New York: Alfred A. Knopf, 1992.

Krull, Kathleen. *I Hear America Singing!: Folk Songs for American Families.* New York: Alfred A. Knopf, 2003.

Kuffner, Trish. *The Toddlers Busy Book.* Minnetonka, MN: Meadowbrook, 1999.

Lamont, Priscilla. *Ring-a-Round-a-Rosy: Nursery Rhymes, Action Rhymes, and Lullabies.* Boston: Little, Brown and Company, 1990.

Langley, Jonathan. *Rain, Rain, Go Away: A Book of Nursery Rhymes.* New York: Dial Books for Young Readers, 1990.

Lobel, Arnold. *The Arnold Lobel Book of Mother Goose.* New York: Alfred A. Knopf, 1997.

Maddigan, Beth, Stefanie Drennan, and Roberta Thompson. *The Big Book of Reading, Rhyming and Resources: Programs for Children, Ages 4–8.* Westport, CT: Libraries Unlimited, 2005.

Marks, Alan. *Ring-a-Ring O'Roses & A Ding, Dong, Bell: A Book of Nursery Rhymes.* Saxonville, MA: Picture Book Studio, c1991.

Matterson, Elizabeth. *Games for the Very Young: A Treasury of Nursery Songs and Finger Plays.* New York: American Heritage Press, 1969.

Mayo, Margaret. *Wiggle Waggle Fun: Stories and Rhymes for the Very Very Young.* New York: Alfred A. Knopf, 2002.

McCracken, Marlene J., and Robert A. McCracken. *Spring.* Winnipeg, Canada: Portage & Main Press, 1987.

McCracken, Robert, and Marlene J. McCracken. *Tiger Cub Books: For Beginning Readers: Animals.* Winnipeg, Canada: Portage & Main Press, 1989.

Mitchell, Donald, and Carey Blyton. *Every Child's Book of Nursery Songs.* Rev. ed. New York: Crown, 1985.

Moses, Will. *Will Moses Mother Goose.* New York: Philomel Books, 2003.

National Gallery of Art, Washington. *An Illustrated Treasury of Songs.* New York: Hal Leonard, 1991.

Nelsen, Marjorie R., and Jan Nelsen-Parish. *Peak with Books: An Early Childhood Resource for Balanced Literacy.* Clifton Park, NY: Thomson Delmar Learning, 2002.

Nelson, Esther L. *The Silly Song Book.* New York: Sterling, 1981.

Newcome, Zita. *Head, Shoulders, Knees, and Toes and Other Action Rhymes.* Cambridge, MA: Candlewick Press, 2002.

Nichols, Judy. *Storytimes for Two-Year-Olds.* Chicago: ALA Editions, 2007.

Nicholson, John. 1890. *Folk Lore of East Yorkshire.* Google Books, 2005. http://books.google.com/books?id=tw0naTcLHeMC.

Northall, G. F. 1892. *English Folk-Rhymes: A Collection of Traditional Verses Relating to Places and Persons, Customs, Superstitions, etc.* Google Books, 2006. http://books.google.com/books?id=UiwiAAAAMAAJ.

Opie, Iona, and Peter Opie, ed. *A Nursery Companion.* Oxford, UK: Oxford University Press, 1980.

Opie, Iona, and Peter Opie, eds. *Oxford Dictionary of Nursery Rhymes.* Rev. ed. Oxford, UK: Oxford University Press, 1997.

Opie, Iona, and Peter Opie. *Oxford Nursery Rhyme Book.* New York: Oxford University Press, 1955.

Opie, Iona, ed., and Rosemary Wells. *My Very First Mother Goose.* Cambridge, MA: Candlewick Press, c1996.

Orozco, Jose-Luis. *Diez Deditos, Ten Little Fingers & Other Play Rhymes and Action Songs from Latin America.* New York: Dutton Children's Books, 1997.

Oxenbury, Helen. *The Helen Oxenbury Nursery Collection.* New York: Alfred A. Knopf, 2004.

Petersham, Maud, and Miska Petersham. *The Rooster Crows: A Book of American Rhymes and Jingles.* New York: Macmillan, 1945.

Pollard, Velma. From *Jamaican Creole to Standard English: A Handbook for Teachers.* Brooklyn, NY: Caribbean Research Center, 2003.

Poulsson, Emilie, and Cornelia C. Roeske. *Finger-Plays for Nursery and Kindergarten.* Boston: Lothrop, Lee, and Shepard, Co., 1893. Also available online at http://books.google.com/books?id=oBUIWmAYGV0C.

Rackham, Arthur. *Mother Goose: Old Nursery Rhymes.* Chestnut Hill, MA: Adamant Media, 2000.

Rankin, Jean Sherwood, and Wanda Gág. 1917. *Mechanics of Written English: A Drill in the Use of Caps and Points Thru the Rimes of Mother Goose.* Google Books, 2007. http://books.google.com/books?id=cwJFAAAAIAAJ.

Reid, Rob. *Family Storytime: Twenty-Four Creative Programs for All Ages.* Chicago: ALA Editions, 1999.

Ross, William T. 1890. *Voice Culture and Elocution.* Google Books. http://books.google.com/books?id=vbAXAAAAIAAJ.

Rossano, Joan. *The Instant Curriculum: Over 750 Developmentally Appropriate Learning Activities for Busy Teachers of Young Children.* Beltsville, MD: Gryphon House, 2005.

Rossetti, Christina Georgina. *Sing-Song: A Nursery Rhyme Book.* Rev. ed. New York: MacMillan and Co., 1893. Also available at http://digital.library.upenn.edu/women/rossetti/singsong/singsong.html.

Scheffler, Axel. *Mother Goose's Storytime Nursery Rhymes.* New York: Arthur A. Levine Books, 2006.

Schiller, Pamela Byrne. *Creating Readers: Over 1000 Games, Activities, Tongue Twisters, Fingerplay.* Beltsville, MD: Gryphon House, 2001.

Schiller, Pamela Byrne. *Critters & Company.* Beltsville, MD: Gryphon House, 2006.

Schiller, Pam, Rafael Lara-Alecio, and Beverly J. Irby. *Bilingual Book of Rhymes, Songs, Stories, and Fingerplays.* Beltsville, MD: Gryphon House, 2004

Schiller, Pam, and Thomas Moore. *Where Is Thumbkin?: Over 500 Activities to Use with Songs You Already Know.* Beltsville, MD: Gryphon House, 1993.

Silberg, Jackie, and Pam Schiller. *The Complete Book of Rhymes, Songs, Poems, Fingerplays, and Chants.* Beltsville, MD: Gryphon House, 2002.

Silberg, Jackie. *300 Three Minute Games: Quick and Easy Activities for 2–5 Year Olds.* Beltsville, MD: Gryphon House, 1997.

Silberg, Jackie. *500 Five Minute Games: Quick and Easy Activities for 3–6 Year Olds.* Beltsville, MD: Gryphon House, 1995.

Skinner, Ada M., and Frances Gillespy Wickes. 1917. *A Child's Own Book of Verse, Book One.* Baldwin Online Children's Literature Project, 2000–2008. http://www.mainlesson.com/display.php?author=skinner&book=verse1&story=_contents.

Smith, Eleanor. *Songs for Little Children: Part 1, A Collection of Songs and Games for Kindergartens and Primary Schools.* Springfield, MA: Milton Bradley Co., 1887.

Smith, Jessie Willcox, illust. 1918. *The Little Mother Goose.* Project Gutenberg, 2007. http://www.gutenberg.org/ebooks/20511.

Stelfox, Susan Ann. *Baby Be Loved: Growing and Learning Together during the First 24 Weeks*. Pacifica, CA: Mason, 2002.

Stetson, Emily, and Vicky Congdon. *Little Hands: Fingerplays & Action Rhymes: Seasonal Rhymes & Creative Play for 2- to 6-Year-Olds*. Charlotte, VT: Williamson, 2001.

Stevenson, Robert Louis. *A Child's Garden of Verses*. Project Gutenberg, 1994. http://www.gutenberg.org/dirs/etext94/child11.txt.

Stoddard, Clara B. *Sounds for Little Folks: Speech Improvement, Speech Correction*. Magnolia, MA: Expression Co., 1940.

Stott, Dorothy. *Big Book of Games*. New York: Dutton Children's Books, 1998.

Sutherland, Zena. *Orchard Book of Nursery Rhymes*. New York: Orchard Books, 1990.

Swainson, Charles. 1885. *Provincial Names and Folk Lore of British Birds*. Google Books, 2007. http://books.google.com/books?id=4FAJAAAAQAAJ.

Tabori, Lena, and Alice Wong, eds. *The Little Big Book for Moms*. New York: Welcome Books, 2000.

The Totline Staff. *1001 Rhymes & Fingerplays*. Flint, MI: Totline Publications, 1994

Voake, Charlotte. *Over the Moon: A Book of Nursery Rhymes*. 2nd ed. Cambridge, MA: Candlewick Press, 1985.

Wells, Carolyn, ed. 1910. *A Nonsense Anthology*. Google Books, 2007. http://books.google.com/books?id=_jQNAAAAYAAJ.

Wicklund, Brian. *American Fiddle Method*. Pacific, MO: Mel Bay, 2001.

Wier, Albert E. *Songs the Children Love to Sing*. New York: D. Appleton, 1916.

Wildsmith, Brian. *Nursery Rhymes Mother Goose*. Oxford, UK: Oxford University Press, 1964.

Wilmes, Liz, and Dick Wilmes. *More Everyday Circle Times*. Elgin, IL: Building Blocks, 1992.

Wilmes, Liz, and Dick Wilmes. *The Circle Time Book*. Dundee, IL: A Building Blocks Publication, 1982.

Wilner, Isabel. *The Baby's Game Book*. New York: Greenwillow Books, 2000.

Wright, Blanche Fisher. *The Real Mother Goose*. New York: Cartwheel Books, 1994.

Yolen, Jane, and Adam Stemple. *Jane Yolen's Old MacDonald Songbook*. Honesdale, PA: Boyds Mills Press, 1994.

Yolen, Jane, ed., with musical arrangements by Adam Stemple. *This Little Piggy: Lap Songs, Finger Plays, Clapping Games, and Pantomime Rhymes*. Cambridge, MA: Candlewick Press: 2005.

Yolen, Jane. *Animal Poems from A to Z*. Honesdale, PA: Boyds Mills Press, 1995.

Supplemental Works

Fishman, Stephen. *The Public Domain: How to Find & Use Copyright-Free Writings, Music, Art & More*. Berkeley, CA: Nolo, 2000.

Lima, Carolyn W., and John A. Lima. *A to Zoo: Subject Access to Children's Picture Books*. 7th ed. Westport, CT: Libraries Unlimited, 2006.

Zimmerman, Barbara. *The Mini-Encyclopedia of Public Domain Songs*. New York: BZ/Rights Stuff, 1997.

Index of Authors

Index of Titles

Index of First Lines

Index of Specific Kinds of Rhymes

Bounce and Lift Rhymes

Dog Went to Dover, 94
Hey, My Kitten, My Kitten, 55
Oh, My Chicken, 77
This is the Way the Ladies Ride, 145
This is the Way the Ladies Ride, Nim, Nim.., 146
Trot, Trot to Boston, 146

Call and Response

Did You Feed My Cow?, 85
I Am a Gold Lock, 190
I Went Up One Pair of Stairs, 190
May My Geese Fly Over Your Barn?, 134

Clapping Rhymes

Miss Mary Mack, 116

Counting and Math Rhymes

A Gaping Wide-Mouthed Waddling Frog, 201
Bell Horses, Bell Horses, 146
Cinco pollitos, 78
Elizabeth, Elspeth, Betsey, and Bess, 20
Five Eggs and Five Eggs That Makes Ten, 76
Five Fat Turkeys Are We, 286
Five Little Chickadees Peeping at the Door, 14
Five Little Chickens, 76
Five Little Chickens, 79
Five Little Ducks Went in for a Swim, 109
Five Little Ducks, 113
Five Little Fishes Swimming in a Pool, 119
Five Little Froggies Sitting on a Well, 126
Five Little Froggies, 126
Five Little Kittens Sleeping on a Chair, 54
Five Little Kittens Standing in a Row, 54
Five Little Mice Came Out to Play, 180
Five Little Mice on the Pantry Floor, 180
Five Little Monkeys Swinging From a Tree, 196
Five Little Monkeys, 190

Five Little Speckled Frogs, 126
Five Little Squirrels, 280
Here is the Beehive, 11
Hickory, Dickory, Dock, 184
I Had a Little Cow, 87
Los Elefantes, 117
My Little Bunnies Now Must Go to Bed, 258
Nineteen Birds, 36
Once I Saw an Ant Hill, 3
One Elephant Went out to Play, 117
One Little, Two Little, Three Little Kittens, 235
One Old Oxford Ox, 206
One, Two, Buckle My Shoe, 81
One, Two, Three, Four, Five, 119
One, Two, Three, Four, Five, Once I Caught a Hare
    Alive, 259
Over in the Meadow, 216
The Ants Go Marching, 3
The First Little Pig Danced a Merry, Merry Jig, 247
The Twelve Days of Christmas, 221
There Was an Old Man, 89
There Was an Old Woman Sat Spinning, 89
There Were Two Birds That Once Sat on a Stone,
    37
This Little Squirrel, 280
Three Jellyfish, 172
Two Little Blackbirds, 17
Two Little Dicky Birds, 17
Where Are the Baby Mice?, 181
Wire, Brier, Limberlock, 134

Games

Fox a Fox, 124
Red Lion, 174

Nonsense Verses

Jabberwocky, 234
The Dinkey-Bird, 39
The Whango Tree, 25

About the Author

ELIZABETH COTHEN LOW, a freelance writer, worked as a Children's Librarian at Rantoul Public Library in Illinois, where her responsibilities entailed programming, collection development, readers' advisory, and promotion. She has a M.L.S. from the University of Illinois at Urbana-Champaign. She lives in Queens, New York, with her husband and two children.